ROUTLEDGE LIBRARY EDITIONS:
DEVELOPMENT

DISTANCE TEACHING FOR THE THIRD WORLD

DISTANCE TEACHING FOR THE THIRD WORLD

The lion and the clockwork mouse

Incorporating a directory of distance teaching projects

MICHAEL YOUNG, HILARY PERRATON,
JANET JENKINS AND
TONY DODDS

Volume 63

Routledge
Taylor & Francis Group
LONDON AND NEW YORK

First published in 1980

This edition first published in 2011
by Routledge
2 Park Square, Milton Park, Abingdon, Oxfordshire OX14 4RN

Simultaneously published in the USA and Canada
by Routledge
711 Third Avenue, New York, NY 10017

First issued in paperback 2014

Routledge is an imprint of the Taylor & Francis Group, an informa business

British Library Cataloguing in Publication Data
A catalogue record for this book is available from the British Library

ISBN 13: 978-0-415-58414-2 (Set)
ISBN 13: 978-0-415-59492-9 (Volume 63)
ISBN 13: 978-0-415-84709-4 (pbk)

DISTANCE TEACHING FOR THE THIRD WORLD

The lion and the clockwork mouse

Incorporating a directory of distance teaching projects

Michael Young, Hilary Perraton,
Janet Jenkins and Tony Dodds

ROUTLEDGE & KEGAN PAUL
London, Boston and Henley

First published in 1980
by Routledge & Kegan Paul Ltd
39 Store Street,
London WC1E 7DD,
9 Park Street,
Boston, Mass. 02108, USA and
Broadway House,
Newtown Road,
Henley-on-Thames,
Oxon RG9 1EN
Printed and bound in Great Britain by
Thomson Litho Ltd, East Kilbride

British Library Cataloguing in Publication Data

Distance Teaching for the Third World.
1. Underdeveloped areas - Distance study
I. Young, Michael, *b. 1915*
371.3 LB1029.D/ 80-40368

ISBN 0 7100 0479 6

CONTENTS

A Lion having laid down to take his repose under the spreading boughs of a shady tree, a company of Mice scampered over his back and waked him. Upon which, starting up, he clapped his paw upon one of them, and was just going to put it to death, when the little suppliant implored his mercy, begging him not to stain his noble character with the blood of so small and insignificant a creature. The Lion, touched with compassion, instantly released his little trembling captive. Not long after, traversing the forest in search of his prey, he chanced to run into the toils of the hunters, and not being able to disengage himself, he set up a loud roar. The Mouse, hearing the voice, and knowing it to be the Lion's, immediately repaired to the place, and bade him fear nothing, for that he was his friend. Instantly he fell to work, and with his little sharp teeth gnawed asunder the knots and fastenings of the toils, and set the royal brute at liberty.

(One of the Fables of Aesop)

PREFACE

We have all four been employed for up to seven years, either full time or part time, by the International Extension College. This is the bond between us, and the common experience that has shaped the book. That being so, we should say a little about the college, its origins and its work.

At a stretch, it dates back to 1962 when one of the authors, Michael Young, urged the establishment of an Open University in order to add to the educational resources of Britain. These were then, at the level of higher education, strained to the limit. The essence of the plan, put forward in that form for the first time, was that broadcasting and correspondence should be brought together with face-to-face teaching to produce a new kind of institution for part-time adult students. There was no immediate response to the plan. So, a year later, the National Extension College was established in Cambridge as a pilot for such a university.

When the Open University was eventually created by the British government the National Extension College continued to exist, working at different levels and teaching different students. Once both had demonstrated their promise the next step was to consider how the same basic techniques could be adapted to the needs of countries in the third world. This in its turn led to the International Extension College (IEC) which also has its base in Britain. Its main purpose is to provide advice and support on distance teaching for education in the third world. It provides courses on the subject at the Institute of Education of London University for professionals from overseas.

The first decision taken seven years ago was that, despite the precedent of the Open University, higher education would not be a major concern of the IEC. The developing countries are generally well endowed on that score. The people crying out for attention are elsewhere. This accounts for the fact that, unless the Open University or another institution has made specific advances in technique that can be copied lower down, almost nothing is said in this book about higher education for people other than teachers. Nor, for that matter, is it about the large subject of distance teaching for technical training, although the remarkable work of the Venezuelan National Institute of Educational Co-operation is mentioned.

IEC is a resource centre that can be drawn on by any government or body in the third world that wishes to make use of distance teaching or, if already doing so, change what is being done. Each of the consequential assignments for which we have been asked to take responsibility has, inevitably, influenced our way of looking at our subject. The most telling experience has certainly been gained in setting up the three overseas colleges we have set up for the governments of Mauritius, Botswana and Lesotho - the Mauritius College of the Air, the Botswana Extension College and the Lesotho Distance Teaching Centre - and the one that we helped establish for the training of teachers at the University of Lagos - the Correspondence and Open Studies Unit. One of us, Tony Dodds, also spent many years engaged in adult education in Tanzania and was involved in the early days of that country's radio study campaigns.

We have, however, done our best in this book to stand back and review the experience of other institutions besides those four, drawing on the literature in general as well as on the consultancy and other work we have done in, for example, Ghana, Pakistan, Sierra Leone, Turkey and Latin America. (1) Apart from the exclusions we have mentioned already we have been concerned with the main uses to which distance teaching can be put, in teacher training, in support for schools, in formal education out of schools and, above all, in non-formal education. The main plea of the book is for a new form of institution to which we have given the name 'radio college'.

Three basic views have guided the work of IEC, and also the book. The first is that the traditional methods of education, with a single teacher in a classroom, offer an inadequate solution to the educational problems of the world and that distance teaching can do something to get education to people who would otherwise lack it, or to offer a better education to people than they would otherwise receive. This is because of the economic case for it where large numbers of students are to be served. Distance teaching is generally more useful for offering education to the many than to the few. It is particularly relevant to the poorest countries where, as a World Bank Education Sector Working Paper put it: (2)

the rapid expansion of educational systems has been accom-

> panied by rapid increases in the proportion of public expenditure devoted to education. While the acceptable percentage will vary from country to country, any proportion much over 20% begins to impinge upon the needs of other sectors and services and limits further increases in educational expenditure to the rate of growth of GNP and public revenue.

The second and more general view is that the resources, and the know-how, of the world need to be shared. There is now expertise in various countries on the planning of radio schools, the running of learning groups, the writing of correspondence lessons in agriculture, the organisation of distance teaching colleges and so forth. The experience can seldom be transferred direct: a pattern of organisation that suits Botswana is probably wrong for Mauritius. But anyone has a better chance of getting it right if he knows what others have done than if each starts from scratch. Just as there is scope for sharing experience so there may be for sharing teaching materials. At the very least, it is easier for a Mauritian teacher of woodwork, say, to write a good course in the subject if he has already seen a similar course written for another country or another culture. One of our first moves was to set up a resource centre to encourage and facilitate the sharing of experience.

The third view is that the Western system of education is out of gear with the needs of many countries that have inherited it. Following writers like Dumont, Foster and Coombs we suggested in our first report that in many African countries (3)

> an emphasis on academic subjects imported from Europe is linked to a reverence for academic qualifications. Both have at best a limited relevance to the lives that most students are going to live. They do nothing to equip them to change and improve conditions in the rural areas where most of them are destined to stay. There is little emphasis on technical and vocational subjects or on rural skills, and the pattern of teaching makes few conscious efforts to train students to solve by themselves the practical problems they are likely to face in later life.

Subject always to national priorities, we hoped to show how distance teaching could be used to offer an education for the majority of people who would live out their lives in a village and not for the minority who would make their way through ordinary schools to the town. This was not because we had romantic notions about the inherent superiority of village over town. We wanted to show that distance teaching, like the Mouse of our sub-title, is a creature of comparable power to the Lion of the orthodox educational system.

This book is a review of some of the work that has been done in the past and a proposal about what might be done in the future. The review has one inevitable limitation. Apart from the four African colleges associated with IEC, we have necessarily had to rely largely on published reports, and many of these are now out of date. All we can say is that as far as we know we have used the most up-to-date information that has been published about the institutions we have referred to.

Many people have helped us build up the International Extension College and so gather the ideas contained in this book. They are too numerous to mention all of them individually. But we would like to express our special thanks to our colleagues in the institutions we have been closely linked to - Kenneth Noyau and his staff at the Mauritius College of the Air, Solomon Inquai and his staff at Botswana Extension College, Kenneth Tsekoa and his staff at the Lesotho Distance Teaching Centre together with Paud Murphy, 'Yinka Olumide and his staff at the Correspondence and Open Studies Unit of the University of Lagos, Dick Freeman and his staff at the National Extension College, Cambridge, and Professor Peter Williams, Hugh Hawes and other colleagues in the Department of Education in Developing Countries at the London University Institute of Education. We also could not have gained any momentum without the support of Donald Chesworth, now Warden of Toynbee Hall in London, of Frank Sutton and Mel Fox of the Ford Foundation, and of David Anderson, now Managing Director of the Commonwealth Fund for Technical Cooperation.

NOTES

1 See the directory of distance teaching projects, pp. 162 ff., which consists of a list of institutions, a brief description of their work, and a selective bibliography.
2 World Bank, 'Education Sector Working Paper', p. 21.
3 Dodds et al., 'One Year's Work', p. 9.

Chapter 1

IMPASSE?

'Education for all' still has a fine ring to it. It is a creed that has been embraced by the unlikely trio of Gladstone of England, Nyerere of Tanzania and Gowon of Nigeria, and millions of others besides. And yet in the last few years it has been under attack, in rich countries and in poor, for its failure to meet the hopes and expectations that the prophets of educational expansion had aroused. 'School is dead', say some, 'school ought to be dead', say others, 'school is irrelevant', say yet more. Amid these voices ever-increasing millions of children are trying to get into school. Their aspirations are in contrast with the current fashion to decry education and all its works.

Many of the contemporary criticisms of education have obvious force. So has the case for education, and for its expansion. Nyerere described its liberating potential when he said: (1)

> Man can only liberate himself or develop himself. He* cannot be liberated or developed by another. For Man makes himself. It is his ability to act deliberately for a self-determined purpose, which distinguishes him from the other animals. The expansion of his own consciousness, and therefore of his power over himself, his environment, and his society, must therefore ultimately be what we mean by development.
>
> So development is for Man, by Man, and of Man. The same is true of education. Its purpose is the liberation of Man from the restraints and limitations of ignorance and dependency. Education has to increase men's physical and mental freedom - to increase their control over themselves, their own lives, and the environment in which they live.

* We, too, have used the word 'he' throughout the book although we almost always mean 'he or she'.

> The ideas imparted by education, or released in the mind through education, should therefore be liberating ideas; the skills acquired by education should be liberating skills. Nothing else can properly be called education.

In other words, education is to do with power. People without education are at the mercy of those with it, who can use what they know to their advantage and to the disadvantage of the ignorant around them. Education is a means of gaining power, and hence freedom, something that should be everyone's right and not simply the right of the better-educated minority. On this showing the case for expanding education is a simple egalitarian one. While education alone will not transform the world, or the life of most of those who get it, the provision of education to only part of a community, or part of the world, reinforces relative deprivation. The case for improving education is that the new attacks on it in the 1970s have revealed its inherent weaknesses. For a juster world we need to expand education and at the same time to improve it, using any appropriate tool.

The need to expand education has become so much the new orthodoxy that it is easy to forget how recent a phenomenon it is. A century ago most people in every continent had not been to school. Enough was the informal education they received from parents and grandparents, from craftsmen to whom they were apprenticed, from friends. Within literate cultures schooling was the privilege of the few; in other societies there were no schools in the sense that we use the word. Jomo Kenyatta, forty years ago, described almost nostalgically how Gikuyu education fitted the needs of society. (2)

> The first and most obvious principle of educational value which we see in the Gikuyu system of education is that the instruction is always applied to an individual concrete situation; behaviour is taught in relation to some particular person. Whereas in Europe and America schools provide courses in moral instruction or citizenship, the African is taught how to behave to father or mother, grandparents, and to other members of the kinship group, paternal and maternal. Whereas European schools in Africa provide training in nature study, woodwork, animal husbandry etc., much of which is taught by general class instruction, the tribal method is to teach the names of particular plants, the use of different trees, or the management of a particular herd of sheep and goats or cattle. After this the child is left free to develop his own initiative by experiments and through trial and error to acquire proficiency.

The strengths of that system of education lie in the way it is rooted in the rich Kenyan soil. Its curriculum - a word no one would have used - had to do with the everyday life and needs of the Gikuyu culture and economy. But an informal system of education of this kind does not meet the needs of a rapidly changing society in which an appeal to traditional knowledge or ways of thought will no longer solve all the problems to be faced by a child as he grows up. Traditional, informal systems of education assume that change is a slow process and that values and ways of doing things will change only a little from generation to generation. As the streets of Nairobi have been extended and its towers built ever higher, like those of countless other cities, so it has become ever more obvious that the road to status and power lies through the schoolroom. While we may mourn the informal system of our forefathers, and try to regain some of its benefits, the appeal of the formal is such that governments cannot resist public demands for its expansion.

Curiously, it seems right to talk about a single system of education. For one of the oddities of a world that is 'Incorrigibly plural' (3) is that education looks alike wherever you go. If you go to Murree in the Himalayan foothills you will see the same crocodile of children in school uniform, walking beside the school chapel tower, as by a rice field in Guyana or between cashew-nut trees in Tanzania. And it is not only the trappings that are similar: the essentials are too. Kennedy's 'Latin Primer' used to be one of the keys you needed to unlock university doors at Ibadan in Nigeria and at Mona in Jamaica. Today the English 'School Mathematics Project' textbooks are used in many different countries. Almost anywhere you go you will find children in class sitting at similar desks, going through the same routines, and often learning the same material regardless of its relevance to themselves. The strength of the colonial model of education has outlived the rule of the colonial powers. These striking similarities mean that the same criticisms are now being made of education in the West and in the third world; in both, schools are condemned for their irrelevance, for their archaic curricula, for their alienating effects and for their role in perpetuating inequality.

THE SIZE OF THE PROBLEM

The third world is in far worse plight than the rest. Along with the problems of quality it shares with the West, it also faces ones of quantity of a quite different order. Most rich countries already have ten or twelve years of compulsory education and are now concerned about its quality. But in the third world there are simply not enough schools to go round.

Not even enough poor and inadequate schools. This is how Nyerere described the problem in talking about Tanzania's achievement in its first ten years of independence in expanding primary-student numbers from 486 000 to 848 000: (4)

> Yet these achievements must not blind us to the terrible fact that almost the same proportion of our children now as in 1961 fail to find a place in primary school. We have provided primary school places for only about 52 per cent of the children of primary school age - that is how far we are from our objective of universal primary school education!...
>
> And it is absurd to think that passing resolutions at TANU Conferences, or asking questions in Parliament can solve this problem. There is no short and simple answer to it. Yet it would be criminal if we allowed our failure to be enveloped in a cloud of self-congratulation about what we have achieved in education. Those children without school places must remain as a real challenge to us for the future.

Part of Tanzania's response has been to create a distance teaching programme on the huge scale needed to train teachers for universal primary education.

Nyerere's desire to expand education is echoed in all the development plans of the third world. At the same time it presents a new problem different from that faced by countries like England and the USA when, a century ago, they began to move from offering primary education to half their children to making it universal. Both these countries achieved a sort of educational revolution over the fifty years from 1870 to 1920. In 1870 only about half the children in England went to primary school; illiteracy was still so common that over a quarter of the women married then could not sign their own name in the marriage register. By 1920, 86 per cent of the children between 5 and 14 were in school and primary education had long been compulsory. Similarly, in the USA the proportion of children between 5 and 17 in school went up from 54 per cent in 1870 to 83 per cent in 1920. In both countries the figures crept up over the half century and in the USA the impact of education was reduced by having a very short school year: in 1870 the school year lasted only 19 weeks and the average child attended for only 11 weeks in the year.

But there are important differences between that and what is now being sought in the third world. Demography made it easier in England and the USA in the last century than it is in the third world now. In England in 1870, 23 per cent of the population was between 5 and 14, and the proportion had dropped to 19 per cent in 1920. Over the same half century the 5 to 14 US age group fell from 25 per cent to 21 per cent of the population. In 1971, in Botswana, for example, the same age group made up 29 per cent; 26 per cent in Tanzania were in the same age group and there is little reason to think that this proportion will fall at the rate it did a century ago in England and the USA. The developing countries are trying to move more quickly - to achieve in a decade or two what took half a century in the West.

Their quantitative problems are made greater, too, by a wish to offer education to adults as well as to children: Nyerere has argued for it on the grounds that the benefits can be felt in society straight away without waiting for a generation of school children to grow up. The problems are also aggravated by a general determination in the third world to expand education at all levels, primary, secondary and tertiary, all at once. By comparison, in the West there was a greater concentration upon primary schooling until the point when it became universal. Only then was there a sharp expansion of secondary education, and only when that was complete came the sharp expansion in tertiary education.

Already many educational budgets are absorbing between 20 and 30 per cent of government budgets and it is difficult to see how they can expand further without cutting into other, and perhaps equally vital, services. Unless GNP, and with it government expenditure, can grow more rapidly than the increase in population, then it is impossible to meet the continuing demand for education by using traditional techniques. There simply is not the money available to finance universal secondary schooling, for which a demand will arise as soon as we are anywhere near achieving universal primary education - itself an objective that is already straining budgets, resources and administrative capacity to the utmost.

Then there is the fact that the third world cannot bear with inequality as comfortably as the West used to. In England at the end of the nineteenth century it was possible to hold down expenditure on education because it could be provided more cheaply for the working class than for the middle and upper classes: different types of education were seen as appropriate for children according to their future status in life. The belief lived on into the present century: this conversation took place in the 1940s: (5)

> I saw the headmaster, and I said 'We've got this form with all these schools down, and we don't know anything about any of them.' 'Well', said the headmaster, 'what's his father's job?' 'He's a lorry driver.' 'Well, then you'd better be sending him to Mill Cross.' 'Mill Cross? Why, is that the best school?' 'No, it's not, but it's the best school for you'. 'How do you mean, it's the best school for me? Where would you send your lad?' 'Oh, I'd send *my* lad to Marburton College ... .

Throughout the world today, with minor exceptions like the fee-paying 'public' schools of Britain or the segregated schools of South Africa, it is widely assumed that all children have a right to the same quality of education. Of course they do not all receive it. So the real educational crisis for the third world is about expanding the schools at an unprecedented rate and changing them at the same time. In expanding education the third world is trying to do more with less. But its problems are by no means only quantitative. They are also qualitative.

THE BANKING CONCEPT

A fundamental criticism has come from Paulo Freire. He claims that much education is a process of 'banking', or transferring banks of information from the near omniscient teacher to the empty minds of his students. Freire was a literacy teacher in Brazil; in contrast with orthodox literacy teaching where teacher and students work through a primer, he developed a process based on dialogue. In discussion with his students, Freire and his colleagues identified key words of importance to them - 'favela', a slum, or 'tijolo', a brick, for example - and then used the syllabic units of these words to make others. In this way, from the very outset, illiterate adults were reading and writing words of their choice, rather than words chosen by the primer-writer. And they were using words that reflected the central concerns of their lives. (6) Underlying Freire's work is a belief that education is a process of increasing one's understanding and ability to control the world, rather than a process of mastering a fixed body of subject-matter. While his theories, and his practice, were worked out in teaching adults to read, the ideas behind them are relevant to a broader critique. In contrast with Freire's views, the orthodoxy has been that there is an organised body of knowledge teachers already possess and which students need to master. The hidden assumption is that the set of knowledge an individual needs will correspond with the set defined by the teacher, or the syllabus, although either is a necessarily arbitrary part of the universe of knowledge.

A consequence of this view is that the teacher deserves profound respect and that the printed word, being the source of the teacher's authority, the very repository of the subject-matter of education, deserves the greatest respect of all. This view of the teacher is symbolised by the Italian habit of referring to professors as 'the barons'. If the belief in authority within the school spills over into a more general respect for authority outside then education tends to become no more than support for the status quo. It was an uneducated child who shouted that the emperor had no clothes.

But our objection to the banking process is not on political grounds alone. Burgess's analysis of higher education in Britain - at the opposite end of the spectrum of educational privilege from literacy teaching in Brazil - has shown that its organisation and methods of teaching are not dissimilar. On this view, then, the educational revolution we are seeking will have its impact on education in the wealthiest countries as well as in the poorest. Burgess argues that, in contrast to the view of education enshrined in the division of subjects between orthodox university faculties, there is an alternative view of the purpose of education. (7) He suggests that Popper's description of the processes of scientific method and discovery is a better guide to education than learning organised into 'subjects'. Popper has proposed that the scientific method does not involve arguing from general theory to particular example but is more in the nature of problem-solving. He suggested that all scientific discussions start with a problem (P_1), to which we offer some sort of tentative solution - a tentative theory (TT); this theory is then criticised, in an attempt at error elimination (EE); and as in the case of dialectic, this process renews itself; the theory and its critical revision give rise to new problems (P_2). (8)

Popper's view of scientific discovery is therefore that science proceeds by making new hypotheses to solve problems, and by seeking to prove them false to find the errors in them, so that science and learning are seen as being in a process of continual change. The attempt to disprove hypotheses, rather than to make new inferences from theory, is the method of scientific advance. If this is the way in which science proceeds, in its efforts to increase man's understanding of the world, then it would seem appropriate for us to adopt similar methods in education and concentrate not on passing on accumulated banks of fact, but on the solution of problems. To put the argument the other way round, if education is to help people solve problems, then they must learn the methods of doing so.

Of course this does not mean that we can eliminate the content of education and invent a fact-free curriculum. Many problems cannot be solved, if at all, without access to the accumulated experience of mankind. But the kind of knowledge we are likely to need may lie beyond the limits of traditionally defined subjects. If our educational system is to offer people a guide in their ordinary life then it must move from reliance on the accumulation of information and become based on procedures for solving problems, to give people a chance of increasing their mastery of their own environment. Popper's view suggests a way of doing this and provides another philosophical base for what supporters of discovery methods have believed from Dewey onwards.

This is not all just theory: there are places where the educational revolution has begun. The best English primary schools, to take one example, are a joy, for their children and their teachers; they provide an education that is both liberating and fun as well as teaching basic skills effectively. And it is a different sort of education from the old authoritarian model we have been describing: (9)

> A middle-aged visitor, educated in an ordinary elementary school at the time of the 1931 Report, who visited a good primary school in 1966, would find much to surprise him. If he arrived at the official opening hour he would find that many of the children had been there long before him, not penned in the playground, but inside the school, caring for the livestock, getting on with interesting occupations, reading or writing, painting, carving or weaving or playing musical instruments.... As the morning went on ... he would hear few commands and few raised voices. Children would be asked to do things more often than told. They would move freely about the school, fetching what they needed, books or material, without formality or interference. Teachers would be among the children, taking part in their activities, helping and advising and discussing much more frequently than standing before a class teaching.

A school like that has an inner strength that comes from a commitment to values quite different from those of the schools we have been criticising. The best primary schools are not authoritarian; they do not follow a curriculum laid down long ago or far away; they are not dominated by examinations and by rote learning.

WHAT HINDERS CHANGE?

Such schools are unusual. Faced with a curriculum that has to be learned, and that lies at the limits of their own understanding, many teachers in many countries revert to rote methods, the way they themselves studied. Rote learning has a long history; before the invention of printing it made good sense for the teacher to read from the one, precious, handwritten book and for the student to copy down or learn by heart what was in it. The practice was buttressed by the scholastic belief that knowledge was finite and needed only to be discovered or rediscovered from the ancient authorities. It continued to be used by the European imperial powers. This is how the missionaries used it in Nigeria in 1867: (10)

> We teach them a text, or a verse of hymn, and the last quarter of an hour is always given in all classes to teaching by repetition some catechism, and sometimes for a change we have the whole school together to go over the Creed, the Lord's Prayer, and the Ten Commandments, to make sure they are not forgotten. O what bright, eager, earnest, black, shining faces we have in our African Sunday School!

The methods survived for generation after generation. In the Sudan, for example: (11)

> In the winter of 1931 to 1932, as a new inspector ... I was being taken round by the chief inspector and shown how to inspect the scattered ... primary schools of the northern Sudan.
>
> We would make our way along the sandy, treeless streets of a village to the north edge. There, set against a bare, limitless horizon, would be the brown, mud-brick, verandahed buildings of the village school. As we came near we would hear the loud voices of the children chanting the Quran, or shouting severally the Arabic letters or numerals. Our approach would be signalled to the headmaster by a small boy posted for that purpose; a moment later a hush would descend on the school and a dark-robed figure with white turban would emerge, greet us with dignity, and lead us to his office....
>
> Ahead of us by the blackboard the teacher would be standing, anxiously waiting to begin his lesson. 'Lesson', did I say? Rather revision or display. For it was impossible ever to hear an ordinary lesson, or even a specially prepared new lesson. Whatever we asked for, the teacher knew well that the right thing for an inspector was to show off what the children had memorised. Old reading lessons were repeated, old grammar questions asked again, names of railway stations rattled off.

Things had not changed all that much at a secondary school in Nigeria thirty years later: (12)

> The reader was 'A Journey to the Moon' by Jules Verne. This was printed in a booklet about ninety pages long in a text based on a 400-word vocabulary, with all the new items listed in the back. The method used by my predecessor, which I cautiously followed, was to go through the book chapter by chapter, answering the questions on each chapter at the back of the book. An average lesson covered four pages.... The process was boring to the last degree.

Learning by heart, where you are not concerned with the meaning or the content, is mastering a fixed quantity of subject-matter, chosen, defined and arranged by someone else. It makes life easier for a teacher who feels unsure of his subject-matter: if you teach people to memorise a fixed body of knowledge you can avoid answering, or even provoking, questions that go beyond its limits. This method was functional enough in the colonial period, as it produced more than enough clerks to fill the lower echelons of government. For students with this destiny the content was also functional. If they were to be clerks in government service, working in countries where government dominated the modern sector of the economy, then the skills required were those of mastering and operating a fixed set of rules and procedures. Until the 1960s even the home civil service in Britain was divided into three classes, administrative, executive and clerical, with starkly different functions. The clerk's function was merely to carry out the clerical duties appropriate to his grade, neither questioning them nor understanding them. An education that consisted of uncritically learning by rote a fixed body of knowledge and mastering a limited range of skills was an appropriate preparation for a government clerk, especially when the higher posts were not open to promotion from the ranks below. But an education of this sort is not likely to produce people who can use their learning to change society, or their own position in it, or to take advantage of technical advances in agriculture or health or industry.

Rote learning of a fixed body of knowledge is of a piece with the examination system that leads to what Ronald Dore has called 'the diploma disease'. (13) Many countries in the developing world and in the West lay great emphasis on paper qualifications: entry into many civil services, and the points at which you enter them, depend not on your ability to do the job but on the certificate you possess. In many countries, public examinations are a necessary evil. In a face-to-face society, where we all know each other from birth, an employer does not need a certificate to tell whether his potential employee has had the education necessary to work effectively. But if people move far from home, or move sharply upward in the social scale as a result of their education, then they cannot be judged on the basis of personal knowledge. If we are not to have nepotism, or a society in which opportunities are conditioned by class or caste or race, then public examinations seem to be inevitable. But examinations test only that which is readily examinable: if there are qualities that are valuable, but that cannot easily be measured, then they are likely to get little attention in a system based firmly on qualifications.

Moreover, many curricula at primary and secondary level are designed for the minority of students who will go on to a further stage of full-time education and not for the majority who will stop at that level. And, in a quest for respectability and for qualifications, syllabuses are not based on local life and culture but on what is seen as appropriate measured by some external, often metropolitan standard. The British examining boards that operate overseas have been among the worst offenders. This is what secondary-school students were studying in Nigeria a decade ago: (14)

> The world view presented by the School Certificate history syllabus was almost as preposterous. For the examiners, England was the centre of the universe. Thus a quarter of the paper was devoted to a survey of all the constitutional bric-à-brac of British government: the kangaroo, the guillotine, and the closure, Black Rod, the Mace and the Sergeant-at-Arms, county councils, urban district councils, rural district councils, and parish councils, county boroughs and municipal boroughs. A close acquaintance with the dehydrated work of Messrs Hussey and White, bound in bilious orange by the Cambridge University Press, gave many a West African secondary-school student the belief that he held the clue to the efficient working of a parliamentary democracy.

There are similar stories from all over the third world: of education for future peasant farmers in Madagascar that had to be 'exactly as in France'; (15) of the study of Tacitus and Mme de Sevigné in the West African bush, and of sole being flown from Paris to Ouagadougou in order to meet the requirement of a home economics practical examination that was to prepare 'sole meunière'. (16) In many parts of Africa where most of the children live in small villages and will work as farmers, the subjects taught in school are of more use to future clerks in the city than to future farmers in the country. This is not entirely the fault of the educators: the financial rewards of city life are so great that there is strong pressure from adults and from schoolchildren for anything that will bring them nearer. Attempt after attempt to introduce and re-introduce agriculture as a 'subject' has failed.

In various ways education in many developing countries is dysfunctional. It relies heavily on rote learning, leads to an inappropriate reverence for paper qualifications, and is based on curricula that are irrelevant to the students' future lives. It also creates an imbalance, with many school-leavers unemployed, while on the other hand there is a shortage of skilled and semi-skilled workers.

THE ALIENATION EFFECT

An education that uses rote learning as a technique and an irrelevant curriculum as its guide is not likely to prove adequate for ordinary people. Its strength has been that it provided a route to affluence for the handful of children who could make their way through all the exams, drawn by the pot of gold that would await them in the end. 'In the late sixties', for example, 'the Ugandan graduate just entering the civil service could expect his income to be fifty times the average income per head in Uganda. (17)

The effects of the system, even on those who passed successfully through it - let alone those who dropped out along the way or never had a chance of starting on it - have often been condemned by third world intellectuals. The exiled Ugandan poet, Okot p'Bitek, drew this picture of the African child going through school and university: (18)

> This is the first step on the path that leads to power, money and the good life. A life better than that of those who stay behind.
>
> He comes to the church school dressed in his front-kerchief and bare buttocks, and squats before a nun or a man dressed in a 'kanzu' and they write things in the sand. During the music lesson he is taught to sing:
>
> Baa Baa black sheep
> Have you any wool?
>
> ...
>
> For his secondary education he goes to the big town. There is no traditional music or dance or poetry here. And except during the holidays the young ruler is now fully subjected to the white man's cultural training....
>
> Drama and poetry are taught, not as ends in themselves, but as a means of learning correct English or French pronunciation and as examination subjects. The key to power is the piece of paper they call the Certificate, and the examination looms largest in the educational process. It hangs like the executioner's axe over teacher and pupil alike. He learns by heart poems about the beauty of the snow in winter, although his experience is confined to the destructive nature of hailstones.... Those who score the highest awards in the examination enter the University....
>
> At the end of the third year he dons his black gown and flat-topped cap. In his hand he carries the piece of paper they give him at graduation - the key to power, money and a big car. Over-dressed in his dark suit he walks out of the University gate, out into the world, materially comfortable, but culturally castrated, dead. A lost victim of the school system, he cannot dance the dance or play the music of his own people....

If Okot p'Bitek is right, then an education that should have been liberating succeeds only in alienating man from man, and man from his own culture. Education, as it has developed, seems in this to be perpetuating and increasing inequality rather than fostering the equality we postulated at the outset as the objective that mattered. In most countries rich and poor children get unequal opportunities. The richer children have a better chance of getting to school, and a better chance of getting to a good school. The good schools, with more qualified teachers, tend to be in the larger or pleasanter towns, the worse in remote rural areas or grim urban ghettoes. Inevitably, those who receive a better education at primary level have a better chance of going on to secondary school and then beyond. Thus more public money is spent on the more privileged children and less on the less. Education becomes socially regressive, widening the gap between rich and poor.

It is difficult to see how orthodox methods of educational reform can work in the opposite direction and achieve an adequate egalitarian education for all in our lifetime or in our children's lifetime. The Herculean task of providing primary schools for all is already stretching educational budgets to the limit in those countries where it is being attempted; when educational budgets rise faster than the growth in a country's GNP then improvements in education can be made only by cutting back on something else or by diverting funds from the private to the public sector. Even if money were no object there would be major obstacles to expansion. With traditional schools, in which the teacher has been trained to control a classroom of children, to instruct them and to guide them in their use of textbooks, 'everything in education depends ultimately on the teacher, and everything in educational progress depends on there being teachers with the right qualities, and in the right numbers, to carry it out.' (19) But the number of teachers will not be right, not for many years, especially in the remoter or poorer places where such teachers as are available do not want to work.

SEEKING AN ALTERNATIVE

What is to be done? One proposed solution has been to go for basic education - a sort of four-year primary school - for all, with more selective education for the few who would go beyond that. (20) But even if this is educationally feasible it is politically unrealistic: at a time when governments are attempting to meet the demand for more and longer education, and when primary courses are of six or seven years, it would be a powerful and brave government that talked of cutting back the number of years. A more promising solution is to shift the boundaries between school and work. In China education has been linked to production so that the same social organisation is responsible for the production of goods for sale and for the education of its members. In Botswana Patrick van Rensburg has argued for the creation of a new kind of school-cum-workplace where the farm produce, and building or engineering work, will contribute to the costs of education. Similarly, every US student who has worked his way through college, or British Open University graduate who has acquired his degree without stopping work, has demonstrated in a less radical way that it is possible to combine some kinds of study with some kinds of work. Work does not have to take place at one time in one's life, or in one place, and learning at another. Education out of school is one way of dealing with educational shortage.

Education outside school, or within, cannot be expanded on the necessary scale if it is bound by fixed staff ratios. We have to find a way of offering education with far, far fewer teachers. One way - and the way that is central to the theme of this book - is to take advantage of print and broadcasts to achieve economies of scale. One book, or one broadcast, can reach students in their thousands or millions. If broadcasts and print are yoked to opportunities for face-to-face learning, perhaps in a group without a trained teacher, then a humane and effective education can be made available on a vast scale. At the same time, if the use of such methods separates the function of the teacher in helping students to learn from that of transmitting facts, then we will be on the way to other beneficial changes in educational method.

Distance teaching, using this combination of methods, is awkward to define. To stretch the definition, the author of a book is teaching at a distance if his readers are learning from what he has written. Some of that experience is very old, going back to the invention of printing in the fifteenth century; once books become freely available, then it is more difficult to restrict education to a small minority. The university teachers of Salamanca were well aware of this in the sixteenth century when they protested against books that threatened their livelihood. (21) The invention of printing made dramatic expansion of learning possible; it is no accident that the printers of London were among the most radical groups in the last century or that the book 'still has its enemies. State and Church censorship of books remains commonplace in many parts of the world. The book threatens established monopolies of knowledge and power and truth, since, as Bronowski has said "the democracy of the intellect comes from the printed book".' (22)

Down the centuries there has been a small but important tradition of the self-educated man who learned to read and to learn from books outside the formal system of schools and universities.

THE GENESIS OF THREE-WAY TEACHING

But that is a hard way. Another fairly recent invention, the post, can make the task easier. After the development of a cheap postal service teachers in various countries began to make use of it towards the end of the nineteenth century. In England Isaac Pitman started to teach shorthand on postcards and William Briggs taught his pre-university students by sending lessons through the post when they could no longer attend his college. In Sweden things began in much the same way: (23)

> In the 1890s a young man, Hans Hermod, had opened a small private school in Malmö where he taught languages and commercial subjects. One of his students had to move to another part of Sweden before finishing his course in book-keeping. Wishing nevertheless to complete, he talked the matter over with his teacher. They soon agreed to continue the instruction by mail. This educational experiment turned out successfully and gave Hans Hermod something to think about. Could not the method be utilized on a larger scale, so that those who, for some reason or other, were unable to attend a higher school, might instead study by correspondence in their own homes? Hans Hermod solved the problem in his own practical way: in December 1898, the first Swedish correspondence course, 'Bookkeeping by single and double entry', left the printing press to inaugurate the triumphs of education by mail in Sweden.

Hans Hermod's first course was different from a textbook for it was designed as correspondence - as a way of maintaining a two-way dialogue between student and teacher. The student could react to his teacher in a way impossible with an ordinary book.

Innumerable book-keeping courses have been produced since then, while Hermods grew into the largest correspondence college in Sweden, eventually to become part of the state educational system. In the other major European countries correspondence education remained in the hands of individual companies and commercial colleges and grew up outside regular education. The striking exception was in France in 1939. It was obvious that the war would disrupt education for many children and, as a result, the Ministry of Education created a national centre for correspondence teaching that proved so valuable during the war that it remained in existence afterwards. It thrives to this day. Among its functions is education for handicapped children, or for children in hospital who cannot get to school.

Even more striking innovations were made in Russia, the USA and Australasia. In the late 1920s the Soviet Union seized on correspondence as a way of widening educational opportunity and combining study with productive work. A Central Institute of Correspondence Education was set up in 1929, later to become the All-Union External Polytechnical Institute. By 1969 there were 2 400 000 correspondence students in the USSR as a whole and this route to higher education was a regular part of the state educational system. There is some flexibility built into it: correspondence students have a right to time off from work for examination and, more important, can sometimes switch to being full-time students at some stage in their course. The experience of productive work and of life generally which as adults they bring to their study is seen as being a positive advantage for them and for society. (24)

In the USA a desire for equality led the public educational sector into correspondence study. The idea of university extension - of extending the university to serve the public at large - was central to the conception of much US higher education from the Morrill Act of 1873 onwards. The University of Chicago gave a lead when President Harper set up an extension services department in 1892, offering correspondence courses along with part-time classes. The idea quickly spread to Wisconsin, Oregon and Kansas and by 1919, 73 'institutions of college and university rank' were offering correspondence courses. (25) American universities have continued to offer them to this day and have also provided them at high-school level. These were aimed mainly at small country schools so that the children could study as many subjects as those in bigger schools in towns.

In Australasia correspondence education was also seen as a way of extending the school system to those who would otherwise be deprived: Australia's scattered population meant that there were large numbers of children who could not get to school. In 1914 in Victoria 'several teachers in training agreed to send lessons by post to the children of a parent who had written to the Education Department pleading for something to be done to provide an education for his boys.' (26) This small beginning led to the creation of a state correspondence school, and similar ones were soon opened in other Australian states. New Zealand followed suit and also, in 1937, started providing regular radio support to its correspondence lessons. (27)

By the Second World War such experience had begun to demonstrate some of the roles distance teaching could perform - to offer an alternative route to education for those who could not get it through the orthodox one, and to support or extend the work of schools. But the methods used were inadequate: a correspondence course alone looks a poor substitute for school and in Australasia attempts began to link correspondence teaching with some face-to-face study and with broadcasts. In Western Australia, for example, an itinerant teacher was appointed in 1946 with an appropriate set of qualifications that 'included several years experience in small country schools and ability to handle a motor vehicle on bush roads and effect running repairs.' He carried with him 'strips of coir matting for use in sandy places, built-in water and petrol tanks, emergency rations, and a first aid kit ... the best road maps procurable, and a Government order book enabling him to obtain supplies of petrol, tyres, etc. along the track.' (28) At university level today teachers at the Universities of Queensland and New England, which offer degrees by correspondence, go out on walkabout to visit their distant correspondence students. Itinerant teachers can help isolated students, but this is an expensive method appropriate only to a wealthy country that has already created near-universal primary and secondary education.

The other medium that, like print, can be cheaply and readily available to all is radio. And just as print was used for school books almost from its invention, so radio was pressed into the service of education from the early 1920s onwards. The University of Wisconsin claims to have started the first educational broadcasting service in 1919: curiously, although educational broadcasts and correspondence courses were both run by the extension division of the university, they were not put together for another 45 years. Indeed, except in New Zealand, radio and correspondence education were to develop separately until the 1960s. In Britain the BBC had education as one of its purposes in its first charter and conducted a large-scale experiment in school radio in Kent in 1926. Many education authorities were at first sceptical or hostile: the London County Council rejected the idea of co-operation in 1923 but a couple of years later conceded that children could listen during the last half hour of school on Fridays. Despite the Depression the number of schools listening to broadcasts rose steadily from 220 in 1924 to 9 953 in 1939. (29)

The BBC was interested in adult education, as well as schools, from the same period. There was an article in the 'Radio Times' on 13 June 1924 on 'A Broadcasting University' and the BBC produced plans for a 'Wireless University' in 1926. These plans were to lie dormant for a long time but meanwhile the BBC started adult educational broadcasting. They were guided by the view of Reith, their Director-General, that education was associated: (30)

> with hard benches in schools and colleges and universities, with the cramming of a certain amount of knowledge in order that certain tests may be passed. I wish someone would invent another word to describe the sort of education which makes life so much more interesting and enjoyable than it otherwise would be.

The BBC therefore began to co-operate with the Workers' Educational Association and very rapidly set up listening groups throughout the country who followed broadcasts and discussed them afterwards. There were over 1 000 by the winter of 1930-1 and more in later years. But the alliance between the BBC and the traditional adult education agencies was not a firm one, and school programmes took priority within the BBC. Like the 'broadcasting university', the listening groups were a false start for the BBC and did not survive the outbreak of war. But it was the germ of something important showing how stimulating a regular radio programme could be for face-to-face discussion. It was picked up in Canada in 1940 by the Canadian Broadcasting Corporation, the Canadian Association for Adult Education and the Canadian Federation of Agriculture. They worked together to set up farm forums with the motto of 'Read Listen Discuss Act'. Groups of farmers came together to listen to a broadcast and to study a pamphlet about a problem facing them, to discuss it, and, if possible, to agree on co-operative action to help solve it. The aims of the series were defined in 1940 as (31)

> to make people face their problems. It would be unwise to assume that people are merely receptive and asking for an advisory service of this kind. We should not tell people what they ought to do, but rather it is important to let them find out for themselves what needs to be done. An attempt should be made to make them realise that they must assume responsibility and take action themselves towards a solution of the problems facing them.

The Canadian forums introduced a new element: the idea that a group, inspired by a radio programme, should move on to action. The forums went on for twenty years by which time their relevance to the developing world had become apparent and the idea was picked up again, to be taken further, in India, Ghana and even more widely, as we show in chapter 5.

The cheap post and radio supported the educational system and extended it. But they did not seem of more than marginal importance. In contrast, television seemed for a while in the 1950s as if it might transform education. It was seized upon in the USA as a way of making radical improvements.

From 1957, for example, the elementary schools of Hagerstown in Maryland were largely dependent on television, although they were more visited than emulated. One of the instigators of the Open University in Britain, Peter Laslett, went to look at television in the USA to assess its relevance for Britain and came back impressed with the way it meant that the same quality of teaching could be offered in the poorest schools as in the wealthiest. The money was there: the Ford Foundation poured in large sums and concluded by 1965 that the claim of television to teach as effectively as an ordinary teacher was so well established that no more research funds were needed. (32) There was national anxiety about the quality of education in the USA at that time: the launching of the first Sputnik on 4 October 1957 was seen as demonstrating the technological superiority of the Russians. It resulted in heavy expenditure on curriculum reform and development. But the dream faded fast. Television did not transform the schools and, with hindsight, it has a fairly insignificant part in the educational history of the 1960s. The pendulum swung the other way as a condemnation of bad programmes spread over into scepticism about the medium itself.

But before that had happened the Americans had already begun to export the idea of educational reform by television. Their colony in American Samoa was the first importer and the first broadcasts intended to improve the schools there by means of television took place in 1964. Schemes on much the same lines followed in El Salvador, Colombia and elsewhere. Smaller school television projects followed in many other countries. An alliance between the Stanford Institute for Communication Research, the United States Agency for International Development and the National Association of Educational Broadcasters acted as the imperialists of US educational television. They argued that large-scale television projects could bring about dramatic improvements in education for the third world. US involvement was followed by that of the French, Unesco and then the World Bank. A schools television project began in Niger in 1964, supported mainly by the French Agence de co-opération, to be followed by a much larger scheme in the Ivory Coast in 1971. Expansion in fact outran the evidence. We know now that you cannot reform an educational system just by injecting a new medium into it.

Britain, like the USA, was in a mood to expand and improve education in the late 1950s and early 1960s. In distance teaching for adults Britain had lagged behind the rest of the world. We had left correspondence teaching in the hands of commercial colleges, keen to make as much money cut of their students as possible. We had missed the opportunity to set up a government distance-teaching institution either in 1939, like France, or in 1945 to meet post-war demands. School broadcasting, however, continued at an unrivalled level of excellence. In the early 1960s Britain began to catch up and overtake the rest of the world; plans for an open university were sketched by one of the authors, Michael Young, in 1962 and he next year set up the National Extension College as a pilot for such a university. The 1964 Government accepted the case for an Open University and it was launched in 1969. At about the same time groups in France and the USA were independently experimenting with courses that linked broadcasting to correspondence.

The timing is important. The 1960s were the decade in which many newly independent states in Africa were enthusiastically searching for new solutions. With the winning of independence they wanted also to banish ignorance and illieracy. The experience of using unorthodox and non-traditional ways of expanding education looked like giving them the kind of tool they needed. There were direct links between those who had developed new teaching systems in the rich countries and those trying to do the same in Africa. A team from Wisconsin went to Kenya to launch a correspondence unit at the University of Nairobi. The Malawi Correspondence College was started by a New Zealander who then came to visit the National Extension College to see if he could get help. French educators worked with the Niger and Ivory Coast governments in launching their television projects and French priests set up the Institut Africain pour le Développement Economique et Social (INADES) which runs farming courses by correspondence in much of francophone Africa. The farm forum as developed in India and Ghana was transformed in Tanzania. The University of Zambia was committed to offering degree courses by correspondence from the outset, influenced by Australian experience. The African institutions did not, of course, merely copy what had been done in the West: rather they developed ideas that had been tried out elsewhere, often on a modest scale, and made them more central.

There had been parallel developments rather earlier in Latin America. As in West Africa, radical Catholic priests were in the forefront of educational development, starting Acción Cultural Popular (ACPO) in Colombia, which runs its own radio station. Its broadcasts are supported by printed materials (see Appendix 2). The influence of ACPO spread through Latin and into Central America; radio schools in Mexico offered alternatives to regular schooling, again for deprived children.

There is a contrast between the uses to which distance teaching has been put in Europe, North America and Australia and what it is now being asked to do in Africa, Latin America and Asia. In the West it has been used mainly to extend education to fairly small and well-defined groups of people who could not get access to ordinary education. In Africa attempts have been made to use distance teaching on a relatively much larger scale. The aim has been not to expand education to embrace the last 5 per cent of the population, but to offer something to the half of the population who never get to school as children, or the three-quarters or more who receive no adult education.

Can it be done? That is what the rest of the book is about. First we need to take stock of the present state of the art before considering what it could possibly become in the future. We shall start, in the next chapter, with an account of the advantage that has been taken of the permanence of print, the reach of radio and the intimacy of face-to-face study for the purposes of teacher training.

NOTES

1 Julius Nyerere, 'Declaration of Dar-es-Salaam', pp. 9-10.
2 Jomo Kenyatta, 'Facing Mount Kenya', pp. 120-1.
3 Louis MacNeice, Snow, in 'Collected Poems', p. 30
4 Julius Nyerere, 'Freedom and Development', pp. 297-8.
5 Brian Jackson and Dennis Marsden, 'Education and the Working Class', p. 106.
6 For a further account of this process see Paulo Freire, 'Pedagogy of the Oppressed', 'Education for Critical Consciousness' and on the process of literacy teaching more specifically, see his 'Education: The Practice of Freedom', pp. 41 ff.
7 Tyrrell Burgess, 'Education after School', pp. 129ff.
8 Condensed into the schema $P_1 \rightarrow TT \rightarrow EE \rightarrow P_2$, Karl Popper, 'Unended Quest', p. 132.
9 Central Advisory Council for Education, 'Children and their Primary Schools', para. 736.
10 Quoted in A.B. Fafunwa, 'History of Education in Nigeria', p. 87.
11 V.L. Griffiths, 'Teacher-Centred', pp. 3-4.
12 K. Elliott, 'An African School', p. 20.
13 R. Dore, 'The Diploma Disease'.
14 K. Elliott, op. cit., pp. 202-3.
15 R. Dumont, 'False Start in Africa', p. 259.
16 J. Ki-Zerbo, Education and Development, p. 99.
17 R. Dore, op. cit., p. 3.
18 Okot p'Bitek, 'Africa's Cultural Revolution', pp. 10-13.

19 Central Advisory Council for Education, '15 to 18', para. 625.
20 H.M. Phillips, 'Educational Co-operation between Developed and Developing Countries', p. 105.
21 R. Hooper, Education and the Mass Media, p. 79.
22 Ibid., p. 81.
23 H. Kökeritz, Sweden's Leading Correspondence School, p. 21.
24 V. Zhamin and B. Remennikov, USSR: Comparative Costs and Efficiency of Full-time and Part-time Education, pp. 310-12.
25 W.H. Gaumnitz, Correspondence Education in the United States, p. 125.
26 K.S. Cunningham, Growth and Extent of Correspondence Education in Australia, p. 2.
27 C.S. Forde, The Radio in Correspondence Education - New Zealand, p. 219.
28 C. Eakins, The Use of an Itinerant Teacher Service by the Correspondence School in Western Australia, pp. 197-8.
29 Asa Briggs, 'The Golden Age of Wireless', pp. 189-94.
30 Quoted in ibid., p. 185.
31 J. Nicol et al., 'Canada's Farm Radio Forums', p. 46.
32 J.A. Lee, 'Test Pattern', p. 14.

Chapter 2

LEARNING HOW TO TEACH

As we saw, there is a whole array of charges that can be brought against schools - for their irrelevance, for their poor quality, for their authoritarianism and so on. But the demand for schooling continues; we are in sympathy with it because of the inequity of a world in which some children get to school and others do not. We are therefore brought up against questions about the quality of education and what distance teaching can do for it. Why are many schools so poor? Can distance teaching do anything to improve them?

The celebrated New Zealand educator, Beeby, noticed something that many others have noticed before and after, that schools in many different developing countries are rather the same in their general style. 'The syllabus ... consists of little but completely mechanical drill on the 3Rs, and the memorizing of relatively meaningless symbols occupies most of the time.' (1) But he made a great deal more of the observation than most have done, partly because he coupled it with another about the state of schools in the nineteenth century in what are now the industrial countries. In English dame schools the same completely mechanical drills were the order of each day. An important conclusion followed. If at early stages of economic and educational development the schools of Europe or North America were very much like schools in Africa, Asia and Latin America today, it followed that the educational backwardness of the latter is not due to any characteristic inherent in their societies. The more likely conclusion is that they must be backward for the same reason that Europe used to be 'backward', as seen from the vantage point of today.

STAGES OF DEVELOPMENT

What reason? Beeby suggested, with considerable plausibility, that the vital one is the quality of the teachers. Teaching by rote is endemic because the teachers can manage nothing else. To depart from it is too dangerous. (2)

> The teacher in a village school who has himself struggled only to a doubtful Grade VI or Grade VII level is always teaching to the limits of his knowledge. He clings desperately to the official syllabus, and the tighter it is the safer he feels. Beyond the pasteboard covers of the one official textbook lies the dark void where unknown questions lurk. The teacher is afraid of any other questions in the classroom but those he himself asks, for they are the only ones to which he can be sure of knowing the answers.

A related issue is about the reason why some advance can be made from the dame school stage. That there can be there is no doubt, because it has happened so often. Beeby has chosen to divide up the progress made in primary schools into a number of stages. They are arbitrarily divided but that does not undermine the general thesis. Table 2.1 shows the stages.

Griffiths, writing of the Sudan, has given his own illustrations of similar stages: (4)

> I may illustrate the differences between my Type III and IV by two examples. In III a teacher might require a class of young children to read silently from their readers and answer questions which relate certain words to items in a picture or even to objects outside the classroom in order to establish a habit of looking for meaning. In IV he might in addition ask them individually to choose a similar incident to that described in the book, for example, a thunderstorm, and ask each to try to write his own description of a similar local event. His object would now be to encourage experimenting with words. In commenting on their work he has a more delicate and uncertain task than before and is in a less authoritative position.

This last approach demands confidence, above all, from the teachers, without which they cannot help children beyond the confines of a prescribed syllabus; and confidence depends upon actually having a much better grasp than the children whom they are teaching. Beeby's conclusion is that the quality of teaching depends more than anything else upon the quality of teacher training.

TABLE 2.1 Beeby's stages in the growth of a primary school system (3)

1 Stage	2 Teachers	3 Characteristics
I. Dame school	Ill-educated, untrained	Unorganised, relatively meaningless symbols; very narrow subject content - 3R's; very low standards; memorizing all-important.
II. Formalism	Ill-educated, trained	Highly organised; symbols with limited meaning; rigid syllabus; emphasis on 3R's; rigid methods - 'one best way'; one textbook; external examinations; inspection stressed; discipline tight and external; memorizing heavily stressed; emotional life largely ignored.
III. Transition	Better-educated, trained	Roughly same goals as stage II, but more efficiently achieved; more emphasis on meaning, but it is still rather 'thin' and formal; syllabus and textbooks less restrictive; but teachers hesitate to use greater freedom; final leaving examination often restricts experimentation; little in classroom to cater for emotional and creative life of child.
IV. Meaning	Well-educated, well-trained	Meaning and understanding stressed; somewhat wider curriculum, variety of content and methods; individual differences catered for; activity methods, problem solving and creativity; internal tests; relaxed and positive discipline; emotional and aesthetic life, as well as intellectual; closer relations with community; better buildings and equipment essential.

THE TIME TRAP

It follows that the length of time between Stage I and Stage IV depends in its turn upon the rate at which the quality of teacher training can be improved. There are limits to what is possible for any government. None, however autocratic or enlightened or rich, can command better teachers to come forth from its colleges. The process is inevitably long drawn out. Teachers are usually trained once - if at all - at the outset of their career, and then left to get on with the job of teaching for a working lifetime of thirty or forty years. If they can at best manage to teach in the manner of Beeby's first or second stage when they begin, they are unlikely to change their approach dramatically during a long career. No matter how training colleges change and improve, it takes a long time for cohorts of untrained or under-trained teachers to work their way through and out of the system. Despite her wealth, it took Britain a century, from the beginnings of a system of universal primary education in 1870, to eliminate the last untrained teacher from her schools. There are also other reasons why the process takes so long.

Primary school teachers form the largest part of the educational profession. Consider what happens at the earliest stage of all, when the first primary schools are opened. To begin with, in many countries of the third world, there were no local school teachers, and their place was taken by missionaries from outside the culture. Then there were a few students, a little brighter than the rest, who had struggled through to the end of primary school and returned to it as untrained teachers. Later on, teacher training courses were developed to follow straight on from primary schools; once secondary schools were developed then the training colleges were in competition with the new secondary schools - and the road to power and fortune lay more clearly through the schools than the colleges. Only when there are more graduates at secondary level than the economy can employ in more favoured jobs do secondary graduates begin to enter training for primary schools. And each time there is a demand to expand primary schools there is pressure to lower the qualification demanded from primary school teachers. Unless there is a lot of slack in the system, with enough school leavers at a particular level to meet the demand for more teachers, then the consequence of expanding primary schools is to lower the quality of the teachers in them. The expansion ordinarily proceeds in fits and starts, with sudden expansions and consequent dangers of a reduction in the quality of schools when primary schools are made free, and then again when they are made compulsory, with the same thing happening to secondary schools later on. After each jolt forward there may have to be a wait of ten years or more before some of the additional children in school eventually graduate as trained teachers. Obviously the educational system develops differently in each country, but there is a general tendency for it to grow in this sort of way, so that the basic education of the average teacher is only as advanced as that of those who went to school some years, sometimes a generation or two, back.

There is a certain inexorability about the process. It cannot with ordinary methods be speeded up beyond a certain point. Indeed, some countries are reluctant to speed it up at all, for simple financial reasons. Generally, the more qualifications a teacher has, the more he is paid by his employing government. Dramatically successful teacher in-service projects are therefore likely to be unpopular with finance ministries if they result in vastly increased salary bills for primary school teachers - often the largest single element in an educational budget. In-service training schemes have been halted in the past, in Kenya and in Nigeria, partly because no one was willing to foot the increased bill. But, given the political will, there are various ways in which the process of improvement can be speeded up.

LEAP-FROGGING THE STAGES

One way is to offer a variety of full-time courses so that the untrained teachers, or under-educated teachers, can be taken out of their schools and given the chance to catch up on the education they themselves missed as children. For some teachers this is clearly an ideal solution, but it presents major problems to others, especially once they themselves have families and homes which they cannot easily leave to return to college. This system also means that the ablest teachers - for it is generally the ablest who will be selected for further training - are repeatedly leaving the classroom in order to add to their qualifications. Until there is a surplus of teachers, they are inevitably replaced by teachers less qualified than themselves. A small study in Northern Nigeria of teachers on full-time courses, which is reported in Appendix 1, showed that many of them would have preferred to study part-time. (5)

Part-time and in-service training is certainly a practicable alternative. To achieve higher standards and gain confidence teachers have to acquire a fuller mastery of the subjects they are going to teach and to practise the skills of classroom teaching. Some of the work must be done face-to-face, through residential courses or through effective supervision of trainee teachers in the classroom. But some can be done at a distance and this opens up the possibility of training teachers without taking them out of school. If distance teaching methods can be combined with residential short courses and classroom practice then it should be possible to upgrade large numbers of teachers more quickly and with less disruption of their regular teaching. If Beeby is right about the dismally slow progress possible if we rely on full-time, pre-service, teacher training then this may be an important way of hastening the improvement of schools. A dozen or more countries have been sufficiently convinced of the potential to try it.

SOME INNOVATIONS

One of the first in-service projects was in the camps for Palestinian refugees. In 1963 their educational problems were similar to those of many other developing societies. Nearly 200 000 children of Palestinian refugees were in primary or lower secondary schools, where they were taught by 4648 teachers. But of these only 450 had received any teacher training; most had done a course of secondary education and nothing more. And the situation was getting worse rather than better, as more qualified teachers managed to get jobs not in the refugee camps but in the host countries of the Middle East. The United Nations Relief and Works Agency and Unesco looked at the problem and saw that it could not be solved by the classic methods of pre-service training: if you took the teachers out of the schools to train them, you would have to replace them with less experienced, and no better qualified, teachers. So it was necessary to devise a kind of in-service training which would be as good as pre-service. The two factors in favour were cultural and geographical: teachers in the refugee camps spoke a single language, Arabic, and, while the schools were in Syria, Lebanon and Jordan, they were all close enough together for the project staff to be able to visit them fairly easily.

In 1963 UNRWA and Unesco set up a joint Institute of Education to undertake the job. All students were sent correspondence lessons which covered both academic subject matter and teaching methods. They had written assignments once a fortnight which were based both on their correspondence lessons and on their classroom experience. But these assignments were not posted to their tutors: instead they were used mainly as the starting point for fortnightly seminars organised by the 20 field supervisors on the staff of the Institute. These supervisors have other functions: they distribute correspondence lessons, collect work for marking from the students and also supervise classroom practice. Thus they combine some of the functions of a college of education tutor with those of an inspector of schools. With a teaching load which was for some years 75 students per tutor and now seems to be about 50, they are the lynchpin of the Institute system. Their work, like that of the trainees, runs throughout the school year; for the trainees this is supported also by residential vacation courses.

It appears to have worked well: whereas in May 1964, 2140 primary school teachers out of 2384 (90 per cent) were untrained, by October 1968 only 350 (9 per cent) out of 4090 were still untrained. The main emphasis of the Institute's work has shifted; it is now on courses for secondary teachers and head teachers, and on refresher courses. The shift has thus been away from a crash solution towards a permanent programme of continuing education for teachers. The great strength of the techniques is that they enable teachers at the same time to increase their subject knowledge and their skills in teaching, through their written work and teaching practice, while developing the maturity without which they would never be outstanding at their job. Meanwhile the teachers carry on their ordinary work in their classrooms. Unfortunately the programme has not been evaluated. If it had we would know how far the hopes have been fulfilled. The one thing we know with certainty is that the costs look reasonable. In 1967 comparisons were made between the cost of a student year on the in-service course and a year on the pre-service course. An in-service year cost $341 and a pre-service year $820. (6) The Institute costs seem to have been lower partly because they had not had to put up a college building to house their students, and partly because the staffing ratios were different; in the late 1960s and early 1970s the Institute had a professional/academic staff of some 40 to 50, including 20 field supervisors to look after some 1000 to 1500 trainees. They also employed considerable numbers of part-time staff both to write correspondence lessons and to mark trainees' work. Even though the cost per student year looks as if it rose to between $579 and $776 in 1974, (7) this was still a good way below the figures for straight face-to-face study.

The UNRWA/Unesco Institute was one of a number of broadly similar projects started in the mid-1960s and after, ranging from a scheme for 600 teacher trainees in Botswana to ones launched in Nigeria and Tanzania for the thousands of teachers needed for Universal Primary Education. The projects took account of earlier experience with distance teaching in Australia, New Zealand and North America. And, while the early projects leant heavily on experience from developed countries, as time has gone on the exchange between third-world specialists on distance teaching has become more important.

One important difference between the UNWRA/Unesco Institute and the later projects in Africa is that the latter were able to use radio. The Institute had no access to time on its host countries' radio stations. In contrast the Nairobi Correspondence Course Unit (CCU), for example, had its own radio production facilities and staff, and daily programmes were broadcast on Voice of Kenya. (8)

> Although the written materials which the students receive from the CCU are self-contained and give all instruction necessary, radio broadcasts have been used regularly to supplement instruction in each subject in the same way that a classroom teacher would offer extra help to the slower students to encourage them, sustain their interest, answer their questions and help them solve their problems. The radio programmes have proved to be particularly useful for speech-work in the two language courses as well as for maintaining good *rapport* between the student and the teacher. It has been established that a large proportion of the enrolled students make a point of listening to the radio programmes regularly, although many of them may be working through their lessons either well ahead or behind the radio schedules.

Radio was also used in both Botswana and Swaziland, although in both cases the colleges responsible for teacher upgrading stopped producing radio programmes after early experiments with them. In part this seems to have been because of a shortage of radio producers, in part because those running the projects had their background in orthodox teacher training and in correspondence education rather than in radio. But the experience of Kenya suggests that there can be a major role for radio to play. If an upgrading project is to be successful, and make significant changes to the way in which trainees actually teach, then they need as much support as they can get when back in their schools. A regular radio programme can provide that sort of psychological support, and remind them not only of the subject matter of their course but also that they are not forgotten in between their residential courses. Beyond that, radio can be used for specific educational reasons - where aspects of a subject lend themselves to the spoken rather than the written word. And radio can demonstrate classroom work, showing how another teacher copes with his classes and with his subject matter. All of these kinds of teaching work better on radio than in print. But radio demands time, imagination and devotion to the inexorable demands of a weekly timetable. Neither its benefits nor its costs are immediately apparent; students rightly object if they are not sent their printed lessons on time or if residential courses are not properly organised. They seldom object as strongly if a radio programme does not come over the air or is replaced by music. Radio programmes look more like the optional part of a teaching package, and under pressure are the first things to be dropped.

This may have been less serious in a country as small as Swaziland, with a population of some 600 000 in 17 000 square kilometres, and good communications. It was relatively easy for the staff of the Swaziland college to visit and keep in touch with their trainees. They could visit any school in the country and still get back home the same night. The aim of the project, run from the William Pitcher Teacher Training College, was to cope with the need for teachers provoked by the expansion of primary schools in the late 1960s. Its objectives were: (9)

(i) to improve the teaching strength of the country by training some six hundred primary teachers [now 1200];

(ii) to inculcate modern methods, not only for use by the trainees, but also as a medium for change in others;

(iii) to organise the training in such a way that it caused the minimum of disruption to the staffing of schools at any time.

The students were mainly women, often with fairly long teaching experience, but with meagre previous education and hesitations about their own ability. This is how one described her approach to the course. (10)

> Before I went to the course, two tutors came to advise us to go and learn there. I told them that I could not imagine myself going to learn. But they told me that some aged from 55-60 are learning. They said that I should go and try for once, and if I failed only then should I leave....
>
> Then it really went as I wished. When I got there for my first course, the materials were all new to me and were also above the level of my standard. But I sacrificed myself with all my strength to try, though difficult was to me. I almost got mad because of education height that was new to me. But I sacrificed myself completely so that I should not prove to be the worse ignorant. The English lessons were new to me as I had never learned them at school before.... I can say all the lessons were new.
>
> Though Education was hard I eventually found myself understanding it because the tutor could explain a lot. I thank the patience of the tutors in uplifting the uneducated to the high education.

The course had three elements, apart from the radio programmes. Each student attended three in-college courses, at intervals of about a year, each lasting six weeks. The first in-college course came at the beginning of a student's involvement with the project, so that she could get the face-to-face help and encouragement necessary to keep up her enthusiasm when she returned to school. After this intensive introductory course, students worked at home on the second element of the course - a series of correspondence assignments on five subjects: English, education, mathematics, science and social studies. The third element was a series of visits paid by tutors to their students while they were teaching and working through their correspondence lessons. The tutors making these visits were the same ones who had taught the students in their intensive courses. While this was a distance teaching project, whose costs compared favourably with orthodox pre-service training, the school visits and intensive courses meant that there was a personal relationship between student and tutor. (11)

> The visits to the students have two objectives. They are, first, to see that the teacher is actually employing the methods and apparatus which they have been trained in, during the in-college courses; and, second, to help the teachers to overcome any difficulties they may be experiencing.

Students who worked through the course were awarded certificates by the Ministry of Education on recommendation from the College. Formal examinations were not held, as it was felt that, with the knowledge from three residential courses, seven or eight school visits and the record of students' correspondence work, project staff knew their students well enough to gauge who should and should not be regarded as a qualified teacher.

The course has been successful. About 580 of the original group of 600 students worked their way through to the end of the course, and there is some evidence that their teaching improved. Further students were then following the course. Hawes, when he visited the project in 1976, found that (12)

> Because of these two things - the amount of accompanying teaching materials (schemes of work, supplementary worksheets etc.) supplied to teachers undergoing the course work, and the amount of tutor contact there is a very high degree of enthusiasm amongst these teachers and a high rate of curriculum activity. With teachers from the programme in every school in the country (most average 2) the 'ripple effect' on the curriculum of the schools has enormous potential.

An internal assessment tried to check on how far the course was successful in terms of its objective of 'inculcating new methods'. Without thorough evaluation - such as has been done for few educational projects of any kind - it is difficult to be sure. But as far as it goes the evidence is encouraging. (13)

> The term 'new methods' is, naturally, a relative term. In the context of education in Swaziland, it means two things: the first is a departure from what is still very prevalent in many countries, the type of teaching that is centred on the teacher, who holds forth in oracular fashion, while the children supposedly imbibe the words of wisdom that issue forth. In place of this 'teacher-centred' education, the aim of the project has been to introduce a 'child-centred' education that permits the children to learn individually and in groups through activity methods, and through 'trial and error' methods. In other words, the child is allowed scope for the development of his own personality. The second meaning is that the education offered shall be environmental; it deals with a world that exists in Swaziland, not with a world imported from outside. This does not mean that things outside Swaziland are never mentioned; if they are relevant to life in Swaziland they are, in a sense, part of Swaziland. Probably the best demonstration of the environmental training can be seen when a visit is made to a teacher at his or her school, between courses. Not all teachers exhibit the same ability or diligence, of course; but every teacher will be found to have set up the various demonstrations which illustrate the environmental approach: pictures, diagrams, a 'shop', and the 'tables' which show particular features of life: a 'mass' table, a 'shapes' table, a 'water' table, a 'science discovery' table, a weather chart, items for local nature study and many more. The study of language will be assisted by many wall cards, charts, and pictures. The work being done by the children will be active, not passive; the learning process will be in groups; and for each group there will be worksheets, prepared by the teacher when in college, and simple apparatus, such as cuisenaire rods for number work....
>
> It is not easy to assess what their influence has been on teachers and officials other than the trainees, but it is now felt that the effect is cumulating noticeably. In many schools the practice of 'child-centred activity methods' was the first opportunity for many teachers (not members of the in-service course) to observe them in action. There are now schools, seen by tutors on their visits, in which requests for in-service materials and assignments are frequent. The fact is that the in-service teachers are taking into the schools, as a result of their training, a child-centred environmental form of education, using activity and play methods.

The scheme seems to have gone a fair way towards moving teachers into at least the third of Beeby's stages. It appears that teachers with only a very modest basic education can change the way they teach as a result of a good in-service programme.

SOME LESSONS FROM EXPERIENCE

When we put this evidence together with that from other projects a fairly consistent picture begins to emerge. Table 2.2 sets out the basic facts.

TABLE 2.2 Completion and pass rates in teacher up-grading projects

	Enrolled		Completed course		Completed course and passed exam	
	no.	%	no.	%	no.	%
Botswana: two cohorts three year course[a]	608	100	539	88	no examination	
Kenya: unqualified teachers (1968-74)[b]	8433	100	n/a	n/a	7632	91
Swaziland: first cohort[c]	600	100	580	97	no examination	
Uganda: three-year grade I upgrading[d]	1000	100	948	95	876	88
UNRWA/Unesco[e]: first two year course	862	100	759	88	713	83
Second two year course	592	100	595[f]	100	414[g]	70

a E.D. Hill, 'Final Report on the Francistown Teacher Training Project Botswana', p. 7. Our total (539) includes both those who had completed the course at the time of this report and those then expected to complete.

b David Hawkridge et al., In-service Teacher Education in Kenya, pp. 314, 324.

c C.H. Green, op. cit., p. 8.

d A.E. Kaye, Upgrading Teachers in Uganda, p. 67.

e Jack Lyle, The In-service Training Programme for UNRWA/ Unesco Teachers: Postscript - April, 1969, p. 369.

f Sixty teachers transferred from a three-year course into this two-year course, thus more than offsetting the dropout (ibid.).

g Some of these were expected to pass examinations at later attempts.

One feature the various projects have in common is a very high success rate if it is judged in terms of completing the course or passing the necessary examination. In Kenya, to go by another criterion, examination results for students of the Correspondence Course Unit compare favourably with those of either private candidates or school students - though the latter are at some disadvantage, as they have to take all the their papers at one sitting whereas the correspondence students can do them one by one. The evidence on examination results is meagre but, as far as it goes, encouraging.

In Kenya the effects of the course on classroom practice were investigated. The trainees themselves thought that (14)

> the in-service course had been useful to them professionally. About 99 per cent of them felt that their performance in the classroom had improved as a result of the course. Many of them indicated that they felt greater confidence in their teaching, and that they commanded greater respect from their fellow teachers than before.

Similar questions were put to the trainees' head teachers, education officers and supervisors who (15)

> felt that about 95 per cent of the teachers under their supervision had improved their performance in the classroom after the upgrading course. This was evident particularly in the three subjects they had studied, namely English, mathematics and either history or geography. More important was the observation that there had been visible improvement in the classroom performance and the examination results of the pupils taught by these teachers. The effectiveness of a teacher is still measured in most cases, unfortunately, by the performance of his pupils in the national examinations. Of the cases examined, 90 per cent reported some improvement in the pupils' performance.

The scheme has shifted teachers who took part from the first to the second of Beeby's stages. It may even have helped some teachers to reach the Transitional stage.

Although the evidence is again rather subjective, the Francistown scheme in Botswana seems to have moved teachers from Stage 1, the 'stumbling and lifeless repetition' of the pre-independence schools, to the Transitional stage, and for some of them to the final stage of Meaning. (16)

> The general reaction to the work done by students from the Francistown Teachers' College is extremely favourable. Headmasters have asked that they be given these students in order to strengthen their staffs.... Officers from other projects and prominent educationalists visiting the schools have said that they can always recognise a teacher from the Francistown College up-grading course by the interest of the pupils in the classroom, by the skill in organisation,

> and by the amount of simple teacher-made equipment and apparatus in use. Visits by field tutors from the College have revealed some outstanding work being done by the ex-students.
>
> The general opinion is that, without any doubt, the Francistown students stand out. They are more mature educationally. They are more enthusiastic. They are applying the spirit and practice advocated in the new Primary School Syllabus to better effect than is seen in most classrooms.

Both these projects appear to have changed teaching styles. The evidence is much too subjective and impressionist, but not much worse than that on much orthodox, residential, teacher training.

More recently, Tanzania has adopted distance teaching methods on a very large scale. In order to speed up the introduction of Universal Primary Education the government recruited in 1976 and 1977 two huge intakes of untrained teachers. They were deployed immediately into the schools with somewhat less than full-time teaching loads. At the same time they were enrolled in distance teaching courses which would eventually offer them the normal teaching qualifications. There are several features of the Tanzanian system which are significant for our argument. First, this was initial teacher training, but made available on the job, and able to cope with very large numbers. Second, the radio and correspondence courses were supported by a system of village-level professional study centres. Here the trainee teachers attended for one or two days a week, and received tuition from a local experienced and well qualified teacher seconded to the centre. His role, and that of the trainees' headteacher, was to guide and supervise their development of teaching skills as well as mastery of the subject matter. Finally, the trainees attended regular vacation courses in the teachers' colleges each year.

There may be advantages in adopting this model, even where the pressure of numbers does not mean that it is forced on to a government unwilling to remove teachers full-time from the classroom. Hawes, in the light of his survey of development in primary education in Africa, suggested that (17)

> First of all, the conventional idea of a course in a teacher-training college followed by teaching practice or short spells in one or two schools, is no longer the only practical way of organising teacher training. Teachers are now being trained in sandwich courses where the student teachers teach full-time for one school year and follow courses in education at a training college at other times, mainly during the vacations. There is a growing number of

> projects for in-service training of unqualified teachers where correspondence courses are combined with residential courses.... I am coming to believe that a curriculum reform project run in harness with an in-service programme would have considerable advantages.

What is needed is to take advantage of the particular strengths of the different elements within a three-way teaching package. Correspondence and radio can teach people facts, and, especially where radio is used imaginatively, can stimulate them at the same time. As for face-to-face teaching, this has an essential part to play. In any method of training teachers, the most important job is to help with the practicalities of teaching. But classroom skills and human relationships in the class are essentially something to show and to feel, rather than something to write or broadcast about. In college, or in teaching practice in a nearby school with supervision from the college, the trainee has a good chance of acquiring these skills.

Traditionally, at least in Britain and North America, the individual teacher has been in sole control of his classroom, subject to the limits set by a government or examination syllabus. This is still very much part of many educational philosophies, and means that a new teacher is left more isolated than is appropriate if he is learning how to teach in an in-service programme. The effects of isolation, no matter how you learn to teach, can be crippling. (18)

> How often are the bright enthusiasms, born in the good teachers' college, dimmed in the first year and extinguished in the second, by the daily reminder of poverty - no maps, no books, no paper, not even newspaper, no crayons, no cardboard, no wood, no needlework material - only chalk. And how much easier is this decline accomplished in the loneliness of the rural schools and the booklessness and darkness of the tropical night.

Distance teaching obviously cannot overcome all the isolation. But if linked with the trainee teacher's work in school it can do something to help. More important, the ideal teacher-upgrading scheme will move away from the assumption that the teacher should be left to work out his own salvation, confined within the walls of his classroom. Rather it will require that head teachers and education officers work closely with a trainee teacher in order to support and reinforce the distance teaching institution. If the distance teaching materials are to be directly relevant to the trainee's classroom work, then he will learn as he is teaching to rely to a considerable extent on materials coming into the classroom from outside. The relationship between himself, his class and outside materials will consequently shift. He may learn from the outset to see himself as someone with the function of encouraging learning among his students, but not as the person who knows all the answers - especially if he and they are together working on materials some of which he prepares and some of which come from outside the school.

There is some evidence that this has happened in Botswana and Kenya. Similarly in Swaziland there are good grounds for hoping for a new style of teaching. A few years ago one of the authors (19)

> saw some of the first batch of [correspondence] students... in a science course being excellently and imaginatively taught. If this example sticks it will be just the kind of thing that is needed to improve the liveliness of the primary schools. The shadow of examinations which, the world over, hangs over what should be 'education' seemed for these few moments to have been blown clean away.

Of course difficulties remain; the design of a distance learning system for training teachers demands that good teaching materials should be distributed regularly, and to the remotest parts of the country. If teachers are to use resources sensitively, they will need this support to continue after they have finished their training course - all the more so if they are edging towards teaching in a new and freer way. Without support from outside, teachers will naturally find it almost impossible to teach in ways other than they themselves were taught. But with such support, it is clear that they can do more than this.

Training teachers in this way may train them for something closer to the sort of school discussed in Beeby's fourth stage than is possible under the present system of pre-service training. This will mean that the trainee is closer to being an apprentice than a student. The implications are far-reaching.

NOTES

1 C.E. Beeby, 'The Quality of Education in Developing Countries', pp. 58-9.
2 Ibid., p. 61.
3 Ibid., p. 73, slightly abbreviated.
4 V.L. Griffiths, 'Teacher-Centred', p. 131.
5 Appendix 2, pp. 143-7.
6 Jack J. Lyle, The In-service Training Programme for UNRWA/ Unesco Teachers, p. 206.
7 E.A. Pires with B. Bartram, Teachers for Refugees, p. 294.
8 P.E. Kinyanjui, The Use of Radio and Correspondence Education for the Improvement of Teaching, p. 258.

9 C.H. Green, 'The Story of the In-service Teacher Training Project of Swaziland', pp. 1-2.
10 Ibid., p. 16.
11 Ibid., p. 5.
12 A. Aarons and H.W.R. Hawes, 'An African Primary Curriculum Survey', p. 22.
13 C.H. Green, op. cit., pp. 6-7.
14 P.E. Kinyanjui, op. cit., p. 261.
15 Ibid., p. 262.
16 E.D. Hill, op. cit., p. 8.
17 H.W.R. and C.R. Hawes, Réformes des enseignements primaires, p. 15 (our translation).
18 E.B. Castle, 'Growing Up in East Africa', p. 112.
19 Michael Young, 'Multi-Media Education in Swaziland', para. 9.

Chapter 3

CLASSROOM SUPPORT

The image of school, common to a hundred thousand cartoons, has three elements - a teacher, a blackboard, and rows of children. Since education is most easily, if least philosophically, defined as what happens in school, this is also the common image of education. The teacher writes on the blackboard, the children copy. Of course they do other things - dance, play, sing, fight - but that picture of the teacher, the blackboard and the rows of children remains. The stereotype, and often the reality, has changed little in a century. And yet, once broadcasting was invented to complement print, there was the possibility of creating a different sort of school, in which radio or television as well as books and pamphlets replaced at least some of what was on the blackboard. The question was whether we could move faster than Beeby thought possible, not just by training teachers more effectively, but also by providing them with more help in the classroom.

This is a practical problem of logistics as well as of education. There is no need to underestimate the practical difficulties, and the costs, of providing all schools in any country with radios, with batteries for the radios and with repairs when they go wrong. These difficulties are obvious, and are compounded by the need to produce and distribute books or notes to go with broadcasts, and to do so on a regular basis. Unless there is a consequential saving on primary teachers' salaries, the costs are likely to be additional to the regular costs of education. Primary school salaries are often so low that to try and economise on them means having less well-educated teachers, or worse staffing ratios. The educational problems are even tougher. They demand more than logistical solutions.

Our approach is not original. It is not very different from that of Illich and the de-schoolers. But we are not going as far as they did: whatever our reservations about schools the demand for them continues. Most parents want their children to go to them. And the demand for de-schooling has, for the main part, come not from the most deprived but from the most privileged. Others see schools, whatever their faults, as a way of increasing their children's control over their lives and life chances. They are right to do so, and schools are here to stay. To begin with, there must be more of them. At the same time they must change, as we have already argued. Then they must provide an education which in its style is near to Beeby's fourth stage, and which enables people to cope with their present environment and the kind of changes in it which are bound to affect them. In most countries, and at most times, it is the teachers who must change before the schools can. It is only in a cultural revolution, or in Paris at a time like 1968, that it is students who spearhead change. For the most part, the path is laid down by the teaching profession.

BROADCASTS AND TEACHERS

As schools have developed, so has the professionalism of the teacher, claiming intellectual as well as disciplinary control of his classroom. The process has been particularly marked in England, and has an important bearing on the way educational broadcasts have developed. Whereas under the monitorial system of the early nineteenth century the head teacher decided what each monitor should teach, the teacher in England now has great power to decide exactly what is taught within his classroom, as well as how it shall be taught. This freedom has led to a dilemma about the best way to use broadcasts for improving schools. On the one hand it has been argued that the function of broadcasts is to support, but in no way to replace, the teacher. When educational broadcasting in Britain began, for example, (1)

> The BBC in 1925 appointed Miss Mary Somerville to its educational staff, with a special responsibility for broadcasts to schools.... (She) saw the new medium as ... placing at the disposal of the teacher an instrument that would neither do his work for him nor even share with him the burden of his straight-forward curricular teaching. Its task would rather be that of bringing to every classroom a kind and quality of experience that would be otherwise unattainable.

Schools broadcasting was thus created as a way of enriching and improving schools, rather than as a way of replacing teachers, getting them to teach in a radically different way or offering education out of school. The limitation of this approach is that broadcasts are seen as an interesting peripheral piece of the educational system, not as something which could lead to major changes in the schools. Under any sort of pressure, enriching broadcasts are the first thing to go, with teachers reverting to their more traditional chalk and talk. In Britain, for example, secondary schools have been growing bigger as large comprehensive schools have replaced smaller, selective schools. Timetabling has become more problematic as the schools have grown bigger, and the use of broadcasts has dropped away simply because of the greater difficulty of fitting them into the timetable.

But broadcasting for enrichment has not been killed off. The quality of much educational broadcasting by bodies like the BBC and the Canadian Broadcasting Corporation has been very high, and their methods of working have had a wide influence. In the third world, educational broadcasting has developed firmly within that tradition of enrichment. It has been at its best, of course, not when slavishly following the BBC but when directly gearing to the interests of its own listeners. In Papua New Guinea, for example, a radio series (2)

> written by a teacher working in Papua and New Guinea and produced locally using some Papuan and New Guinean actors, was immensely successful. The stories contained emotional and mysterious situations which appealed to the local children. This intense, emotionally involved, listening situation was a far more favourable learning climate. Stories were serialised so that there was a continuing motivation and children would often remind their teacher if he looked like forgetting to have the radio ready and tuned in. Production of this series was not nearly so good technically, with more limited facilities and with only amateur actors, but the children were unaware of these sorts of imperfections. The story came alive in their minds because it was acceptable and appealed to their emotional tastes.

Kenya has a quite different success story. In the later 1960s, Voice of Kenya began to use a radio series called 'Beginning Science' to improve science teaching in the upper classes of primary schools. By 1971 'probably 80 per cent of Kenya's upper primary children in registered listening schools now learn their elementary science through this radio series'. (3) Radio seems to have been successful in getting schools to approach science in a new way. The broadcasts were supported by pamphlets, and there were regular visits to schools. (4)

In 1968, the number of schools to which pamphlets were sent

was doubled to 800, and in 1969 a further 400 were added. The full cost of the pamphlets was now carried by the Kenya Government. By this time, about 100 000 pupils' pamphlets had been issued free to schools and several thousand sets of teachers' notes. Continuous school visiting during 1967, 1968 and 1969 showed that the teachers using the series were gaining in confidence and so were making better use of the notes, pamphlets and experiments. This was most evident when visiting the same teachers over the three years - a very hesitant, unsure teacher in 1967 had become a competent, practical one by 1969.

The real test of the popularity and success of the series came in 1970. For this year, it was decided that the notes and pamphlets would be placed on the Kenya School Equipment Scheme list for sale to schools. No more free issues were to be made. The notes were taken out of the general book and published separately. The pamphlets were bound into three termly booklets instead of six subject ones....

The sale price of the notes was 25 cts. each and of the pamphlets Sh 20/- for a set of 30. For 1970 the schools ordered and paid for 3 000 sets of notes and 24 000 sets of pamphlets. For 1971 the order is 3 250 sets of notes and 27 000 sets of pamphlets. About 2 000 primary schools now take the series and the number is steadily increasing.

There have been similar stories from many other countries. The successes are certainly modest in comparison to the hopes for some of the world's spectacular educational television projects. But successes they are. Where enrichment broadcasts have succeeded they have generally used broadcasting stations which already exist, and studios and transmitters which would otherwise be under-employed during the daytime, so that their costs have been low. In these circumstances it is reasonable to attribute to educational broadcasting only the marginal costs - the costs incurred through using the studios and transmitters for a few extra hours a day - rather than the costs that would properly be borne if equipment were provided on a large scale mainly for education. In the third world, radio has generally been used, and costs have been kept at about one-tenth of what they would have been with television.

This kind of broadcasting is educationally successful within its limits. A broadcast which assumes that the teacher can effectively follow it up assumes that the teacher has the necessary pedagogical skills for this purpose. More fundamentally, it assumes that there is a teacher: broadcasts to support class work are not likely to be of much use for the children outside school who have no teacher at all. Broadcasters have bent over backwards to insist that they are not trying to replace teachers - even where there are no adequate teachers to be replaced. In Nova Scotia in the 1960s, to take just one example from many, it was decided to teach spoken French throughout secondary schools. The department of education came (5)

> up against the solid problem of finding competent teachers who can speak fluently the language to be taught. Of course, it has not been possible to find teachers fulfilling the last stipulation and it was necessary to devise another solution, that is to say, to do the work of several teachers by a single fluent teacher through the aid of television. Our television French course was born.

While this looks like an appropriate substitution of television for teacher, the Nova Scotia television producer hurries on to add carefully that 'even if the class teacher is relieved of part of his burden, he is still indispensable....' (6) So there is a curious modesty about the aims of supporting broadcasts. While they undoubtedly can make improvements to the quality of schooling, they are a long way from confronting the major problems of quality and quantity - of poor teachers and of the shortage of teachers.

TEACHING DIRECTLY

It is a bold step, then, for a broadcaster to go one stage further and suggest he should not merely support the teacher, but replace him by offering direct teaching in the classroom. On the face of it, it should be possible to use broadcasts for distance teaching of this kind, especially where we know that teachers themselves lack experience and training. And there is research evidence to show that, in theory, broadcasting can be an effective means of teaching. Research in the 1930s and 1940s showed that, if you taught the same subject matter by radio and in the traditional way with a classroom teacher, you usually found no significant difference between the results. (7) Similar results were found with adults, when Trenaman of the BBC established that differences between subject matter affect learning far more than the differences between the media used to present it. (8) He was followed by a small army of research workers who compared teaching by television with face-to-face teaching and, time and time again, found no significant differences between the results. (9)

If the research findings can be trusted then it looks as if broadcasting, especially when supported by other media, is an effective tool for changing school curriculum and methods. In the past, following Beeby's analysis, it looked as if a generation or more would have to pass before new ideas, new ways of teaching, could shift from curriculum developers to teacher training colleges and thence into the schools. If, however, broadcasts could bring directly into schools a better style of teaching and a new curriculum, then reform and dramatic improvements would be possible far more rapidly than Beeby's model would allow. At the same time the universality of broadcasts might reduce the differences between good schools schools and bad: this is how one British observer saw television's potential in the early 1960s, when American schools had embraced it with optimism. (10)

> Television, with other visual aids, is helping transform American education; it is already doing there what previous innovations failed to do, and will do much more; it may yet out-date the printed word as a teaching instrument for many purposes....
>
> It is successful in all subjects, but it is most successful in the hard ones, above all in mathematics. Television courses in history, or literature, even in science, are sometimes taken one year, but not continued the next. But very, very rarely are courses in mathematics dropped. Once a teacher sees that this instrument can do the really taxing job of expounding things like systems of numbering to the base of five instead of ten, then he almost always stays with it....
>
> Television can teach languages, too. Everywhere I went I was shown classes of children, aged seven, eight or nine, who could handle numbers, dates and conversational phrases in French which was recognizably Parisian, French which was frankly confessed to be better than that spoken by the classroom teacher. In the rich, white suburbs of Detroit it was impressive, yet appropriate enough, that the neatly dressed children could already use the Spanish they would need to go to Spain or South America, but it was even more impressive that the negro children in their shabbier clothes, their poorer schools, were just as quick with the same skills, chanting away the same phrases to their much less qualified teachers. From this I learned of a property of television teaching which I had not even thought of. It can really share the resources of a district between rich and poor, between every school and every child.

With that sort of optimism, broadcasting projects, usually based on television, have been set up in many countries. Distance teaching in the classroom has, for example, been seen as the best way of teaching French in secondary schools in Glasgow, most subjects in Samoa and the Ivory Coast, mathematics in Nicaragua. The variation has been from programmes dealing with just a few subjects to large-scale television ventures in which the whole curriculum was covered. Curiously, the grander and larger projects came first: a handful of countries leapt straight from the idea of broadcasting for enrichment to the idea of television as a major tool. But it seems more logical to start with the more modest programmes, where distance teaching methods have been used with limited aims. The experience of the Mauritius College of the Air (MCA), for example, suggests how distance teaching can be used in a small way to improve the quality of school education.

The College was set up in 1972 and its methods were based on the experience of other countries with distance teaching. At that time the quality of secondary education was the severest problem identified by the ministry of education in this small and densely populated island. Nine children out of ten already went to primary school: a fortunate 6 per cent of them then went on to government secondary schools and 9 per cent to grant-aided ones. The rest of the children went to less well-endowed, less well-equipped and inadequately staffed private schools, or did not go to secondary school at all. MCA's first move was to try to improve quality in the secondary schools, partly by making the curriculum more relevant. An initial programme of courses was drawn up to test the methods of distance teaching during an experimental year in 1973. Of these the first two were General Certificate of Education 'O' Level or School Certificate subjects aimed at fifth formers and private adult students. One was English language, which Mauritians do not normally use in ordinary conversation but which is vital for passing exams and for getting jobs: the second was human and social biology, a new subject for secondary examinations and one which lent itself to MCA's stated intentions, being at once an introduction to a scientific discipline, to a future career and to home-making and parenthood.

In February 1973 these two courses were launched. Of the island's 130 secondary schools, 34 enrolled for the English language course, and 26 for human and social biology. Nearly 2500 students took English and approximately 1000 biology. Demand in the second year was much greater, so much so that MCA's plans for courses with out-of-school students had to be delayed. More courses were added in the second year, each one organised slightly differently, according to subject requirements and support facilities. They enabled schools to add subjects like agricultural science and woodwork to the curriculum which could not otherwise have been introduced.

With the English course MCA set out to provide something which would certainly cover the syllabus but would at the same time provide a culturally appropriate setting in which to practise English. The materials consisted of correspondence units, television and radio programmes, and in-class teaching.

The whole process was co-ordinated by MCA tutors who kept in regular touch with the classroom teachers.

It turned out that the function of the television programmes in stimulating interest could be performed as well by radio. Often the radio set out to lead drills in language patterns which students were likely to find difficult. It also included aural comprehension passages in which they were given a chance to hear and try to understand a continuous passage of English. Almost by accident the tutor discovered that these comprehension passages could stimulate writing projects. Two such passages became instalments in a Mauritian suspense drama, and some students could not wait for the next instalment. They were encouraged to produce their own conclusions, and their eagerness to do so resulted in a writing competition, with the best results read out over the radio. The radio programme also served another purpose: every fourth week it was devoted to recordings of students together with advice to them. (11)

Mauritius showed that the teacher could support a child following a correspondence and radio course while improving his teaching at the same time. The MCA materials were locally produced, and because they consisted mainly of print they were relatively cheap. The broadcasts added dimensions of their own. All the time there was feedback from the children to the teacher, and to MCA and back again, so that the programmes and texts could be constantly adjusted to fit the needs of the schools.

The Mauritian experience was not unique. There is evidence from Nicaragua which confirms much of what the MCA found. There radio was used to improve mathematics teaching in schools, again with direct teaching over the air. (12)

> The Radio Mathematics Project assumes responsibility for all the mathematics instruction children receive. A daily lesson consists of a thirty-minute radio presentation, followed by approximately twenty minutes of teacher-directed activities, for which instructions are contained in a project-developed teacher's guide. Children use either printed worksheets or their own notebooks for written responses. Teachers are asked to supply simple materials such as bottle caps and sticks....
>
> During the broadcast part of the lesson, the children are asked to respond orally, physically and in writing, and they do so 50 to 60 times during each thirty-minute lesson. Sometimes children handle concrete materials during the broadcast - for example, counting or grouping bottle caps. After the radio transmission the teacher continues the lesson, following the directions given in the teacher's guide.

So far this project appears to have been going well. Efforts were made to train the teachers, and to support them generally in their use of radio. As the project was introducing new mathematics, which the teachers could not readily have taught without support from outside, and as it was dealing with only one subject, it was not too surprising that teacher opposition was not reported. The early results suggested that children were learning effectively - as the research suggested they would - and more tentatively that repetition rates within primary school might be falling after the introduction of the mathematics project. (13)

GREATER AMBITIONS

The aims of these two projects were quite modest: MCA began by introducing two courses for one year of secondary education, while the Nicaragua mathematics project was concerned only with mathematics teaching. Such projects are untypical. When television was introduced some educators saw it as an instrument of far-reaching reform. As we saw in chapter 1, large and expensive projects were launched in turn in American Samoa, in El Salvador and in the Ivory Coast. They were launched because they looked as if they might be the only way of achieving the dramatic changes needed. The Samoan educational system, for example, had suffered from decades of neglect. A new governor regarded television as the sole solution. (14)

> There was no time for waiting, no time for 'armchair patience' - there has been too much of that for sixty years, he has been quoted as saying.... He was turning over in his mind a daring idea: could television be used to share the best teaching, and to spread the use of English over the islands?

His was a bold enough vision of a new kind of school, and he had the means to realise it. The capital outlay on the project was enormous. A national television transmission system had to be built, which was no easy job given the nature of the terrain. A huge school rebuilding programme was started. The aim was over 60 hours of programming each week, with support materials and support staff. The programmes were made and the schools equipped to receive them. The foremost American educational broadcasters came to advise, and vast numbers of dollars were spent on the first major attempt to reform third world schools through distance teaching. And yet, despite the efforts and the imagination, opposition to the project by teachers and parents built up to such a point that, after ten years, it was dead. By 1973 - with a new governor in post - the service was redefined as a classroom enrichment support service. (15)

Just as the Samoan dream was changing to a nightmare, television projects elsewhere rose and fell. A closed-circuit television service was launched in Glasgow in 1965 to overcome the teacher shortage; it closed down in 1975. Television was used to teach physics in Sierra Leone, then totally abandoned. In the Ivory Coast, launched on a scale comparable to that in Samoa, it survives, but appears to be adding to the cost of education rather than reducing it, (16) and in 1975 depended on the employment of 187 expatriates. (17)

But while the picture is depressing it is not entirely dark. Though grand attempts to reform education through television have achieved very little, often at great cost, this is not to say that television cannot be used effectively. In El Salvador television was introduced in 1969 as part of a general programme for reform of secondary education, including changes to the curricula, school buildings and the organisation of the ministry of education and teacher training. As in Samoa and the Ivory Coast, the idea was to use television for direct teaching in the classroom. Television sets were installed in over 80 per cent of secondary schools by 1971. It was possible to use existing television transmitters, and there were no problems of getting a television signal to remote schools in a country of only 22 000 square kilometres. In contrast to Samoa and the Ivory Coast, control of the project remained firmly in Salvadorean hands and policy decisions were made locally, not by expatriate advisers. At an early stage, for example, the United States Agency for International Development (USAID) wanted to concentrate on primary schools, although El Salvador's priority was to raise quality in the lower years of secondary school. The Salvadoreans won the argument. Another positive feature was that they put efforts into supervising the work of teachers using television in the classroom, and provided in-service training for them. By 1972 courses were being offered in all three junior secondary grades to some 48 000 students.

Yet despite the attempts to train teachers in the use of television, and to involve them in the reform, reactions against it built up to the point where, in 1972, there was a teachers' strike. (18) It was not just against television: as a result of the reform work-loads were increased, and teachers were in danger of losing out financially. Examining fees they could previously earn were no longer available, as children were promoted from grade to grade automatically instead of by examination. But the reform survived the strike, and there is evidence that children learned more under the reformed system than they had done previously. The project was thoroughly evaluated, at least in its early stages: tests compared the work of groups of students following the old curriculum and the new curriculum both with and without television. Although at first there was no significant difference between the latter two groups, (19) over a longer period students on the reformed curriculum with television support performed slightly better than those with the same curriculum and no television. (20) The way the teachers taught in the classroom changed too: they used visual aids more, dictated to the class less, and got more lively responses. One observer commented that after the reform (21)

> Salvadorean teachers were in Beeby's 'transitional' stage. They were beginning to rely less on lecturing or rote learning and more on student activity; they were asking more 'thought' questions (that is, questions with more than one correct answer); and they were encouraging students to ask their own questions, state their own opinions, and work on individual projects. These characteristics were all observed frequently enough to suggest that El Salvador's classroom teachers are changing, but also that they have far to go if the Reform's ambitious goals are to be achieved.

Perhaps more remarkable still, rural children, usually at a disadvantage compared to urban children, gained comparatively more than urban children did. (22)

So there have been some successes and some failures in the application of distance teaching to schools. There is enough evidence both ways for us to be able to sketch out conditions for the success of a distance teaching project to improve schools - conditions which need to be met if unorthodox methods are to be used with any hope of success.

CONDITIONS FOR SUCCESS

The first condition is that the support of local teachers and administrators be won. A project must be designed so that it is appropriate for the teachers who will work with it. It is significant that the El Salvador project matched the stage (in Beeby's sense) that its teachers had reached. And it is here that the Samoan scheme went spectacularly wrong. All initiative was taken away from the teachers: the children were taught by television, detailed notes for teachers and worksheets for students defined how the rest of the time was to be used and a non-Samoan educator was posted in each school to supervise activities. Nothing was given back to the teachers in terms of new status, or new subject matter to teach. Not surprisingly, they rebelled against the scheme. And not surprisingly they benefited little from it: rote learning, criticised in 1961 before the television reform, was still a feature of the schools eight years later. (23) Perhaps the project would have survived if there had been local support for it from administrators, but their feelings were neglected in the same way: (24)

> the Samoan counterpart to the American assistant director of elementary education, a man who had been elected chief of half the island of Tutuila and certainly a skilled diplomat and administrator, was given a desk in the outer office with the secretaries.

In contrast, the more successful projects embraced both teachers and administrators as partners. Teachers in El Salvador were trained thoroughly in the use of broadcasts, and were closely supervised as they worked in the classroom. Each classroom was visited once a week by a supervisor whose job was to help and advise the teacher. Once initial problems were solved about the exact role of the supervisor, this seems to have been an effective method and one that for the most part ensured teacher support rather than opposition to the reform. There was, too, fair success in getting teacher support in Mauritius and Nicaragua.

Nursing teachers along in this way is unlikely to work if their confidence and competence is too limited. Direct teaching by broadcast is then seen by them as a threat to their autonomy and their expertise: teachers with little training, working at the level of either of Beeby's first two stages, have particular difficulty in switching their role to that of counsellor and guide to the television programmes, although this was implicit in the design of all the grand projects. There is a general problem here. Any large educational project relying heavily on teaching materials produced centrally has a tendency to be authoritarian and tightly controlled from the centre. It has been suggested that many of television's (25)

> inherent characteristics are those which tend to reinforce hierarchically arranged learning patterns and student passivity - a one-way communication, authoritative teachers as role models, and self-contained instructional units with follow-up activities designed to reinforce a message. The assumption in the whole model is that learning results from the transmission of knowledge and information in a direct line from television set to pupil, who forms part of an inert mass quietly imbibing the information.

If this were the whole story it would imply that the best that distance teaching can do is to create a dame school of the air.

An unwilling partnership between teacher and television

does little more than duplicate the pattern of rote learning. Where distance teaching methods have been used in this way, they have not moved the education system very far in the directions we suggested that we wanted to go. And, just as they have demanded a limited and predictable response from the student, so they have reduced almost to a cipher the role of the teacher.

Not surprisingly, teachers have often rebelled against the role assigned to them in attempts to improve schools in this way. The Samoan teachers' successful demolition of the project as originally planned, and the Salvadorean strike, are the more dramatic examples of a common reaction. If distance teaching methods are to be used effectively in school, then a new relationship is created between the children, the teacher and the media which are bringing teaching into the classroom. Neither the traditional model, with the teacher as the main source of knowledge, nor the Samoan model, with the teacher reduced to the role of slave to television's magic lamp, is the right one. The new-model education will need a new-model teacher. There is all too little evidence from the history of distance teaching in schools so far about what sort of teacher he will be. But it is clear he will be moving towards being a manager rather than a source of information and that, in encouraging such a move, administrators must be sensitive to his existing skills and background.

So our first condition is that the relationship between class teacher and distance teaching must be one that the teachers approve. Since such a system is one which improves schools by adding extra teaching elements, the second important condition is that the results justify the extra costs.

The size of the extra cost obviously depends upon the choice of medium. One commentator has concluded: (26)

> Too often technology selection has preceded the examination of a country's educational needs (and, further ... the selection of educational television itself usually occurred with, at best, only a cursory and inconsequential look at other possible approaches for meeting the educational problem). In essence, then, the 'solution' to the problem was chosen before the nature of the problem was properly identified or at least subjected to critical scrutiny.

The unthinking choice of television has had two effects. First, it means that there has been a comparative neglect of radio, although recent experience suggests that what television can do can often be done as well by radio and at a tenth of the cost. The second effect is financial: many projects have cost far more than they might, because of the high expense of television. The costs are, of course, much higher where a television system has to be created, as in

Samoa or the Ivory Coast, than in countries where it exists and can be used at marginal cost only. In the Ivory Coast the television system is now expected to cost 20 to 50 per cent more than traditional teaching. (27)

Unfortunately most of the evidence on costs concerns television, and for anyone who identifies distance teaching with that medium, distance teaching can be damned on cost grounds. That would be unfair. Distance teaching does not have to use television at all. But of course we have to accept that, whether or not television is incorporated, the costs of distance teaching were additional to the regular costs of schools in most of the projects discussed.

There are exceptions to this general rule. In El Salvador, the whole process of educational reform resulted in larger classes and a longer working week for teachers. Television was seen by the ministry of education as providing help to teachers who saw themselves as overburdened. As a result, the cost per student after the educational reform may well prove to be lower than it was before, despite the introduction of television. (28) The Salvadoreans may have found a way of getting better education on the cheap, if they can only maintain the support of their teachers. In Nicaragua the cost of producing high quality teaching material was such that the radio mathematics project increased costs dramatically, but also reduced the dropout rate from schools. As a result, the cost for each student completing the course may finish up no higher than before. (29) Evidence from Mauritius confirms that the cost of the MCA courses is additional to the costs of ordinary schools. But the extra cost per student is lower than the amount parents are willing to pay in private tuition fees, seen as an alternative way of improving the quality of their children's education. (30) The general conclusion must remain that distance teaching usually adds to the cost of schools, although these three projects are exceptions to that rule. If fewer children drop out of school or repeat classes then the additional cost may be justified. And distance teaching may also be a cheaper way of improving schools than the alternatives.

All in all, the evidence about distance teaching in schools is not encouraging. But problems of quantity as well as quality are facing us and, in theory at least, it ought to be possible to use distance teaching to extend schools to people who would not otherwise reach them. And offering opportunities to people who would otherwise not have them is one way of creating a more egalitarian system.

CREATING SCHOOLS

In the West, the British Open University and similar institutions are providing such opportunities at tertiary level. In the third world, distance teaching has been used more often to create new institutions at the primary and secondary levels. As with attempts to improve schools, television has been a key element in many of the programmes. One of the most interesting attempts to create schools where there were none before was in Niger. While - once again - it looks like a grand failure for television, the project was imaginative, and points a way forward to the use of distance teaching methods to create a different kind of educational system. In 1962 only 5 per cent of the children were actually attending school, and there was no prospect of being able to find enough teachers to expand the schools on anything like the scale needed. At the same time as the president was beginning to explore the idea of using television to substitute for the missing teachers, Unesco and the French aid agency (Agence de co-opération) were beginning to contemplate the use of non-traditional methods. The three interests came together in a plan to ensure that 30 per cent of primary-school-age children would be in school ten years later.

The new schools were to be quite new. The children would be taught entirely by television, not by teacher. But they would not be a passive audience; the programmes would demand an active response from the children, and would teach them how to discover and learn things for themselves. They would have the support of adults in the classroom, but these would be monitors - young, untrained primary school graduates. To sidestep the problem of multi-lingualism, all the teaching was to be done in French.

The project got off to an excellent start. In 1964, 22 pilot classes started work. Two of these were attached to the television studios at Niamey so that the children's reactions could be carefully observed, and the other 20 schools were rural but near to the capital. By 1972, 510 of the original 800 children had graduated from primary school without ever having a face-to-face lesson from a trained teacher. This proved that the system worked. Also remarkable was the children's attitude to learning. In traditional society in Niger the elders have authority, and children are expected to ask no questions; these children were taught to question, to find out for themselves, and were soon doing so enthusiastically. One of the things that made this possible was that the curriculum was closely tied to the children's environment. Although the project got off the ground very quickly, time was made for a careful study of local village life, including an analysis of the agricultural cycles, so that the themes of the television programmes fitted in with what was actually happening in the villages. The role of the monitors was particularly interesting, pointing to a new pattern for distance teaching. Most of the monitors were young, about 20 years old, and they were not seen as threatening authority figures. Their job was to organise the children's activities throughout the day. They were helped by their own television programmes before the start of each day in the classroom, and a manual which laid down procedures for that day in very great detail. (31)

Interesting light is thrown on the monitor's role by an experiment conducted in 1971. (32) For one week, the children were left to run the classes on their own. All went smoothly; some of the older children came early to watch the monitor's programme, and they managed to follow the day's instructions in the manual. But although everything was apparently functioning normally, at the end of the week they showed signs of fatigue and stress. There is no reason to suppose that the children were less competent than the monitors in following the day's instructions; on the one hand some of the monitors had difficulty in doing this well all the time themselves, while on the other, some of the brighter, older pupils by this time knew more than their own monitors. What this finding points to is the importance of the adult's presence for motivation and support. Perhaps the children would not have continued coming for much longer without their guide. As one child commented, 'the television set doesn't breathe'.

So far this account has been a success story: young children learning in a foreign language directly from television. But something went seriously wrong. The original plan had been for 30 per cent of the primary age children to be in school by 1973, with television as the main organ of expansion. A few dates and facts tell a very different story: (33)

- 1967 Still only 22 classes: the 'plan' was re-named an 'experiment'
- 1968 Still only 22 classes: original target 500
- 1970 5th year class added
- 1972 Beginning of expansion of television transmission network
- 1974 Television signals now reaching 200 kilometres from Niamey: 122 television classes
- 1975 214 television classes serving 9000 children (10 per cent of those of primary age)

The 30 per cent target was far from being reached.

What went wrong? There was a complete lack of integration

with existing facilities in the country. Tensions between expatriate and Nigérien staff on the project were compounded by the opposition from the existing broadcasting and education services. These were probably the main causes of failure to expand. There were also logistical difficulties in extending the television system over the whole country. Moreover, the costs of this were so great that the project showed no chance of making economic sense. Although the system could, potentially, save on teachers' salaries, the cost of television was such that the scheme would have been economic only if at least 100 per cent of children of primary school age were to go to television schools. Television, with its heavy capital cost and dependence on sophisticated support, looks once again like a false start for any general reform, despite the attraction of its glittering screen.

And yet the Niger scheme cannot be written off, for it succeeded educationally, despite its catastrophic failure economically. The ideas behind the project - of using monitors, and of enabling them to relate centrally produced materials to the children's own experience - are relevant to the analysis of educational problems with which we began. It suggests that one could conceive of a different sort of school, relying on distance teaching. This suggestion is supported by evidence from Mexico - a country in which such projects make better economic sense, as there is already widespread television coverage. A distance teaching system has been created there at secondary level. This was done to provide an alternative to the normal three-year secondary course for some of the 180 000 primary school graduates who had no access to secondary schools. The problems were in the countryside where in many areas there were too few primary graduates to justify opening secondary schools. It was decided to try television schools.

In 1968, 304 classrooms were opened in eight different states of Mexico. Children from all three 'years' of the secondary cycle sat in the same classroom. Each hour of television was divided into three 20-minute sections, one for each of the three school years. The children were supposed to watch only their own year's programme, spending the next forty minutes studying their workbooks. Despite the difficulty of learning in this way, there is no doubt that 'Telesecundaria', as the scheme is called, gave the opportunity of secondary education to thousands who would not otherwise have received it; by 1976, 50 000 students had graduated and 61 000 were studying under the system in 16 states. The scheme was also fairly cheap; in 1972 it cost 25 per cent less to produce a Telesecundaria graduate than a graduate from a normal secondary school. If the comparison was with the costs of extending ordinary schools to remote rural areas with a small demand, the savings were even greater. (34)

The 'teachers' in the television schools were monitors, ex-primary school teachers who were given three weeks training and were then supported by their own television programmes, and by printed guides and schedules. The monitors were to supervise learning in all the subjects of the secondary cycle, and it was hoped they would adopt more modern methods of teaching, but this has not happened. In a study of classroom activity it was found that in 80 per cent of the classrooms the students never asked a question, the teachers never asked a question that required opinion rather than fact, and in all the classrooms the only learning aid in obvious use, apart from the printed texts, was the blackboard. (35) This confirms our earlier hypothesis that teachers cannot bypass Beeby's stages, they can only move through them. However, the monitors did not, apparently, resent the system, perhaps because they had been promoted from primary teaching.

Despite the disappointing standard of class teaching, the children in television schools did about as well as children from ordinary schools. Rural children generally had a poorer home background and lower performance at school. But though the urban children still did better, the gap was closed a little between urban and rural. The evaluators suggested (36)

> The apparent answer is that the instructional television of Telesecundaria makes a difference in learning; that a less talented and disadvantaged group given the chance to learn by instructional television and a classroom coordinator can overcome the disadvantage and achieve equally with regular secondary students.

It would be an exaggeration to attribute all the success to television. Probably contributory factors are that classes were small (average 23) and that those few rural children who actually got as far as secondary school were very keen.

'Telesecundaria' was far from being revolutionary. Children received a formal education whose meaning lay mostly in the graduation certificate, seen as a passport to jobs in town - even if there were no jobs available. The curriculum offered was a formal one, relevant only to urban white-collar jobs, so that in rural areas the end result of the project was to help the drift to the towns.

The evidence on extending schools, like the evidence on improving them, comes mainly from television. Economically it looks a bit better: if you can economise on buildings and on salaries, then you may be able to afford the heavy costs of television. But it is worth asking whether it would be possible to use radio with as grand ambitions as those of the big television projects and with a greater chance of success. The economic arguments are all on the side of radio. And it is easier to maintain a radio than a television set. If a radio project could work out the right relationship with its participant teachers, is there a chance for achieving large-scale educational reform?

THE PROBLEM OF SCALE

There are two last points we want to make in this chapter. The first is about scale. A project as small as 'Telesecundaria' could not create a rural curriculum in a country where the prevailing mode was quite different. There is a dilemma here. It is often the small projects that have the greatest appeal. It is easier to reform small corners than to make a wholesale reform. Tiny Niger television with its handful of schools is educationally more exciting than the huge Ivory Coast scheme 800 kilometres to its southwest. La Voz de Atitlan, a Guatemalan radiophonic school for adults, keeps close to the interests of its peasant students by concentrating on a community of 50 000, when it would be ineffective or politically unacceptable if it tried to reach the whole of Guatemala. The other horn of the dilemma is that it is extremely difficult for a small project to influence a whole educational system, or to work in a different direction from that of the system as a whole. Where an educational system is dominated by examinations, as for example in Mexico, it is virtually impossible for a school or group of schools to fight against the diploma disease by itself. It is especially difficult when the school is teaching a group of students who are already educationally deprived: they are the most vulnerable to the disease. In Botswana, the Brigade Movement, which has tried to combine work and learning in a new combination for secondary age children, has been tolerated within the school system, and provided a useful and interesting alternative secondary route for thousands of children. But children and parents alike see it as a second best for those who have not managed to get into regular secondary schools, and its effect on the regular school system has been minimal.

In theory the dilemma - small enough to be easy: big enough to change the system - has often been tackled by setting up a pilot project which then could be replicated on a larger scale. This is the approach we favour, but only if the pilot has the potential to solve a major educational problem if all goes well.

Much recent educational thought has suggested that the teacher should be more of a manager than a source of information, more someone to help children as they learn than someone who instructs them and provides them with memorised information. Among the resources which such a teacher should be able to command are those provided through distance teaching. Experience from a handful of broadcasting projects has suggested that ill-equipped and under-trained teachers can use distance teaching resources in this way and offer an education which is in principle the same as that offered by the best teachers in very wealthy child-centred educational systems. But many educational projects using broadcasting have in practice gone wrong over the relationship between the teacher, distance teaching methods and the student.

This view of the teacher is also the only one appropriate to education outside the walls of the school. As his job is to guide learning rather than to provide information on subject matter, he requires different skills from those of the traditional teacher. This shift in function suggests that one can sometimes use, quite effectively, monitors or helpers with less training than is necessary for an orthodox teacher. Or - to look ahead to the latter part of the book - if we are concerned with education for adults, we can contemplate designing an effective educational system without creating huge cadres of adult educators, by using as counsellors, or group leaders, or tutors, people with the relevant human skills rather than people with specialist subject knowledge. The social organisation within which such tutors will be working, at least with adults, will be something quite different from the orthodox school or even the school helped along its way by distance teaching. And so we turn next from the schools to the people outside.

NOTES

1 John Scupham, 'Broadcasting and the Community', pp. 167-8.
2 B. Halesworth, Radio Broadcasts for Schools, p. 58.
3 John Ball, Beginning Science, p. 79.
4 Ibid., p. 82.
5 L. Graham, Pupil Participation in the Teaching of Languages by Television, p. 267.
6 Ibid., p. 267.
7 The research is summarised in, for example, N. Woefel and I.K. Tyler, 'Radio and the School'.
8 Joseph M. Trenaman, 'Communication and Comprehension'.
9 Godwin Chu and Wilbur Schramm, 'Learning from Television'.
10 Peter Laslett, Teaching by Television, pp. 4-5.
11 Tony Dodds, 'The Mauritius College of the Air: The First Two Years', p. 21.

12 Barbara Searle and Patrick Suppes, The Nicaragua Radio Mathematics Project, pp. 78-9.
13 Dean T. Jamison, 'Radio Education and Student Repetition in Nicaragua', p. 29.
14 Wilbur Schramm, Educational television in American Samoa, p. 14.
15 Agence de co-opération culturelle et technique, Samoa.
16 Martin Carnoy, The Economic Costs and Returns to Educational Television, p. 47.
17 A. Kaye, The Ivory Coast Educational Television Project, p. 156.
18 El Salvador has long been ruled by one of the most repressive military oligarchies in Latin America (Rutilio Sanches, 1972). Strike action must therefore have been taken only under extreme pressure. While the television reform remains interesting as a possible model for other countries, one should bear in mind the unpublicised effects of the totalitarian political situation.
19 Wilbur Schramm, 'Instructional Television in the Educational Reform of El Salvador', p. 45.
20 Henry Ingle, Reconsidering the Use of Television for Educational Reform, pp. 126-7.
21 Ibid., p. 132.
22 Robert C. Hornik et al., 'Television and Educational Reform in El Salvador', p. 44.
23 Lynne Masland with Grant Masland, Some Cross-cultural Implications of Educational Television, p. 187.
24 Ibid., p. 185.
25 Robert F. Arnove, Sociopolitical Implications of Educational Television, pp. 10-11.
26 William Perron and Michael Kirst, 'Organizational and Administrative Considerations', p. 78.
27 Martin Carnoy, op. cit., p. 47.
28 Dean T. Jamison et al., 'The Costs of Educational Media', pp. 161-2.
29 Dean T. Jamison, op. cit.
30 Tony Dodds, The Mauritius College of the Air, p. 392.
31 Arlette Bienfait, L'Ecole et la télévision, especially pp. 113-23.
32 Arlette Bienfait, Recherches Pédagogiques, pp. 107-24.
33 Data derived from Agence de co-opération culturelle et technique, Niger - télévision scolaire en marge.
34 John K. Mayo et al., 'The Mexican Telesecundaria', chapter 2, especially p. 27.
35 Ibid., p. 23.
36 Ibid., p. 66.

Chapter 4

CORRESPONDENCE COURSES

In the mid 1980s, ten million children will finish primary school in Nigeria with no chance of going on to secondary school. Of course, many will go into employment, many will have benefited from a better primary education than their parents or elder brothers and sisters, and many will later enjoy opportunities for further education as adults. But hundreds of thousands will want an immediate chance of some alternative to the education obtained by the more favoured million and a half who get into secondary school. Advertisements like this from Lagos will assure them that there is an alternative in correspondence education: (1)

Exam Success Correspondence College
(AFRICA'S MOST SUCCESSFUL POSTAL COLLEGE)
believes in your future

FOR A BRIGHT FUTURE
YOU
NEED A SOUND EDUCATION
AND
FOR A SOUND EDUCATION YOU NEED A TOP GRADE
PASS AT FIRST ATTEMPT IN THE G.C.E. OR W.A.S.C.

TO US IN 'EXAM SUCCESS' IT DOES NOT MATTER WHAT YOUR PRESENT EDUCATIONAL QUALIFICATION IS OR WHAT TRADE OR PROFESSION YOU ARE IN OUR SCIENTIFIC TECHNIQUE TAKES GOOD CARE OF EVERYBODY

The College's name, 'Exam Success', and their advertisement, reflect the public image of correspondence education as a way of becoming qualified - with stress on the qualification - and so gaining personal advancement.

It is a far cry from Nyerere's vision of education as a

prerequisite for group action for social development. (2) But correspondence education, and distance teaching which has correspondence lessons at its heart, has been widely used to offer alternatives to school. This is relevant to our theme in two ways. First, whatever their failures and excesses, correspondence courses have offered a route open to those deprived of secondary education, and so have done a little to redress the balance of equity between those selected and those rejected. And, second, the experience of distance teaching for school qualifications suggests ways in which it can be used for other purposes also. (3) For generations to come there will be numbers of people, in town and country alike, who want to study for school qualifications, even though they have left school without them, or cannot get to school.

IS CORRESPONDENCE EDUCATION ANY GOOD?

Correspondence has been attractive as a way of expanding education because it looks simple and straightforward. (4)

> For its main advantages relate directly to the source of the problems. First is its economy: school buildings are not required and teachers and administrators can be responsible for many times more students than they can accommodate in a school. Its second main advantage is its flexibility: people who have got jobs can study in their own time, in their own homes, without being removed from their work for long periods. Its third advantage is its seven-league boots: it can operate over long distances and cater for widely scattered student bodies.

Correspondence was widely adopted in the newly independent nations of Africa in the 1960s as a way of offering alternative routes to education; it was assumed - although there was then little hard evidence on the point - that it was an economic way of teaching people, as well as an effective one. In Kenya, Malawi and Zambia, for example, governments established correspondence units working at secondary level between 1964 and 1967. Other African countries, English and French speaking, were to follow.

Acceptance by ministries of education was eased by the first-hand experience that many civil servants had of its effectiveness: in most developing countries the passport for many of them had been correspondence education, especially during the colonial period when orthodox opportunities along orthodox routes were even fewer.

Two kinds of objections have been brought forward against correspondence education - first, that it is essentially impersonal, missing the human communication which is the essence of good learning, and second, that it is inefficient with appallingly high drop-out rates. The first argument is on the face of it a strong one, but looks a bit irrelevant when there is a shortage of teachers and the alternatives are packaged learning or none at all: if it is turned into a question about the best way to use printed resources and living teachers, then one may perhaps produce a better pattern of use for both. But this is to anticipate: if the method is no good because of inherent inefficiency, it may not be worth bothering with at all.

There are a number of difficulties about answering even apparently simple questions. How many people complete correspondence courses or drop out of them? How many pass their examinations at the end? Courses vary enormously in length, so even where we have statistics from more than one institution we often cannot compare like with like. Nor does information from colleges about the number who have completed courses give an accurate picture. Many correspondence students work through only part of a course, or work through it all but make little or no use of their tutors. These students may still pass the examination, but from college records it looks as though they have dropped out. Also, examination results do not tell the whole story of a student's achievement or lack of it. Apart from the fact that they are a somewhat arbitrary measure of achievement, many adults discover as they study (as with any sort of education) that their personal reward has very little do do with the barren certificate they were pursuing at the outset. In discovering themselves and their interests they may turn in a completely new and unexpected direction.

All the same, examination results are often the only measurement we have. But correspondence students generally enter public examinations as private candidates, and cannot easily be distinguished from others. If you rely on students telling you their results, then you build in a favourable bias, for since people are reluctant to admit to failure, it is mostly the successes which are reported.

There is less reliable information from the poorer countries than from the rich, but we do have a little, such as the pass rates in the Kenya junior secondary examination for students at the University of Nairobi's Correspondence Course Unit (CCU). These look better than the figures for children in school, with a pass rate of 51 per cent for CCU students in 1970, compared with 47 per cent for government-aided schools and 13 per cent for private candidates. (5) But the school students had to take all their subjects at once, where the adults could do them one at a time, which makes direct comparisons hazardous.

At the Swaziland International Education Centre, a new correspondence college, pass rates in the first year (1975-6) for a growing range of Junior Certificate subjects were between 50 and 93 per cent.

These examples of high pass rates, higher than at school, are paralleled by the evidence from Europe. Figures for pass rates in secondary subjects or complete courses (for example the French 'baccalauréat', the secondary school leaving certificate which acts as a qualifier for entrance to university) show between 70 and over 90 per cent of entrants passing. Telekolleg, a Bavarian college using television, print and group teaching for secondary equivalence examinations for adults, had in 1969 a pass rate of 96.5 per cent. (6) That these are not exceptional is shown by Hermods Correspondence College in Sweden. With 75 years experience and an excellent reputation, they are able to state that students who do take their examinations 'do somewhat better on average than comparable students in traditional schools'. (7) It is certainly possible to learn by correspondence, if you keep at it.

But many do not, and it is here that the statistics are most inadequate. Many commercial colleges simply do not reveal them. Swedish and Russian experience suggests that drop-out rates of 50 per cent are normal, even with very considerable support to students through methods other than correspondence. (8) The French figures, which are difficult to interpret, may show a similar figure for the 'baccalauréat'. And some drop-out figures are undoubtedly nearer the 70 to 80 per cent range. In Norway of a sample of 1417 adult students at the respected NKI Skolen, 283 (20 per cent) were still active two and a half years after starting. Forty-nine or 3 per cent had completed their course and 77 per cent had discontinued their studies. (9) These were, by our standards, unusually long courses, virtually all of them having more than 32 lessons. At Telekolleg, despite the pass rates of over 90 per cent, only 28 per cent of those enrolled for its first two courses had got their passes after three years. (10)

The evidence from the Swaziland International Education Centre compares favourably with this. Between February 1973 and August 1976 only one third of all the students had ceased work. Total enrolments over that period had been small, only 477 students altogether. Of these, 31 had been suspended for non-payment and 40 had not sent in work for a long time and were assumed to have discontinued. A further 86 had not sent in work for between two and four months. Some of these may have resumed work later, so the drop-out rate may have been even lower. Often drop-out figures are difficult to calculate, because people work at different rates, and in fits and starts. One person may complete what was meant to be a year's course in three months, another may work on slowly for three years.

So the evidence is patchy, especially for courses at a modest educational level in the third world. We have concentrated on this level, as the problems of higher education look somewhat less severe than those for schools or adult education. But the one institution on which there is a wealth of data is, by contrast, the Open University in Britain, working at degree level in a rich country. Given all these advantages, the Open University ought, if anybody can, to show good results. If it were failing, economically or educationally, then the traditionalist argument that education must be done in orthodox classes would be immensely reinforced. Happily, the early evidence from the Open University is encouraging. Students have been graduating; drop-out rates have been kept down; Open University degrees have been accepted as of a quality and standard comparable to those of other British universities. The two key studies on the Open University's costs showed that it was continuing to provide graduates more cheaply than other British universities. (11) While these successes reflect the strength of the University's methods as a whole, the core of its teaching is offered through correspondence courses, the main element in its teaching system.

Two general conclusions emerge. First, in so far as one can generalise from this mainly Western experience, it seems that enabling people to pass examinations is not the problem. The rigour that is involved, both for the writer in creating a correspondence course and for the student in following it, is such that it will get you through the examination it is aimed at. But, second, drop-outs are a much greater problem, and it looks as if one must expect these to be between 50 and 60 per cent of those who start out on secondary schooling by this method. Despite this, there is a case to be made for it on grounds of cost-efficiency.

Again, evidence about costs is scattered and by no means clearcut. For distance teaching to be economic, there must be enough students to justify the cost of writing the courses and setting up a system to produce and distribute them. Where there are only a few hundred students, then costs can easily exceed the costs of conventional, face-to-face study. In Kenya, for example, a programme to provide secondary equivalence courses to teachers cost more for each successful student than regular schools. (12)

Telekolleg in Bavaria, West Germany, takes adults from elementary school-leaving level to the examination which is a passport to college for technical, economic, social and arts professions. Traditionally, this is a three year course, two years in evening classes followed by one in full-time further education. Telekolleg teaches instead by a combination of television (carrying the core of the teaching), printed texts (containing enrichment material and exercises) and regular Saturday group meetings. The scheme started in 1967, and in that year there were two intakes, totalling about 17 000 students. In November 1969, 2983 of these took the examination and 2878 passed.

The costings available for this period (13) are rather confusing, but if we take as a base the number who passed (although research showed that several of the television series had a regular audience of over 200 000, who must have thought they were benefiting too) the cost per student per year to the state (which organised the groups and the examinations) was DM 434 ($109), and the cost to the broadcasting service (who produced the television programmes and printed materials, and distributed the latter) was DM 1600 ($400). This does not take into account transmission costs, nor does it account for the DM 144 ($36) each student spent on texts over his period of study. However, it gives us a figure of DM 2043 ($511) per student per year; the cost of one student per year in a Bavarian secondary school was DM 2240 ($560) and in the sixth form was DM 2280 ($570). So the system is slightly cheaper for each graduation, and much cheaper if you attribute some of the costs to the non-completers and the 'invisible' audience.

But such figures themselves are not the end of the story. First, there is an opportunity cost to full-time education: if these students had stopped work for a year in order to study, they would not have been contributing to the national economy during that time. There is thus a hidden saving to the state if people are in employment rather than studying full-time. Second, the system yields another saving in the form of buildings. It is not necessary to provide extra colleges for extra students. In the main, they study at home, and the regular Saturday group meetings for students do not need special buildings either; existing educational - or non-educational - buildings can be used. And so distance teaching programmes regularly save money in ways which do not show in the accounts. Such savings are difficult to compute accurately but are of economic importance.

Some schemes look even cheaper. Nippon Hoso Kyokai (NHK), the Japanese state broadcasting authority, offered upper secondary education to adults, again presenting the bulk of the teaching through broadcasts, this time using radio as well as television. With drop-outs running at or just above 50 per cent the cost per student per year was still (1971 figures) $308 compared with high-school costs of $540. (14) In South Korea an Air Correspondence High School has offered an alternative route to secondary school qualifications and produces results at less than half the cost of regular high schools. (15) In the Dominican Republic the radio school Radio Santa Maria, which used distance teaching methods, had costs per enrolment about half those of more traditional adult education. (16)

Quebec Province's Tévec (1967-9) shows even more spectacular savings. (17) Designed as a pilot project to give lower secondary education (seventh to ninth grades) to adults in an area of the province where 90 000 adults had only had primary education, it offered a combination of television and correspondence teaching with strong face-to-face; there were 70 'revision' centres for group meetings and one home visitor employed to support 80 students. The whole project cost 3 000 000 Canadian dollars. Of the total population of the area (250 000):

52 500 watched the TV programmes regularly;
35 000 enrolled for correspondence work;
29 700 followed the course to the end (drop-out was only 15 per cent, and over 50 per cent sent in correspondence work regularly);
12 000 passed the final examination.

Traditional education for the same course would have cost $25 000 000 for 25 000 students. Leaving aside the benefits to the rest of the audience, those that passed had cost the state only 25 per cent as much as school completers.

The Tévec project was notable for more than its cheapness and efficiency. The curriculum offered was not based on the school curriculum. It was modified so that what was learnt was linked with the life and problems of 'Québecois' adults. The way it was taught was different from school, too, in that participants did not learn passively but were encouraged to define local problems, and to do something about them. (18)

> The Tévec staff talk ... of changes to communities like one where an unemployed Tévec student successfully ran for the office of mayor in place of the holder who had been in office for 25 years. Tévec groups gained the confidence necessary to summon before them the mayor, or the president of the school board or the curé: in one case a successful appeal to the bishop meant that the curé was drummed out of town.

Part of the cost-saving here comes from the fact that adults have considerable experience anyway. If it can be tapped, and if the learners can realise that their own experience is worth something, then learning becomes easier and quicker. We know of no other project costs that show such outstanding savings compared with conventional education - yet there was no stinting in support services.

As with the evidence on effectiveness, that on costs is

patchy and incomplete. But as far as it goes it strongly confirms the view that there is a case for using distance teaching, so long as there are enough students following courses for there to be economies of scale. Distance teaching can be used to enable people to pass their examinations and to do so cheaply. Within its limits, correspondence education does work.

THE LONELY STUDENT

But the limits are significant. The correspondence student is necessarily isolated; he lacks the stimulus of discussion with his tutor or with other students in his class, and, lacking that stimulus and those points of comparison, finds it difficult to know how he is getting on, and is easily discouraged. The loneliness of the correspondence student is a recurrent theme of discussion. This is how one of the students of the National Extension College, UK, on a residential course run by the College, described the isolation: (19)

> I started this degree lark because I wanted to understand things, understand them more than you could with newspapers and the telly. So I thought; right, Economics - that's the thing, and I've been bashing away at it by correspondence for a couple of years now. But this week is the first time I've ever had a chance to talk to a real economist. Never even seen one before! I just can't describe what a chance like that means.

The isolation from a tutor means that, even when a student's work is marked promptly and returned to him, there is a considerable delay between learning or practising something and getting informed feedback on it. This can have a number of unfortunate effects. First, the student may not be able to get on with his course at all. If he cannot do a problem in mathematics, for example, he may not be able to do anything more until he gets help from his tutor. Or, second, if he is working in a less sequential subject, he may actually learn something which is wrong, and find it hard to unlearn owing to the delay in feedback from his tutor. In either case he may get so frustrated with waiting for a response from his tutor that he simply gives up. The problem of delay is, of course, far worse in a country with a slow postal service.

A third and worse effect of the separation of tutor from learner, inevitable if printed correspondence lessons alone are used, is that the method of study will lead to a passive form of learning. If the correspondence student has only his correspondence text to rely on, then he will tend to follow it slavishly and uncritically. A major problem for correspondence writers is to produce lessons which help the student and inspire his confidence, but at the same time encourage him to develop a critical attitude to the subject matter and even to the course itself. This can be done, for example, by asking the student to make his own observations and experience part of his work, so that his communications with his tutor become a dialogue, instead of a corrective monologue. But this is very difficult to achieve, and it is particularly hard for the isolated learner to gain confidence in what he is doing. Thus, while we have criticised rote learning, it is difficult to avoid the conclusion that correspondence courses actually lend themselves to it. While we have criticised the diploma disease, correspondence courses are undoubtedly used as a way of catching it. In folklore, and probably in fact, you can pass examinations most easily by trotting out platitudes about the prophets or the mores of the British constitution that you can mug up from any half-decent textbook or correspondence course. For such reasons, religious knowledge, defined as a knowledge of Christianity, is very popular among Hindu and Muslim students in Mauritius. There is therefore considerable pressure on students to learn by rote, especially if they have learned that way at primary school, and to believe that to satisfy the examiner all they need do is reproduce what is in their course.

So there are inevitable limits to the value of correspondence. In practice, many courses have been even worse than they needed to be because they have been left in the hands of commercial interests. As in many other social services, the needs of the market place and the needs of education are in conflict. The higher the drop-out rate, the less work a correspondence college has to do for its students and so the higher its profits. Conversely, the more services it offers to students, the higher the ccsts. Even where correspondence colleges are honest, and conform to a code of ethics, there is a fundamental contradiction between maximising profits and providing the best service to students.

One disadvantage of commercial colleges relates to the linking of correspondence with radio and face-to-face teaching. In Britain, for example, there was no non-profit multi-media college offering examination courses to the general public until 1963; and no action by the state educational system in this field. At the same time, adult education was generally in state hands and broadcasting was run as a public service. This meant that there was no obvious body to link correspondence teaching with the work either of adult and further education centres, or with radio, until the National Extension College was set up in 1963. As a non-profit college it was in a position tc build up these links.

Not only had the commercial colleges no incentive to link their work with broadcasts or evening institutes, but they would have found it constitutionally most difficult to do so.

CORRESPONDENCE AND OTHER MEDIA

Yet it is in the links between correspondence and other modes of education that we can see a way out of the problems inherent in correspondence teaching on its own. This is how it works in Lesotho. The Lesotho Distance Teaching Centre (LDTC) was set up by the International Extension College in conjunction with the government of Lesotho to provide formal and non-formal courses, aiming to improve the quality of life in Lesotho generally and to provide courses for formal qualifications. There is considerable demand for the latter. With as much as 80 per cent of primary age children starting school, and only a very small percentage of these going on to secondary school, there are many children and adults who have not had a chance of a full school education. Opportunities for employment for them are starkly limited. The mountains that cover much of Lesotho, and the soil erosion which eats away much of the rest, leave only 15 per cent of cultivable land. The alternative to living on the land, if you lack formal education, is to sell your labour to the gold mines of South Africa. Secondary-level qualifications are seen as a route away from that sort of life. LDTC therefore responded to requests for secondary-level courses.

The Centre arranged for courses to be written in the major school subjects, and began to provide weekly radio broadcasts to support them. Some of these were on the techniques of study, in order to help people learn more effectively. More of them were about the subject matter of the various correspondence courses, teaching through radio what could not readily be done by print alone. In English, for example, they provided practice in using and understanding spoken English; in agricultural science they dramatised the issues involved in agricultural change by means of a weekly dialogue between old and young farmers. The broadcasts were to stimulate and encourage the students, pacing their work, week after week. The combination of broadcasts and correspondence looked like a more hopeful way of offering education out of school than either medium by itself. But LDTC soon decided that they must do more than provide just these two elements. Their reasoning went like this: (20)

> I assume that written materials alone will not help the majority of students in Southern Africa to pass academic examinations. The reason for my assumption includes the following:

a) language. All students will be studying through a second language. Comprehension of written materials will be poor.
b) environment ... Most students study at home without electric light. The size of the family and the size of the house usually have an inverse correlation and students can't find a quiet place to work.
c) learning habits ... Students in primary schools are for a variety of reasons (including big classes, teachers' learning habits etc.), taught using rote methods. They are not taught to handle written materials.

Reasons which apply in every country - such as unrealistic assessment of the work involved, the difficulty of working without help etc. - also apply in Southern Africa.

For all these reasons, many students in Southern Africa, as in other countries, find learning by themselves difficult. LDTC therefore set up study centres where students could come once or twice a week, work in adequate comfort and good light by themselves at their courses, and seek help from an 'elbow-tutor' as they needed it. The function of the tutor was not to teach, so it was not necessary to staff study centres with a full complement of subject specialists. Rather it was to be at the student's side, encouraging him and suggesting ways around problems that were proving too difficult. The tutor was a guide to the written materials and to study techniques, rather than someone who was himself providing information about the content of lessons. This pattern of study groups was closely modelled on a similar scheme in Zambia where, under the auspices of the ministry of education's Correspondence Course Unit (CCU), (21)

> students work in groups during the daytime under an administrative tutor. They follow a set timetable and use the CCU courses designed for home study. Worksheets follow each lesson in these courses and these are sent in to the CCU for marking and returned through the supervisors. There are about thirty lessons in each of the six subjects in the three years course.

In Lesotho then, the Distance Teaching Centre has moved a long way from simply providing correspondence courses, and has used other media to overcome their inherent disadvantages. In particular, the use of study centres looks like providing the human element lacking in much distance teaching in the past. But problems remain; in Lesotho they were severe enough for the Centre to have moved towards running weekend courses at regular schools. There, as elsewhere, not all students can get to study centres and not all want to. Half the students of the Open University in Britain make no use of study centres. The evidence on their effectiveness suggests that it is very difficult to run a study centre which does not soon turn into an imitation school, and a poorly endowed one at that. Tutors expect to teach and not to be tutors or guides to learning; students expect to be taught, not to be helped in some different style. But despite the problems, the shift in focus from an individual learning by himself to a group coming together to study may be an important clue to the future of distance learning.

The group study idea has also developed elsewhere in the world, from a different starting point. Since 1947 radiophonic schools have been operating in Latin America, offering a basic education to peasants. They use a somewhat larger amount of radio than African correspondence colleges (many radiophonic schools own a radio station), printed materials and study groups with monitors (the 'schools'). In the next chapter we will look more closely at these. Here we describe the operation of one school in the Caribbean which offers an efficient alternative primary education to young adults who have not been to school or have dropped out of it. Most radiophonic schools work at primary level because this is the most immediate need in the countries where they operate. But the methods they use are equally applicable to secondary level.

Radio Santa Maria (RSM) in the Dominican Republic was started in 1964. The aim was to provide literacy courses and the equivalent of primary education in rural areas where educational opportunities were far worse than they were in the towns. Attempts were made to rework the curriculum so that it avoided the tendency towards rote learning, and related more closely to the educational needs of rural people. This is how the system works: (22)

1 The basic educational aid provided for the student is a weekly set of six to eight attractively printed lesson sheets, one for each subject, carrying on one side an outline of the material to be explained in one week of radio broadcasts and on the other a series of written exercises. These lesson sheets, which over the twenty-three weeks of a course form a combination text and workbook, are distributed to the student each week for work in the home. Thus, the system of Santa Maria resembles a correspondence course with broadcast explanations and a weekly meeting with a field teacher.

2 Second in importance is a one-hour daily broadcast (Monday through Friday) explaining the material in the lesson sheets; one half hour is given to explanation and one half hour to working the exercises.

3 Supplementing the lesson sheets and daily broadcasts is a field teacher who is to correct the written exercises,

answer student questions, and detect weaknesses of individual students so that help may be given if necessary. The field teacher also performs administrative tasks of enrolment, giving examinations, and forwarding student fees to the central office. Through the field teacher, the student receives personal guidance in his or her own studies....

4 As a communitarian dimension of the learning process, the field teacher holds a weekly meeting with the students of his or her 'sector' to answer questions in a group context, explain material which is a problem to the whole group, provide general reviews for examinations, and give the examinations. An important part of this weekly interchange is the discussion of a social question which has been the 'central theme' of the various subject matters during the week.

5 Radio Santa Maria provides other general cultural and educational radio programs for different age and occupational groups which are designed to provide a cultural and educational support to the more formal educational process.

6 Although Radio Santa Maria maintains no staff for promoting organizations at the community level, its educational programs work through existing organizations, and the activities of these organizations are looked upon as an extension of the more formal educational courses. It is expected that students of Radio Santa Maria will consider active participation and leadership in community organizations as part of their education. According to a survey in 1975, some 60 per cent of the students were participating in some community organization, especially in the neighborhood youth clubs.

The pattern of organisation developed by RSM differs from most radio schools in the large part played by the field tutor. It looks as if the key to success may lie in the link between his role and that of the print or broadcast produced centrally. The evidence of its success is that RSM gets people through the equivalent of primary school more cheaply than orthodox education, and with fewer drop-outs. As usual the figures are patchy and difficult to interpret, but a study in 1974 suggested that RSM schools had a drop-out rate below 10 per cent per annum, while in the regular primary schools 70 per cent of students left without getting their leaving certificates. (23) The costs are thought to be 50 per cent lower than the costs for regular schooling, and 60 per cent of RSM's income was accounted for by the fees paid by students in the radiophonic school. (24) Comparisons, using official sixth and eighth grade examinations with school and RSM students, showed that the latter performed as well. (25)

The Latin American radiophonic schools and the African distance teaching units have very different starting points. The former began with a priest using radio to reach his flock, while the latter decided to use correspondence courses in order to make good the deficiencies of colonial education. But over the last ten years both sets of institutions have moved closer in their thinking, and both now see group learning as a central part of their work. While it remains vitally important to get the quality of printed materials or broadcasts right, this shift in focus suggests that the even more difficult and important job is to get the face-to-face element of distance teaching organised in the best way. The Latin American radiophonic schools have all used monitors or auxiliaries to support the work of the groups: these are not teachers but people from the area where they are working, who have received a short training on ways of supporting and helping their groups. This may be a more useful guide to the future than the attempts to get teachers to work as elbow-tutors for correspondence students. In either case, there are striking advantages in trying to study within a group rather than as an individual. It is a way of overcoming the isolation of the lone student, and a way for him to get help from his family or his neighbour. Potentially, once we move away from the equivalent of formal primary and secondary courses, it is also a way of trying to move from group learning to group action.

Indeed, you can be even more visionary and suggest that this is the way much adult education ought to be organised: with groups of individuals coming together to study something of common interest and benefit, and to do so free of the restrictions of schools, syllabuses or examinations. Neither the correspondence-based groups nor the radiophonic schools are quite that sort of institution. Perhaps the nearest things to it are the Swedish study circles, which play such a central role in adult education there that one in every four adults belongs to a circle.

These study circles began in the last century, when Sweden was a thinly populated country with few opportunities for education in rural areas. There were not many teachers, and certainly not enough to supply adult education groups. The study circles began as reading groups; each week the participants read part of a book and then came together to discuss it. There was no teacher, and no need for one; the meeting was led by one member of the group who simply acted as discussion leader. Quite often the members of the study circle took it in turns to act as leader. (26)

> The study circle organizers, the participants and the circle leaders were themselves able to dedide upon the

> methods of work to be practised in the study circle. In study circles one was taught how to use co-operative techniques, how to train one's capability to present points of view and to debate, one was trained in writing and summarizing answers (correspondence circles, training in letter writing). This type of study circle was mainly used within the Labour Movement when training members and officials. In the study circle it was also possible to be trained in those subjects needed for their own profession or work. A person dealing with the co-operatives read economy and accountancy; the farmer studied questions concerning husbandry and animal-breeding; the trade union leader studied social science and questions regarding agreements etc.

The Swedish study circle movement has developed to the point where it enjoys considerable state support. Government grants are paid to any study circle provided it satisfies some simple conditions, mainly that it has at least five participants, that each participant has access to study material and that the circles must meet for at least 20 hours altogether. Each circle decides for itself what it wants to study, and there are no limits imposed by the state on subject matter. Members are recruited in any way that seems appropriate. Most are organised by unions, church organisations or adult education bodies who encourage their own members to take part. But they also use newspaper advertisements, distribute brochures, and employ outreach workers whose function is to seek out potential students and encourage the organisation of circles which will meet their educational needs.

Study circles now use many other resources besides books. One of the major Swedish correspondence organisations, Brevskolan, produces study materials mainly directed towards the needs of the circles. They are designed to be used in groups as a basis for discussion, and then for individual study between circle meetings. Similarly, study circles have used radio and television series as a basis for their work. The variety of materials available in this way, with Brevskolan's 350 different courses, means that the individual needs of circles can be met, while the numbers are great enough for the economic production of good support material.

This ought to work well, and in many cases it does. But there are problems, which come from the role of the leader - or rather the circle members' perception of his role. (27)

> Circles can develop into a form referred to as the 'school class', with recipient pupils and an instructing teacher. Another deviation from the ideal is the 'coffee party', in which a great deal of emphasis is put on the camaraderie of the circle and discussion centres round things which have nothing to do with the members' studies.

A third deviation is said to be the 'therapeutic group', in which activities concentrate unduly upon individual mental or social problems. Personal problems are then liable to stifle the acquisition of other knowledge.

Of these three deviations, the 'school class' appears to be the commonest.

When members of a study circle come from an orthodox school background, it is inevitable that there will be a tendency for them to see the circle leader as a teacher.

There is an obvious parallel here with the history of study centres in southern Africa: in both cases the temptation to try to re-invent the school seems always to be there. Though we may try to create an education outside school with the advantages of a non-institutional environment, the teacher is still likely to be treated as a source of authority and knowledge. This is one aspect of a general problem. As we saw in previous chapters, one of the changes we have been looking for in education is a movement away from an authoritarian view, whether this emphasises the authority of the teacher or the authority of the textbook, and towards education 'to increase men's physical and mental freedom' as Nyerere put it. We want to create an educational system which helps people to solve problems for themselves, but calling for appropriate resources from outside their environment when they need them. To do this, we have to abandon the 'banking' concept in which the teachers' didactic and authoritarian role is emphasised. The Swedish study circles, like the study centres in Africa and radio schools in Latin America, have moved in that direction, but all are still struggling with the assumption that teacher must be there as an authority figure.

Individual correspondence students are faced with a similar problem. In the absence of a teacher they may endow their printed lessons with the same sort of authority. Part of the shift in educational philosophy which we are seeking involves a move away from rote learning and from the irrelevant acquisition of trivial information - those bric-à-brac of British constitutional history or the details of the geology of the Thames Valley we have mentioned before. One of the ways of making that shift is to use distance teaching materials: you can use them in order to make relevant information more widely available and give students an alternative to what is in a pile of mouldering textbooks or in the head of the nearest teacher. But this is to be idealistic: in practice, as we have seen, distance teaching can too easily degenerate into rote learning. So there is an apparent contradiction here. We are suggesting that distance teaching methods can be used as a way of liberating education, when we know that in fact they have been used as a poor substitute for the worst sort of the education we have been criticising.

The resolution lies in using distance teaching imaginatively and in drawing on the experience of group study. If the ideas presented in a correspondence course are used as a starting point for group discussion, then participants will use and criticise the ideas, not merely reproduce them unthinkingly. In this way you can meet educational needs and at the same time minimise the risk of 'banking' and of rote learning. The group activities are essential. In many distance teaching institutions they have been seen as a useful optional extra, while the main burden of work has rested on the correspondence lesson and the work the student does on paper in relation to it. The emphasis needs to shift away from the individual to the group if we are to create a genuinely liberating educational system. This means that correspondence and radio lessons need to be aimed at groups of people rather than at individuals, and need to be designed to open up discussion rather than foreclose it. This reminds us that it is not possible to reform an educational system simply by manipulating distance teaching methods. If the examinations which people have to take as a means of social mobility demand the reproduction of irrelevant trivia then it is impossible to write good correspondence courses for them. But with a better formal education system, or outside the formal system altogether, distance teaching methods linked with group study can be used for different educational ends.

None of this is easy, but the experience we have quoted shows it is possible. Distance teaching can be organised in a variety of ways to help people get formal qualifications. But it is less educative, and less fun, without a face-to-face element.

Where correspondence courses are used to compensate for a lack of formal education, there is always a danger of emphasising the worst sides of schooling - rote learning, reliance on the authority of the teacher, worship of certificates. But correspondence education can be the bridge between formal and non-formal education. The students are outside the walls of an educational institution, although learning school subjects. The way forward is to use group study methods that are the foundation stone of good non-formal education.

Distance teaching can clearly be used to extend formal education to people who otherwise would have no chance of getting it. The experience that has been gained over the last quarter century, however, is more significant than that, because it suggests ways in which distance teaching could also be used for education of a different kind - for vocational skills, for agricultural improvement, for rural development and for helping people to gain a more immediate control over their own environment. We look next at the potential of distance teaching for grappling with these fundamental tasks.

NOTES

1 Nigerian newspaper advertisement.
2 See chapter 1, p. 1.
3 Experience from university-level correspondence study in the West also confirms but adds little to our arguments. It is only quoted where other evidence is lacking.
4 Tony Dodds et al., 'One Year's Work', p. 10.
5 Peter Kinyanjui, Kenya: The Use of Radio and Correspondence Education for the Improvement of Teaching, p. 260.
6 TRU Commission, 'Distance Education Systems in a Number of Countries', p. 27.
7 TRU Commission, 'Distance Education', p. 26.
8 Ibid., p. 26 and V. Zhamin and B. Remennikov, USSR: Comparative Costs and Efficiency of Full-time and Part-time Education, p. 309.
9 Torstein Rekkedal, Correspondence Studies - Recruitment, Achievement and Discontinuation, p. 22.
10 TRU Commission, 'Distance Education Systems in a Number of Countries', p. 25.
11 Leslie Wagner, The Economics of the Open University and The Economics of the Open University Revisited. Although Mace (Mythology in the Making) has pointed out that the value of an Open University degree in terms of increased earnings is lower than the value of a conventional degree (because OU graduates are typically older than conventional university graduates), his critique does not dispute Wagner's thesis that the methods used by the OU are cheaper than those of conventional universities.
12 David Hawkridge et al., In-service Teacher Education in Kenya, and Dean T. Jamison and François Orivel, The Cost-effectiveness of Distance Teaching Projects, p. 59.
13 TRU Commission, 'Distance Education Systems in a Number of Countries', p. 26 and Wilbur Schramm, 'Big Media, Little Media', p. 210.
14 Wilbur Schramm, ibid., p. 212.
15 Dean T. Jamison and François Orivel, op. cit., p. 59.
16 Ibid.
17 Agence de coopération culturelle et technique, Les Systèmes multi-média utilisés pour l'éducation des adultes, p. 36. Tévec is a modified acronym for Télévision éducative en Québec.
18 Tony Dodds, 'Multi-media Approaches to Rural Education', p. 31.
19 Jenni Gunby, The Open University, p. 23.
20 Paud Murphy, Study Centres, p. 16.
21 Sheila Reid, Study Centres - a Report on a Seminar, p. 10.
22 Robert A. White, The Use of Radio in Primary and Secondary Formal Education, pp. 175-6.

23 Antonio Cabezas Esteban, Documento Informativo sobre Radio Santa Maria, p. 8.
24 Robert A. White, op. cit., p. 185.
25 Ibid., p. 187.
26 Gunnar Andersson, The Study Associations in Sweden, p. 6.
27 Jan Byström, The Study Circle as a Pedagogic Situation, p. 14.

Chapter 5

RURAL DEVELOPMENT

For millions of people, education means primary school. A generation ago in Tanzania there were two Swahili words for schools - 'shule', adapted from the German 'schule' before 1918, which usually meant a primary school, and 'skuli', a less usual word adapted later from the English 'school', and meaning a secondary school. 'Shule' came first and appropriately remains the general term for any sort of school today. In reshaping education we have to think first of the primary school. It is seen as the basic educational institution by the majority of those in the third world who have never been to any sort of school, as well as by the minority who have. The evidence, sketchy as it is, shows that distance teaching methods can be used to raise the quality of schools even at the primary level, extend their numbers and increase the number of competent teachers. Their capacity to do this springs in part from mechanisation - particularly that of radio and its far costlier partner, television.

But 'mechanised education' has an Orwellian ring to it. It sounds as if content and method alike are to be centrally controlled, and a single national or universal type of education forced on to a huge mass of children. Such a vision is a vision only of inhumanity. We are not advocating the mass-production of materials which preclude any active role for the learner. Our hope is quite different. It is one of a community, whether of children with a teacher or adults with a group leader, using information from outside its own experience, but using it to reduce its ignorance and dependence on external authority. If we can combine opportunities for face-to-face learning with the use of radio and print, then we may be able to get the best of both worlds, both adding to schools and improving on them. The unassuming mechanised mouse of our sub-title can perhaps become strong enough to help the lion of orthodox education escape from its trap.

The fact that has to be faced is that even if distance teaching were used to improve and expand schools on a far larger scale than has yet been attempted, there would in many countries remain millions upon millions of children who would never get more than the bare minimum of primary schooling, if that. For generations to come there will be adults who have had no education at all. The creation of an alternative route to secondary qualifications, such as we considered in the previous chapter, may open doors to a few, but not to the many. To find ways of doing this we turn our attention away from school, and instead look at non-formal education for adults - adult literacy, the work of rural extension officers, radio rural forums, radio study campaigns and finally the radiophonic schools of Latin America.

ADULT LITERACY

In many countries the education of adults has meant, almost exclusively, teaching them to read and write. It has usually been done in primary school classrooms, or in no rooms at all, by volunteer tutors who have themselves received no more than primary schooling. Usually they have had no books except, if they were lucky, the primers written for children of 6 or 7 years old. It is not surprising that their efforts have had little effect. One result has been the belief that literacy should follow rather than precede an adult's initial involvement in education. Most people want to learn how to improve their standard of living, to earn money, to have better health. Only when literacy is shown to be one of the means through which such goals can be achieved will most of them be prepared to make the effort to learn to read. In the last 15 years two important new approaches to literacy have come to the fore.

The first is functional literacy. It has depended on teaching materials about practical subjects, addressed to people's down-to-earth interests. In the conclusions of the World Conference of Ministers of Education on the Eradication of Illiteracy, which met in Teheran in 1965, the purpose of functional literacy was described as follows. (1)

> Rather than an end in itself, [functional] literacy should be regarded as a way of preparing man for a social, civic and economic role that goes far beyond the limits of rudimentary literacy training consisting merely in the teaching of reading and writing. The very process of learning to read and write should be made an opportunity for acquiring information that can immediately be used to improve living standards; reading and writing should lead not only to

elementary general knowledge but to training for work, increased productivity, a greater participation in civil life and a better understanding of the surrounding world.

The concept is illustrated by the way one of the Unesco Functional Literacy Pilot Projects, in Algeria, set out to integrate the content and the skills it was teaching. (2)

In both [the agricultural and the industrial] sectors the same pedagogic approach was followed, beginning with the introduction of a theme of professional interest presented through posters or films and followed by group discussions of possible solutions to the problems. The actual learning of reading, writing and arithmetic was integrated with these discussions and corresponded to the problem situation under review. For the agricultural sector this could mean a discussion of various plant diseases, harvesting, irrigation, the introduction of new techniques and the improvement of techniques already acquired. For the industrial programmes, actual parts of machines and tools were utilized in the discussion. The main themes of the common industrial programme prepared during the first phase of the project included an introduction to technological knowledge, social education, general education and knowledge related to industrial development.

Another example comes from Zambia, where a traditional literacy campaign had started in 1964 with the target of eradicating illiteracy by 1971. (3) By 1971, however, only 10 000 illiterates out of an estimated total of 1 200 000 (1969 census) had been reached. At that rate and by the traditional methods it would take nearly 400 years to complete the task. So a pilot project aimed at functional literacy was launched in the same year. Its objective was to train 5000 people annually to the point where they could read local vernacular newspapers, write in the same language and be competent in basic arithmetic. At the same time they were to be helped to increase their yield of maize per acre, thereby achieving self-sufficiency in maize production. In the first year nearly 3000 peasants were enrolled, in the following year more than 4000. Approximately 60 per cent of them were women, partly because the illiteracy rate amongst women was higher than amongst men. Most of the learners were between the ages of 20 and 35, and they met in classes with an average of 11 members. At first the teachers were volunteer part-time staff, trained in short courses by the literacy officers who recruited and supervised them. From 1973 onwards, however, the majority of the teaching appears to have been carried out by the officers themselves.

The programme was divided into two stages. From March to October, in the first stage, the main emphasis was placed on practical training in improved methods of maize production. It consisted of three parts. In classes, often held in the open, the students studied basic literacy texts about the new methods, together with posters and flip charts illustrating them, listened to radio programmes, and then discussed them. Concurrently, on a demonstration plot they watched and practised the recommended methods. On their own half-acre plots they could put the methods into practice. Seeds and fertilisers were provided free for the purpose. November and December were the local planting season, and during those two months in the first stage they spent nearly all their time working on their own plots.

In the second stage, from March to October, they learnt about secondary crops such as cotton or groundnuts, and spent much more class time on mastering literacy and numeracy. By the end of this period they were expected to have covered six workbooks, and were tested for their certificates. Throughout they continued to listen to radio programmes and to participate in group discussions on what they were learning. At the same time, on the demonstration plots, they were shown how to use natural manure, how to harvest groundnuts, and how to use insecticides.

The workbooks were written in several languages, and allowed for regional variations. In addition, a series of follow-up books were produced to cater for the students' reading needs. These were published in seven different languages with up to 50 titles in each language. Local vernacular newspapers were also used for follow-up classes, together with a farmers' magazine published elsewhere.

The project seems to have suffered from poor printing and distribution, both for workbooks and follow-up books, and for radios and batteries. But gradually distribution improved. Naturally, both full-time and part-time staff initially lacked experience. This was partly remedied by the in-service training of the literacy officers, and their increasing assumption of responsibility for the teaching itself. The average student's yield of maize had doubled by 1972.

Many other countries have adopted the same idea, despite the inconclusiveness of the evaluation studies that have been made. In Tanzania it seems to have worked. The Cuban literacy campaign of 1961 was the model. There the campaign was promoted politically, and all school and university students were called on to act as teachers. As a result adult illiteracy was said to have fallen from 20 to 25 per cent to 4 to 5 per cent in one year. In Tanzania the same political mobilisation has been allied to the experience of functional literacy. Huge numbers of adults enrolled all over the country in literacy classes - by 1975 over 2 000 000 people had learnt to read. A wide range of functional primers was produced, often related to different regional crops and occupations. The impact on living standards is more difficult to measure, though Unesco suggested there were some successes here. (4)

The second major movement for literacy has a different starting point. Freire saw literacy as a means by which peasants could take the measure of the reasons for their oppression. To 'name the world' is to recognise its nature and to find ways of changing it. Language, and the ability to manipulate it in written form, is a tool of communication. All education should be a dialogue between teacher-learners and learner-teachers. For the peasant that dialogue is about his conditions of life, the tools he needs to change those conditions and his own ability to obtain and use them. (5) Freire developed his 'pedagogy of the oppressed' in Brazil and Chile, and it has had a great influence on literacy teaching in many parts of Latin America, as we will see when we come to radiophonic schools later in this chapter. It has also made a significant impact on adult education in Tanzania. Not only do Freirean methods enable people to become literate, but they arouse their political consciousness - their awareness of their own potential and their recognition of the forces which oppress them. But few countries, least of all the military dictatorships of Latin America or elsewhere in the third world, are prepared to allow this to happen.

AGRICULTURAL EXTENSION

That sort of political opposition has not been encountered by agricultural extension officers. In nearly all countries they act through personal advice and demonstration. Their object is to improve practices in agriculture. Their role is rarely seen as educational: they are usually not expected to develop farmers' understanding of agricultural or scientific processes, or set up a Freirean dialogue with them, so much as to instruct them on what to do. Supported by district, regional and headquarters staff they are supposed to work in co-operation with other mobile specialists - the livestock officer, the coffee officer, the poultry officer and so on.

Agricultural extension works well in North America, where it originated, and now also in Europe. It has done the same in developing countries where governments have brought together manpower and administrative support in large concentrations, as for the Gezira cotton scheme in the Sudan, for intensive maize or rice production in India, for rural development at Comilla in what is now Bangladesh, or for the Upper

Kitete Wheat Scheme in Tanzania. Such concentrated efforts are the exception rather than the rule. More common is the poorly-trained, ill-equipped extension officer on his own, who with only a bicycle for transport can reach no more than a small minority of the thousands of clients spread over the 130 square kilometres or more that he is supposed to serve. (6) As in the Western countries, nearly all agricultural extension officers are men, most of them young, while many of the peasant farmers of the third world with whom it is their job to communicate are women. The extension officers naturally go where they are most welcome and where they make the biggest impact, to the so-called progressive farmers whose education and background are most like those of the extension officers themselves, and who are already the largest landholders and therefore the richest people in rural society.

There is now much disillusionment. Chambers, in a book based on several years' experience in East Africa, summarises the view as a (7)

> widespread conviction ... that the lowest levels of agricultural extension are virtually useless, 'dead wood', incapable of giving the sophisticated advice which is the only advice worth giving, and devoted not to the development of their areas but to their own farms and interests.

He goes on to quote evidence of inefficiency and demoralisation in Kenya, Tanzania, Uganda and Nigeria. He also cites, from the same surveys, the reasons for poor achievement given by the extension officers themselves: poor conditions of service and career prospects; poor communication with farmers, partly because of vast areas and numbers; inadequate or non-existent supervision; and continually changing, and often irrelevant or even incorrect instructions issued from their central offices. Another and crucial reason they could have given is inadequate training. And yet they could do so much. It is they who could communicate to the farmers the ideas and information on which development depends. How can their effectiveness be increased?

Part of the answer, especially where there are simple, cheap improvements to agricultural practice which would have an immediate effect on farmers' incomes, is to improve the organisational structure. The World Bank has recently developed a 'training and visit' system in which the functions of extension agents and their working weeks are planned and specified in much more detail than they have traditionally been. They are supposed to visit a new cadre of village extension workers, who in turn instruct groups of farmers in specific farming practices. The early results are impressive, with dramatic increases in production at little extra cost. (8) They confirm that it would be quite wrong to dismiss the agricultural extension service as an agency of adult education. That is not our intention at all: rather our argument is that the work of agricultural extension can be helped and supported in a variety of different ways, one of which is to use the mass media.

MASS MEDIA

Film, newspapers, magazines and pamphlets, radio and television have all been used to publicise development. Film still has enormous novelty appeal, especially in rural areas where cinemas are few and far between; it can be relied on to draw large crowds. The Ghana Film Unit run by the Ghana Broadcasting Corporation, with only one van, showed locally produced educational films to over 250 000 people in the one year of 1971. (9) The Malawi Extension Aids Department of the ministry of agriculture ran a similar unit concentrating on agriculture and development and was able to draw crowds everywhere. (10) But film is very expensive to produce and distribute, and as a result can make only spasmodic if occasionally spectacular impacts.

Newspapers and magazines can only have limited effect in the largely illiterate societies of most third world countries. Even so, farmers' magazines, such as 'Mkulima wa Kisasa' (Modern Farming) in Tanzania or 'El Campesino' (The Peasant) in Colombia, had large circulations. The language and format were designed for the newly literate. Each of these has achieved by far the widest circulation of any regular publication in its own country. Recent pamphlets from the Lesotho Distance Teaching Centre (LDTC), written after careful testing of language and pictorial comprehension, have produced similar results: very high sales and very large readership. (11)

Radio is, as we have said, the most important of the mass media in developing countries. McAnany, who has studied extensively the use of radio for development, gives the following statistics. (12)

> In 1969 there were over 10 000 radio transmitters around the world (excluding the People's Republic of China) broadcasting to 653 million radio sets in almost 200 countries. ... In ten years the total number of sets had almost doubled. In certain world regions the growth was more spectacular: Africa increased its sets by 271%, Latin America by 155%, East Asia by 100%, South Asia by 380%, USSR by 121%.

Two specific examples show what radio can mean for particular countries. In Tanzania in the early 1970s it was estimated that 60 per cent of the adult population had regular access to a radio (their own or a neighbour's), and this was expected to grow to 80 per cent by 1980. (13) In northern Nigeria it has also been reported that for nearly 50 per cent of farmers, radio is the most important and usually the first source of information about innovation. (14) In these countries, as elsewhere, radio stations carry regular programmes on agriculture, health, civics, nutrition, road safety, first aid, women's affairs and co-operatives, and when a government launches a new policy and wants its citizens to respond widely it usually makes use of radio.

Radio and film carry a glamour and an authority which a young, not very well-educated village extension officer can never command. But both are remarkably unreliable as communicators of complex information. They are ephemeral. One-way communication is always only too liable to misunderstanding. Nor by themselves are they very effective as persuaders. So there is little if any evidence that new or changed practices are adopted merely as a result of broadcasting, or indeed of reading. Of the readers of the first LDTC pamphlet, for example, very few tried out any suggestions that were entirely new to them. (15) In their study of communications for innovation in a number of countries, Rogers and Shoemaker summarise the evidence more broadly by saying that mass media are more important in transmitting information than in encouraging innovation. (16) This is where face-to-face contact comes into its own. We are all more likely to try out something new if we have discussed it with, or been told about it by, our friends or relatives, our neighbours or our colleagues. The other people do not have to be experts. What matters is self-confidence, and this can often be obtained from people like ourselves more easily than it can from experts.

RURAL FORUMS

So in the last few decades the most important step taken has been to connect radio with organised but informal groups. The radio is used to arouse interest and to convey information; the information and the ideas are then discussed by group members; often the local extension officer serves as a group leader. The combination seems to be a powerful one. It allows the technical knowledge of the teachers or experts, usually from outside, to be combined with and adapted to the local knowledge and environment of the students or forum members.

In Canada in the early 1940s, as we mentioned in chapter 1, Radio Farm Forums became the first large-scale effort at carrying education into rural areas by means of self-help groups. (17) Agricultural advice was given. Listeners' questions were answered. The professional extension service was linked with groups of farmers coming together informally in each other's homes, week by week. They discussed and learnt from the broadcasts, and examined the experience and implications of putting those ideas into practice. The radio forums carried large audiences for nearly a quarter of a century.

The idea was taken up in India as early as 1949. During the next two years an enthusiastic start was made by a few of the regional stations of All India Radio (AIR). The initial interest seems to have waned quickly. The transistor revolution had not yet reached India and there were very few radios. (18) But a few years later, in 1956, a new start was made with Unesco support and much greater resources. A pilot project was launched from AIR's station in Poona in what was then the state of Bombay. The evaluation report indicated that in forum villages there was a noticeably greater increase in knowledge that in non-forum villages, and a higher proportion of the villagers put into practice ideas and innovations introduced to them in this way. (19) The result was an ambitious nation-wide plan by AIR. Once again the mammoth organisational and support problems in a country of 500 000 000 people, 14 states and 3 268 000 square kilometres hampered expansion. In 1967 Schramm reported that the resources made available for forum organisation from 1959 onwards nowhere matched those of the Poona project. As a consequence achievement has not matched what was done in Poona and there has been a danger of forums becoming 'clubs for the people who need them least'. In spite of these setbacks, however, he concluded from several studies of Indian forums carried out after Poona that they were still a positive force in improving the livelihood of the peasants. (20)

The movement survived. In 1977 Khan, then the director of AIR's Farm and Home Broadcasting Department, reported that there were currently 22 500 registered forums. He had been convinced that, rather than being abandoned, forums should be reorganised and made part of a more comprehensive programme of rural education. They should be linked with programmes for functional literacy and with the new Farm-School-on-the-Air project. In this scheme, courses dealing with agricultural problems or development plans were written and broadcast at the same time as extension support and supplies of seeds and fertilisers were made available. After nearly 30 years the India radio farm forums seemed likely to survive. (21)

The first African forums were started in Ghana in 1964. They have put down firmer roots and lasted longer than in Zambia, Malawi, Nigeria and elsewhere in Africa where they have been tried. The pattern was basically the same as in Canada. But an important variation in India, which was also adopted in Ghana, was to move away from an exclusively agricultural content to a more general one.

Ghana had the advantage of a Rural Broadcasting Unit which had been preparing educational programmes since 1961. The organisation of the forums was left in the hands of this Unit. It worked in co-ordination with the agricultural extension service as well as with the extension units of the ministry of health and community development. This concentration of responsibility on a single institution has had disadvantages as well as advantages. The lack of a village-level organisational network has been a severe restriction on the number of forums. By 1972, after eight years, there were still only 325 registered forums.

The unit was established under the Nkrumah regime, along with the forums project. In January 1972 it was in the middle of a campaign boosting prime minister Busia's call for a new national discipline. By the time the campaign was due to finish Busia was no longer in power. Nevertheless, the Ghana radio rural forums and the Rural Broadcasting Unit which runs them have survived for 13 years and through four different political regimes. (22) They are still as relevant as ever to the drive for self-sufficiency in food production and accelerated rural development, and to the new interest in non-formal education.

A parallel development in francophone West Africa, the radio clubs, derived from the French 'Télé-Clubs'. Considerable emphasis was placed by both on the involvement of the members of the clubs in making the programmes, choosing topics for discussion and collecting local suggestions for the solution of local problems. This concern with stimulating and transmitting rural opinion is the most important feature which distinguishes the radio clubs from radio forums. The difference is described by McAnany in this account of the radio clubs of Niger. (23)

> Programs do not consist of information but rather of feedback from interviews of local people about a certain problem. Thus, the animateur or group leader of each club is asked to survey a certain number of people.... The answers are tape recorded and sent to the production center in Niamey. This kind of opinion survey forms the basis of a weekly program that will spark the village discussion of the problem to be focussed on.... The kind of philosophy behind such a development project sees the first stage of change not in giving out information 'useful' for a solution that others have found but for local people to see the problem in their own context. Once the group recognizes

the problem, it will then seek the necessary information for a solution.

Senegal's Radio Educative Rurale (RER) was launched through a pilot project at the end of 1968 in three administrative regions. These regions were largely dependent on the production of groundnuts. Their price was low at the time the programme was launched. What was worse, production was low as well - an unusual combination. The crop was being seriously hit by the drought which that part of West Africa suffered for several consecutive years. The programmes therefore concentrated on groundnuts. Through literate club members, the groups wrote about their own opinions and experience in letters sent to RER. They did not mince words. They attacked central policies, local officials and their own fellow-villagers alike, and presented their plight in the most dramatic terms. RER then invited officials and even ministers to attempt to answer these criticisms on the air. Since the president was in support, senior government officials were forced to pay serious attention to this 'voice of the peasants' and to participate in the dialogue. It became the means of expression for widespread peasant discontent and led directly during 1970 and 1971 to government and even international action. An exceptional bonus was paid on all groundnuts delivered, varying according to the amount of damage caused by the drought and the efforts made to repay debts. A reform of the co-operative movement was set in motion. And eventually the government announced an annulment of debts incurred for seeds, equipment and other agricultural supplies. The peasants therefore saw direct results; they realised they had a third way of making themselves heard in addition to the normal political and administrative channels. They could now speak directly to senior officials, ministers and even the president himself.

From its initial success with 57 radio clubs, RER grew to serve much larger numbers of informal and self-organised listening groups. Cassirer noted in 1972, however, 'a lack of systematic effort to promote group listening ... RER is too busy just producing programs ... group listening has not kept pace with the spread of individual listening.' (24) His most recent reports nevertheless suggest that the popularity of RER and its radio clubs has been maintained. Radio Educative, as it is now called, reaches out to many more regions of Senegal with different languages and different agricultural and climatic conditions.

Despite all their successes, neither the forums nor the clubs have achieved what it once seemed they would. Many of them are in danger of losing the excitement and the sense of direction which marked their early years. (25) They seem to have failed to attract or hold widespread organisational support. Communication between individual forums and the centre has been inadequate. They have, moreover, concentrated too much on radio as their medium of information and instruction. They have made too little use of print. At best, their selection of subjects has been commendably related to the farmers' seasons and to matters of urgent topical interest. At worst, it has been guided by a more spasmodic response to problems as they chanced to catch public - or at least the producers' - attention. Basic educational skills such as literacy and numeracy have not been encouraged. As a result there has been little or no systematic or cumulative learning.

Several attempts have been made to remedy some of these shortcomings by creating variations of the radio forums or clubs. A few institutions have designed simple correspondence pamphlets, relying heavily on illustrations, using a limited vocabulary, for use by literate group leaders and 'animateurs'. One of these, the Institut africain pour le développement économique et social (INADES), with its headquarters in Abidjan but operating in most francophone and some other countries in Africa, believes as a basic premise that scientific facts can always be explained in a language and content which the peasant farmer can understand. A similar approach has been adopted for teaching basic technical and mechanical skills by the Instituto Nacional de Cooperación Educativa (INCE) in Venezuela, and by the Co-operative Education Centre in Moshi, Tanzania, for teaching basic economics, co-operative management and book-keeping. The same techniques have been applied by the Mauritius College of the Air to health education and family planning, and by the Botswana Extension College to Village Development Committee training. What distinguishes the materials of all these projects from the support pamphlets of the forums or the clubs is the attempt to use carefully designed printed materials both as self-study discussion manuals, and as a system of two-way and individualised communication within and between groups and with course tutors.

These same institutions have also attempted to reach people already organised in groups. They have designed courses to meet the needs of existing organisations, such as co-operatives, young farmers' clubs or the churches. The primary purpose of these organisations may not be educational, but that does not mean they do not welcome education. The courses are then distributed and run through the organisations' local branches.

Two of the bodies mentioned, INCE and INADES, have recognised the need to provide some form of sequential learning materials which lead on from each other, from one level of difficulty to another, and which taken together begin to offer a more comprehensive understanding of a particular body of knowledge or set of skills. Each of INCE's courses on motor mechanics, for example, deals with a different part of the car - the brakes, the gears, the electrical system - graded in difficulty. A student who has taken all of them, and has worked through them at the same time as getting practical experience, will have a good understanding of the skills he practises. (26) Similarly, INADES's courses in agriculture each deal with a particular crop or agricultural activity. The various courses are, however, grouped together in a loose curriculum. Students are expected to complete one group of courses before they move on to another at a higher level. (27)

RADIO STUDY CAMPAIGNS

In Tanzania the radio study campaigns, which embody a different approach again, began on a very small scale. From the start they were an attempt to learn from, and improve upon, the farm forums, the study circles of Sweden, and the adult education campaigns of Cuba.

Most of the early campaigns were on political themes. A small pilot project was run in 1967 which included series on politics, agriculture and English. This was followed in 1969 by the first campaign on Tanzania's Second Five Year Development Plan, 'To Plan Is to Choose', and in 1970 by a somewhat larger one on the national elections held that year. It reached nearly 4000 people in more than 150 study groups. In 1971, the year in which Tanzania celebrated the tenth anniversary of its independence, a campaign was held which reviewed her development achievements and policies during the decade, called 'A Time to Rejoice'. Partly because of the enthusiasm aroused for the celebrations, and partly as a result of the creation during 1970 and 1971 of a nationwide network of specialist adult education officers, 'A Time to Rejoice' reached out to nearly ten times as many groups as its predecessor. In 1973 and again in 1975, much more significant campaigns on health education and nutrition were launched on a much wider scale still. These were called 'Man Is Health' and 'Food Means Life' respectively. Both were supported fully by adult education bodies and the political organisations. It is thought that in 1973 nearly 2 000 000 group members participated; in 1975 more than 1 500 000.

Unlike the forums or the clubs, Tanzania's campaigns have not been organised by a single institution. The early experiments arose from the initiative of the university's Institute of Adult Education and of the Co-operative Education Centre, and from the beginning they were dependent on the co-operation of Radio Tanzania. From the election campaign in 1970 onwards, both the ministry of education and the political party TANU were deeply involved in the organisation of study groups. This pattern of co-ordination reached its peak in the 'Food Means Life' campaign when the ministry of health and the ministry of agriculture were also involved. Their specialists at headquarters helped in the preparation of materials and radio programmes; their extension officers worked with the village adult education officers and local party officials to organise and to service the study groups.

The experience of the early projects underlined the importance of study-group leaders, and the need to train them in their unusual educational role as leaders of discussion between members rather than as transmitters of information. In order to cope with the enormous task of training sufficient group leaders for the campaigns, 2000 for 'A Time to Rejoice' and 75 000 for 'Man Is Health', a multi-stage strategy was devised. The Institute of Adult Education and the Co-operative Education Centre each set up training courses at key points throughout the country where district adult education officers and similar officials were introduced to the methods and materials of the campaign. The discussion group method was itself used extensively at these training seminars, and the materials used in them were designed to help the district officers to conduct training sessions in their districts. At these, the divisional adult education officers and ward or divisional party officials were trained in the same methods and to use the same materials, and they in turn passed on the skills to the group leaders selected to put them into practice during the campaign itself.

> Here is described a typical group in 1970's campaign. (28) The typical group had twenty-four members. Thirteen were men and eleven were women. Seventeen were farmers, three were teachers, two were locally-employed labourers, one was a government official and one was a local official of the political party. One had been to secondary school, six had had at least six years of primary education, six had had four or less years at primary school, and eleven, of whom four were illiterate, had never gone to school at all. The group's leader and organiser was the local primary school head-teacher (though in many groups a separate chairman, either a local leader, or sometimes other members of the group in rotation, was selected by the group) and he was assisted by his fellow-teachers, one of whom usually acted as group-secretary. News of the campaign had come from the District Adult Education Officer and from the local office of the Institute of Adult Education.

> Printed materials - a booklet prepared for the course, which included study-guide questions for discussion, and notes and hints for group leaders - were distributed by the Institute through the District Adult Education Officers. A pictorial *History of Elections* had been prepared by TANU and was also distributed to groups. In the end about half of the group members received copies of one or other of the booklets. The radio series proper lasted for ten weeks, though there were two introductory programmes and three repeats. The group met on eight occasions, and was able to listen to the radio programme on seven of them. Meetings lasted, on average, for an hour and a quarter including ten minutes of introduction and revision, thirty minutes listening to the programme, and thirty-five minutes of discussion. The group leader/chairman launched the discussion by reading out the questions printed in the booklet, sometimes together with selected passages of the booklet which he summarised or read aloud for the sake of illiterate members of his group. He then invited members to comment or ask questions.

An important development during the growth of radio study-group campaigns in Tanzania was the increasing emphasis on group action based on decisions taken during the study sessions. In the 'Man Is Health' campaign, groups were urged to leave monuments of better health practices. (29)

> A second activity stimulated by the campaign was the building of latrines. While the sample of supervisors' reports showed that 20% of the groups visited engaged in building or repairing latrines, in some parts of the country the building of latrines took on truly miraculous proportions. In one district reports showed that every house had its own latrine! This particular latrine-building campaign was started off by local TANU officials, who included the goal of a latrine for every house amongst their development targets for the district. The campaign was strengthened when the dry season came and the vegetation which had provided privacy previously was harvested. Irritated reports from villagers were heard about neighbours who slipped into nearby latrines at someone else's house rather than build their own. In one village a man discouraged his neighbour's use of his latrine by putting a padlock on the door. The neighbour promptly built his own. In another area, people decided that having a latrine at every house still left many areas lacking. What, for example, could travellers use while waiting along the side of the road for buses? It was agreed that one latrine should be built at each major bus stop in the area....

> Other types of activity carried out in the spirit of 'Mtu ni afya' were limited only by the imagination of the groups. Some collected money to buy mosquito nets or malaria tablets. In one town the market place is now closed twice a week for a general cleaning by voluntary workers. Another town is shut down occasionally so that everyone can take part in picking up rubbish and general cleaning.

Campaigns in Botswana have been strongly and directly influenced by Tanzania's experience. The first campaign was in 1973, about Botswana's National Development Plan. Based on the success of this project and the experience gained from it, a much larger campaign was run in 1976 on a major new government initiative, known as the Tribal Grazing Lands policy. In Botswana land was traditionally held by the tribe in common. By the early 1970s the tribal system of holding land was breaking down. The increased number of cattle and the uncontrolled use of communal grazing were beginning to cause severe problems of erosion. The government therefore decided to divide tribal grazing land into three categories: communal land which would continue to be farmed communally as before, commercial land to which leases would be provided and reserved land which would be reserved for future use.

Before deciding on the details of the policy and its implementation the government decided to inform and consult people about its proposals. Plans for a radio learning-group campaign were drawn up as one part of the process of consultation.

An important feature of the Botswana campaigns has been their attention to the recruitment, training and support of the study-group leaders. In 1976 these were recruited at village meetings organised by the extension officers in the traditional 'kgotla' assembly. The leaders were unpaid volunteers, and the core of their training was to equip them to serve as facilitators, not teachers. They did not necessarily know anything more about the subject matter than their fellow group members. Here is how the training system has been described by two of the campaign organisers: (30)

> In ... the 27 [training] courses in 1976 the training programme began with a dramatised demonstration of a Radio Learning Group session. Then participants broke into groups for the remainder of the training course, each trainee having the chance to lead the group through a simulated study session. Each of the groups was assisted by a field worker who helped evaluate each practice simulation. Very short versions of the campaign materials were used in these practice 'drills'. Courses contained no theory and allowed trainees to feel rewarded by performing a manage-

> able set of steps.... At the end of each course the campaign study materials were distributed to the leaders.

The study materials consisted of a study guide with 10 sections, one for each of the radio programmes, a flipchart with sets of illustrations related to the topics covered in each session, and a popular version of the tribal grazing land policy proposals.

The evaluation of the campaign shows that there were more than 3000 radio learning groups of which nearly 2000 met throughout the campaign. The audience reached by the campaign was more than 55 000, or approximately 15 per cent of the total adult population of Botswana. 25 000 report forms were received from the groups, containing questions and comments about the government's plans. A supplementary series of radio programmes was broadcast to answer some of the most common questions raised by the groups, and their views were taken into account in the final formulation of the policy.

The teaching methods in these campaigns were much the same as those employed for radio forums. The radio was, again, the focus. It was supported by supplementary printed materials. Both were used as the basis for group discussion. Every effort was made to direct the discussion towards decision and action. The campaigns like the clubs stressed the importance of group leaders. This was a serious limitation in the expansion of the clubs. Tanzania and Botswana, on the other hand, developed multi-stage training for leaders which appeared to be effective. Training manuals were carefully prepared which made it possible to train large numbers of leaders in a short time.

There are, however, two important differences between the campaigns and the clubs or forums. In the campaigns, the energies both of teachers and learners have been concentrated into short sharp bursts and discussion has been centred around single subjects or topics. This is an attempt to keep motivation at its highest level and to avoid the loss of momentum. The second difference is the scale of the supporting organisations. The response in Tanzania was due to the active support of Tanzania's political party and of the adult education network; to the central production and co-ordination role of the Institute of Adult Education, the ministry of health and Radio Tanzania; and also to the overall political priority attached to adult education. Botswana does not have Tanzania's network of village-level political or adult education workers. The campaign organisers therefore had to call into being an alliance of government extension agencies for the period of the campaign, and this imposed considerable and unwonted strain on the individual ministries and their local staffs.

The radio study campaigns have in each case been successful in carrying non-formal education to very large numbers of people. In both Tanzania and Botswana the central themes of the campaigns have been vital ones for everyone. Their most significant achievements have been the community action which has followed upon the discussions, and the extent to which the popular response has been fed back to the central authorities. But, like the forums and clubs, the campaigns have ignored two basic educational requirements. They have given inadequate attention to the design and use of permanent support materials, through which the learning, so admirably begun, can be reinforced. And short spells of teaching about individual topics have not been properly related to each other. They did not form part of a comprehensive and continuing curriculum of any kind. The campaigns stimulated very large numbers of people to want to learn, but then 18 months, or two or three years, later a new, not necessarily connected campaign was launched with a renewed outburst of exhortation and activity.

The objectives of the campaigns were severely practical; but basic education was largely ignored. The final institution we want to examine, the radiophonic school, brings these two concerns together.

THE RADIOPHONIC SCHOOLS

It all started with a radiophonic school in 1947 at Sutatenza in Colombia. The founder of the school, Father Salcedo, in fact drew his inspiration, as did the founders of the rural forum and the radio campaign, from the Canadian Radio Farm Forums, but he went for a more radical adaptation than elsewhere. He believed that basic education based on literacy and numeracy was essential for the progress of the peasants in Colombia. But it had to be basic education which embraced the health, family, communal and vocational needs of peasant life, as well as their spiritual needs.

A quarter century later, Acción Cultural Popular (ACPO) had a budget in 1972 of US $4.2 million, serving thousands of rural Colombians. (31) Today, not only does ACPO run a radio station, a publishing house, and several thousand radiophonic schools in Colombia, but the idea has spread to some 25 countries in South and Central America. The radio programmes are designed to provide information which will help people in their everyday life - towards better health, better agriculture and so on - and also to provide the equivalent of primary education for people who have had little or no formal schooling. Radio programmes are supported by printed lessons and by monthly newspaper-style magazines. The work of the radio schools, small informal groups who are often all members of one family, is supported by a network of monitors and supervisors who advise and encourage the groups. The movement retains its religious character, and, as a result, parish priests play an important part in forming groups and encouraging them to keep working. Groups are more successful where the parish priest is sympathetic, and where he is relatively young. If he is too old he cannot easily climb up the mountains to visit nearby schools.

School meetings are informal, adapted to the monitor's household, as one of the writers found when he visited a Colombian school. (32)

> We were not expected. The mother who greeted us when we branched off the main path wore a blue cracked hat, a whitish shirt and yellow trousers. It turned out she was the 'auxiliar' (or monitor) for that particular radio school. The radio lying on the ground near the baskets was the only product of modern industry to be seen apart from a poster issued by the Mision Biblica Catolica and another advertising we did not know what. A chair and a stool - the only ones? - were brought out from the house for us to sit on; and we were told a little about the school.
>
> Its meeting place was the ground in front of the house. The members were the other members of the family who attended as they could, her father and mother, her two brothers who worked in a village some ten miles away, and her sister, together with young children from other families who came to get a good grounding before they entered the primary school. How often and how many of them settled around the radio depended on the demands of work. On that day they were not going to listen at the usual evening hour of 5.30 because it was a day for basket-making. An Indian woman under a much broader black hat was squatting on the ground busily splicing canes for the mother and daughter to dye and fabricate. She was an employee to do this particular job.
>
> The mother said they had learnt from the radio school to make a latrine at a distance from the house; to grow vegetables that they hadn't before; to organise a basketball team which played against others on the pitch at the primary school; to have catechism classes on Sundays, and to discuss the Bible. There were 25 other 'auxiliares' in her 'vereda', the neighbourhood made up of similar homesteads grouped along a particular network of mountain paths.... Since it was one of her busy days and darkness was near we did not stay for long before returning down the (literally) breathtaking hillside to the van. A dog

> barking and snapping at the moving wheels seemed to fall off the road and disappeared.

There is probably no 'typical' radiophonic school, neither this one nor any other. The model of learning groups, following regular radio programmes and using printed materials, has been adapted to the differing educational needs of other Latin American countries. As part of the process, many of them have gone much further than either the correspondence colleges we looked at in the last chapter, or the radio forums and campaigns, in creating a curriculum to meet the needs of out-of-school students in rural areas. They are not interested in providing a duplicate of formal primary education, but set out to provide an alternative whose subject matter is agriculture and family life in rural communities. They also put great emphasis on the face-to-face support they provide to groups, though in virtually all cases this support was given by monitors, counsellors or other non-professional helpers rather than by ordinary school teachers.

Radiophonic schools differ in placing emphasis on the education of the individual or on the development of the whole community. The radio schools of Acción Cultural Popular Hondureña (ACPH) in Honduras are amongst the latter. ACPH has taken a radical political stance in relation to the purposes and content of the education it is offering. Its programmes have been strongly influenced by Freire. Having started in 1960, very much on the model of ACPO, it has increasingly adopted a more aggressive political position and has identified itself closely with peasant co-operative and political movements. To this end it has offered itself as a communications network between the development agencies and the low-status highland 'campesinos' (peasant farmers) who are its students.

In 1972 it set out to apply this radical philosophy to its more formal radiophonic schools, and developed a Primary School Equivalency Programme (PEPA). It devised curricula which were officially recognised by the ministry of education. Its courses led to the award of official diplomas to successful students, but at the same time concentrated on raising their political and economic consciousness and equipping them to analyse and solve their own problems.

A typical afternoon in the life of a radiophonic school following PEPA courses looks like this: (33)

> School starts at 4 p.m., which is the hour when most 'campesinos' return home from the fields. The place is usually the house of one of the monitors, the man or woman in charge of the school who has received some three weeks training. He has his own special manual which tells him in advance what is going to be broadcast and what he will

be expected to do on each day. There is also a 30-minute radio programme on Saturdays expressly for monitors, 20 minutes for 1st level monitors, 10 minutes for 2nd level. The monitor, or one of the members of the group which may have up to about 20 people in it for Levels 1 and 2 taken together, mostly heads of families between 20 and 35 years of age, starts the afternoon with a prayer before the radio tutor comes on the air. Both 1st and 2nd level students are in the same room together - the 1st level being concerned mainly with the attainment of basic literacy and numeracy skills. How many students can already read and write? Most have had some primary education, but usually long ago - most of those who do become functionally literate have retained at least something from previous educational experiences....

The first 20 minutes on the radio are given over to the 2nd level. First there is music, varying from day to day, not a signature tune but something popular. Then comes the radio tutor with something to this effect, 'Good day, fellow "campesinos". We are meeting today to continue our fight against ignorance, poverty and exploitation.' After a few more introductory words he says, 'I will now ask the monitor to show you Picture No. 12', from the batch circulated to the schools, one for each week of the 8 months. This particular lesson that we were taken through was largely about the history of Honduras. Picture No. 12 depicted a richly clad Spanish Don with his ship in the background alongside Indian slaves with yokes and chains. When the radio tutor hands over to the monitor the radio emits gentle background music (like western 'piped' music) which we were told the 'campesinos' did not find distracting. After a few minutes while the monitor is talking and asking the students what the picture suggests to them, the tutor is back on the air to draw attention to the Indians in chains and to their hands which are breaking the chains. From there he raises the question of independence, what it means and whether today people are genuinely independent, and again to the music which is the signal for group discussion. Again he refers the group to a certain page in their textbooks and asks them to read a passage and complete a particular exercise, usually a comprehension test of what has just been read, by filling in blank lines in the books. Level 2 now proceed to work on their own or in groups from the exercise books, often moving outside to a corridor or another room; and the radio turns for the next 80 minutes to Level 1, the beginners who are usually the more numerous of the two sets.

From 1969 on ACPH has stressed the causes of peasant

poverty and economic dependency and the need for co-operative action to overcome them. Parallel to PEPA, therefore, it has developed a Programme of Agricultural Promotion (PPA). (34)

> Instead of agricultural education being the force-feeding of technology to meet national production goals, in the PPA context it means developing a critical analytical ability in defining the causes of agricultural and agrarian problems and in deciding to integrate new factors of production. The basic premise is that the small farmer is an expert in his own enterprise, and the aim is to develop the values of experimentation, innovation and creative satisfaction in small farmers who generally have a derogatory image of themselves as agriculturalists and as a social group. Communal activism is stressed, and directed specifically towards training in the management of communal production enterprises, working closely with the regional marketing and supply co-ops.

PPA is based on study groups very similar to those we have seen in radio forum and radio campaign programmes. Technical advice, as there, is given by radio and in print. But it is supported by a network of para-professionals. They visit, provide for the study groups' administrative needs and give basic agricultural guidance. An important additional motivation for the groups is that through them credit facilities are made available to their members, especially for activities carried out on a co-operative basis. The groups are strongly encouraged to affiliate with a major 'campesino' federation and to support its local and national political activities.

The intention to provide an equivalent to primary school is one important difference between the radiophonic schools and the various other kinds of non-formal education we have looked at. Basic literacy and numeracy, an understanding of the basic concepts of science, and an appreciation of the moral and political values of society are their goals, just as they are of primary schools. But the radio schools set out to teach through discussion of agriculture and how to improve one's income from it, how to improve the health of oneself and one's family, religion, basic politics, civics and economics. It seems to work. Many students, both young and adult, expressed strong preference for the radiophonic schools over the ordinary primary schools. This very approach, however, gives rise to the main dilemma which the radiophonic schools movement faces. Non-formal education which attempts to help students to liberate themselves from poverty, ignorance and exploitation, and an elite political and economic system which seeks to maintain itself and its privilege cannot be in harmony with each other.

The conflict has sometimes flared. In Brazil in the mid-

1960s, for example, the Movimento de Educação de Base ran foul of political authorities because it encouraged and supported school members in improving their living conditions by direct action. (35) Such policies inevitably risk closure. Confrontation is to some extent avoided since radiophonic schools have remained private institutions and have the powerful support of the Catholic Church. But without active government commitment and involvement their impact is inevitably either restricted or revolutionary. Nevertheless the radio schools, or at least some of them, however hesitantly and imperfectly, have felt their various ways towards a system of non-formal education which has both catered for the immediate needs of members of rural societies and gradually made available to them a comprehensive education comparable to that provided in schools.

CONCLUSION

Where then does the experience of non-formal education and its use of distance teaching methods lead us? Can we find here any of the answers to the limitations and false starts, the irrelevancies and failures of the formal system? Is it possible in this way to harness education to the twin, though not always linked, processes of development and liberation? For it is only of importance if it shows new ways of overcoming the educational deprivation of the vast numbers of third-world citizens of this and future generations whom the schools will hardly touch.

The examples we have looked at certainly show that adults with little or no formal education can benefit. They also show that this can happen without large-scale investment in teachers and in specialised institutions. What is more, some of them prove it can be done for large numbers of people, tackling problems fundamental to development in their various settings, while others show that such learning can be fitted together into a comprehensive curriculum. 150 000 latrines built by self-help in Tanzania, new marketing channels established by villagers for their produce in Ghana, more careful and systematic sowing techniques adopted in Mali, the attention of government drawn to corrupt and wasteful practices in the co-operative movement in Senegal, 25 000 questions and suggestions on the way to implement new land policies in Botswana - all these have followed upon non-formal education using distance teaching and group discussion.

We have identified some of the characteristics of success which the different projects have displayed, and the limitations which have held them back. From the extension movements we have learnt of the importance of personal advice and human contact, and the limitations placed upon them by having too few people, too little training and too much bureaucracy. From the forums and clubs we have learnt that study groups, without expert instructors, can become the interpreters and users of new knowledge, but that such a process requires support and servicing beyond the capacity of any individual institution. The campaigns have demonstrated that what the forums have achieved on a limited scale can also be achieved on a larger one, especially by working through existing organisations. They have suffered from lack of continuity and regularity. The radiophonic schools have at their best produced a comprehensive and sequential curriculum by means of which adult students can become educated to understand and to change their societies. They also illustrate the limitations of private organisations attempting to do so without government support and commitment.

So none of the projects have found all the answers, by any means. They have either found ways of reaching and teaching quite a small number of people cheaply in scattered and isolated places over long periods of time, or they have mobilised very large numbers for quite a short time. They have mostly relied on the dramatic impact of radio or on the less dramatic impact of print, instead of using both in tandem. They have depended either on the guidance which can be given by extension officers or the persuasive powers of group discussion. They have capitalised on the motivation which comes out of immediate needs or on the comparability to traditional schooling of a wide-ranging and sequential curriculum. Yet between them they illustrate that non-formal education making use of distance teaching has great potential.

Our final conclusion is that the organisers of the different projects could learn more from each other than they have. Out of their combined experience, by bringing together the various elements we have just listed, it should be possible to create a whole system of non-formal education which would complement the formal. In our next chapter we will attempt to show how such a system might work.

NOTES

1 World Conference of Ministers of Education on the Eradication of Illiteracy, 'Final Report'.
2 Unesco/UNDP, 'The Experimental World Literacy Programme', p. 21.
3 Mushtaq Ahmed, Country Report, ZAMBIA, p. 345.
4 Unesco, op. cit., p. 110

5 Paulo Freire, 'Pedagogy of the Oppressed'.
6 Guy Hunter, 'Modernising Peasant Societies', pp. 172-8.
7 Robert Chambers, 'Managing Rural Development', pp. 57ff.
8 Daniel Benor and James Q. Harrison, 'Agricultural Extension', p. 48.
9 Tony Dodds, 'Multi-media Approaches to Rural Education', pp. 18-20.
10 Ibid., p. 40.
11 Lesotho Distance Teaching Centre, 'Learning from a Booklet'.
12 Emile McAnany, 'Radio's Role in Development', p. 1.
13 Budd Hall, 'Adult Education and the Development of Socialism in Tanzania', pp. 76-7.
14 Imrana Yazidu, 'The Study of Radio as a Means of Communicating Agricultural Information to Farmers in Northern States of Nigeria', p. 51.
15 Lesotho Distance Teaching Centre, op. cit., p. 45.
16 Everett M. Rogers and F. Floyd Shoemaker, 'Communication of Innovations', p. 255.
17 Nicol et al., 'Canada's Farm Radio Forums.
18 N. Kumar, 'Educational Radio in India', p. 59.
19 Wilbur Schramm, Ten Years of the Radio Rural Forum in India, p. 132-4.
20 Ibid.
21 A.W. Khan, 'A.I.R.'s Non-formal Education Broadcasts for Rural Development', and comments in discussion of this paper.
22 Tony Dodds, op. cit., pp. 11-15.
23 Emile McAnany, 'Radio Clubs of Niger', pp. 3-4.
24 Henry R. Cassirer, Radio in an African Context, p. 311.
25 For example, see Wilbur Schramm, op. cit., and John F. Ohliger, 'Listening Groups'.
26 Jenny Fakes (ed.), 'Technical Education at a Distance', pp. 15-20.
27 Tony Dodds, INADES - A Case Study, in A. Kabwasa and M.M. Kaunda (eds), 'Correspondence Education in Africa', pp. 13-30.
28 Tony Dodds, 'Multi-media Approaches to Rural Education', pp. 16-17.
29 Budd Hall and Tony Dodds, 'Voices for Development', pp. 40-2. 'Mtu ni afya' is the Swahili title of the campaign 'Man Is Health'.
30 David Crowley and Ross Kidd, 'Radio Learning Group Campaigns in Botswana', p. 7.
31 Stephan F. Brumberg, Colombia, p. 12.
32 See appendix 2, pp. 149ff., for a longer account.
33 Michael Young, 'Note on the Honduras Radio Schools', pp. 2-4.

34 Ibid., p. 18.
35 Emanuel Jehuda de Kadt, 'Catholic Radicals in Brazil', chs 7-14.

Chapter 6

COULD IT ALL BE CHANGED?

Now that we are coming towards the end of our book we need to return to our starting point, and our reason for writing it: the multiple educational crisis we spoke about then. Even a few years ago it did not seem too optimistic to believe it was only a matter of time before most of the poor countries possessed the rudiments of a school system. No doubt they would remain, for as far ahead as anyone could see, behind the rich countries, with the gap between them at worst widening, at best staying the same. The poor countries would only be able to do better if they managed to attain faster rates of educational expansion than the rich countries and this seemed highly unlikely. But it was expected that they would in the foreseeable future have primary schools for the great majority of their children, and secondary for many. As a result, before too long the schools, with the aid of adult education, would at least have eliminated illiteracy.

Now, as we said in chapter 1, that guarded optimism has been destroyed by the population explosion. Every poor country has strained to put more of its budget into education, regarded as the gateway to modernisation by the one great alliance of parents and governments which has, on this issue, stood firm almost everywhere. More schools have been built. More teachers have been trained. More children have been enrolled. But not enough for these countries to do much more than hold their own.

Illiteracy figures are bound to be suspect, especially when the counts made on many different bases by governments who all have an interest in underestimating run into hundreds of millions. Given the bias of the arithmeticians, the real situation is likely to be worse than that displayed by Unesco; and that is bad enough. The Office of Statistics contributed its conclusions to the Unesco report, 'Learning to Be'. (1) The absolute number of illiterate adults rose between 1950 and

1970 from 700 to 783 millions. Though the proportion of people who could not read had decreased, world population was rising too fast for the teachers to keep up with the demand. Looking forward from 1972, the report was more gloomy about the decade to come. It said that (2)

> The effect of the huge increase in the adult population in the seventies of 536 million - as against 418 million in the sixties - will continue to undermine all the efforts made by Member States to undermine illiteracy.

This has become an ever more common refrain. It is almost conventional to say, as the World Bank did later on, that 'there is a prospect not only of stagnation in progress toward universal education, but even of a retrogression which would leave larger numbers and proportions of the populations of many countries without even a minimum education.' (3)

To pick up one of those figures, if for no more than illustration, what is to happen to those 783 000 000, to the still larger numbers there may be to come who have never been to school, or to the great numbers who have been to school but then dropped out?

It is not just a question of numbers. We need an approach which will not only make it possible to reverse the trend towards growing illiteracy, but will do so by giving students a chance to learn how to improve the quality of their lives and of their societies. This cannot be done by setting up for adults and adolescents who have not been to school something which is a poor image of what goes on in it. The 'banking' system, where students are led to store the pearls of wisdom which their teachers give them (and which they themselves learnt by heart from the teachers who went before them), produces submissiveness, not the search for new ways of doing things. If people are to learn to control and change the world in which they live, they need to learn through dialogue and participation. Can the techniques of distance teaching be used to this end?

The previous chapters indicated that there are answers which seem to us to give some reason for hope, when it is only too easy to have none. By a development of non-formal education, on the more systematic lines which we suggested were possible, that frightening number of illiterates might be reduced; in their place might emerge more people educated to help themselves.

But the last chapter pointed to the precedents. It did not show, or indeed try to show, how the new model might work in practice. That is the purpose of this chapter. Before we go further we should underline one obvious point - we are generalising, as we have been doing throughout the book, but even more obviously. We recognise, of course, that what might be in one place could not be in another. There can be no one blueprint for the future of non-formal education in the third world, or any other world for that matter. The differences between countries, and districts within countries, are far too great for that.

But if there has in effect been a single blueprint for schools, both primary and secondary, why not for adult colleges as well? The third world has taken over many of its notions about education from Paris, London, Moscow, Washington, which are themselves sufficiently similar to make it quite sensible to talk about 'the school' as though it were one animal. But this clearly will not do for adult education. Adults cannot or do not want to go to school. Learning for them only makes sense if it springs from issues in their own lives which matter to them. These issues differ immensely from one country or one district to another.

Yet there is, we assert, some value in generalising; not in order to lay down what should be done in any one place, nor even in some dream-house of education, but in order to suggest the agenda, a list of check-points, to anyone who wants to change the existing provision for adult education or add to it. An agenda is always a kind of generalisation, until it is known who is going to propose exactly what, on each item. We know now what the agenda is for. It is for a system of radio colleges which could be an alternative or complement to the schools which so many people have never been inside.

We use the term radio colleges because we know that the majority of the 800 000 000 people who have never been to school, as well as those who have started but have dropped out, live in villages and homesteads. They have been deprived of education because of their remoteness from schools, or even extension services. There is not enough money to build the new schools or to train and pay additional teachers or extension officers. An alternative system must reach them in spite of these constraints. We believe that distance teaching might do so. Distance teaching, that is, which rests on the three-legged stool of broadcasting, print and study-group meetings. And from the examples we have looked at we draw the conclusion that radio is the focus around which the study groups should meet.

What then are the questions on the agenda? There are, we think, three main ones:

1 Who will the students be?
2 What will the organisation be?
3 What will they learn?

1 Who will the students be?

We have been concerned throughout the book with people deprived of education. The first target of an alternative must therefore be the millions who have never been to school at all. But in some societies now, and in many in the future, where universal primary education has or will have been achieved, the educationally underprivileged are those who have been to primary school but dropped out, or 'failed' the primary school leaving exams. Our system must also be able to offer them a chance to build on what they have learned, or to relearn what they have mislearned or forgotten. These two groups, the wholly unschooled and the school-leavers or dropouts, have at least one major difference. The latter will have acquired the basic skills of education; they will have learned to read, write and count, whereas the former will not.

The system must therefore provide a chance for some to acquire these essential skills of learning from scratch, while allowing those who have them already to practise and improve them. The Freirean concept of dialogue between teacher/learner and learner/teacher, and the Laubach 'Each One Teach One' literacy method, might consummate a marriage. Those with some schooling, while continuing to be students for part of the time, could become the monitors and group leaders, and even the literacy and numeracy tutors, for those who are just starting. As in the radio schools of Colombia, their role would be to guide and tutor rather than to teach. Their own lack of expertise should be more than counterbalanced by the printed and broadcast lessons. Literacy and numeracy apart, these two groups of potential students would have very similar learning needs. They share the same village societies, they struggle with the same economic necessities, they bring up families in the same conditions of life, whether or not they have been to school. The really important differences will reflect the differences between their economic and social roles. The majority, both men and women, will presumably be farmers. But the skills and knowledge needed by farmers vary enormously from one ecological district to another. There will also be carpenters and carvers, builders and technicians, housewives and mothers, traders and businessmen. Our colleges must offer each of them the chance to master the skills which they need to build a better life for themselves and for their families, including educational skills.

Most of the students in the radio colleges we propose will be adults, or at least adolescents who are beyond the normal school-leaving age. For it is highly doubtful whether distance teaching can provide children with sufficiently structured learning: it has not done so yet. Strong personal motivation is a condition of successful learning with these techniques, and such motivation requires maturity; it is for adults who have been persuaded by life (rather than by teachers) that it will be of advantage to them to have some education. This is not to say that young children could not benefit from a radio college as long as there were adults in it. This seems to have worked well on occasion in the Latin American radiophonic schools. But we expect that the radio colleges will be mainly for adults.

2 What will the organisation be?

The study group will be essential to the system - or any variation of it - which we are proposing. The radio programme and the correspondence pamphlets are, by their very nature, likely to be centrally produced - although it would be a great advantage if they could be adapted regionally and, if necessary, to each main ecological environment. Even so they are bound to be generalised, whereas the problems to be solved, and the circumstances in which they must be defined, are local. The study group, in which families, neighbours or members of local communities meet as colleagues for the purpose of learning together, is a local institution, built and dependent on local resources, and in which the information and ideas received from a distance are related to local development and local realities. It is there that new knowledge and new skills from outside can be synthesised with local understanding and experience. The study group would, for the non-formal system, become the organisational equivalent of the school. But a study group does not need a separate building, trained teachers or extension officers, the main constraints upon orthodox expansion. It is these characteristics which make expansion by study groups economically attractive.

Such groups cannot, of course, be entirely self-sustaining. They need stimulation and organisational support. These can most conveniently be provided by the existing educational and extension officers - the primary school teachers and the health, community development, co-operative and agricultural officers. The value to them is that they can reach larger numbers and a wider cross-seciton of their potential clientele than they can ever hope to reach by individual visits. They can be relieved of the task of being the primary transmitters of information, and can concentrate on the human support and interpretation which they are best able to provide.

We have looked at the study group in several different forms in the previous chapter. There are very attractive features to all four variants. An alternative system should attempt to retain all these features, the permanence of the forums, the consultation of the clubs, the mass mobilisation of the campaigns and the clearly-defined role of the monitors in the radiophonic schools. But on one point there is a basic choice between the radio forums and the radio clubs on the one hand, which are new and separate groups, and the campaigns and the radio schools on the other, which graft study groups on to existing organisations. We believe that the latter approach is generally preferable. The campaigns in Tanzania were directed at groups set up by the political party, local government and educational organisations. Existing groups became the vehicles for the campaign. In this way they reached out to large proportions of the total adult audience. Some radio schools used the family as the only appropriate base on which to build study groups in the most remote areas, others the farmers' co-operatives and federations. Both relied on the Catholic Church for distribution of materials and local support.

Attaching study groups for particular courses or campaigns to existing social organisations - youth clubs, sports clubs, women's clubs, church groups, adult education classes, co-operatives, trade unions and local party branches - takes people where they are, and approaches them where their involvement and loyalty are already present. (It can present problems where only the most prosperous belong to such groups.) But it is then possible to operate on a much larger scale than new and separate groups can, if, like the clubs and forums, they are entirely dependent on a single central institution, whether or not it is attached to the broadcasting organisation.

One point to make about study groups is that their members should be given the fullest possible opportunity to plan for themselves. All too often the political elites of third world countries, and the first- or second-world experts who run the development programmes of international agencies, determine the sort of change they think best for the rural areas where other people live. This is not too likely to be what the others really want. There is a much better chance of providing what ordinary people want if they are involved in making the plans.

Despite the difficulties of involving learners in the production of centrally made broadcasts and correspondence lessons, there are three ways in which study group members can and should participate. The first is by expressing their needs and becoming aware of their own ability. We have seen how in Senegal radio clubs led peasant farmers to define for themselves the reasons why they were kept poor. They realised that they could make the authorities listen to what they said. This in turn gave them the confidence to consider and use the advice they were offered, instead of reluctantly submitting to orders from above. In Tanzania likewise: the radio campaigns mobilised millions of people to discuss their own health and food habits critically. They then decided, community by community, what they could and should do to change them. These examples show that distance media allied with local study groups can help people with little or no schooling to a 'deepened consciousness of their situation' which, as Freire says in a different context, 'leads men to apprehend that situation as an historical reality susceptible of transformation'. (4)

In two other countries we have also seen how study group members can say what they want to learn. In Botswana one of the objectives set for the radio learning group campaign on the Tribal Grazing Lands policy was to find out from group members what topics they would like to know more about. Enormous numbers of questions were sent in which were the basis of a further radio series of 'Answer Programmes'. It should be possible to analyse listeners' questions so as to plan follow-up courses to meet what is a proven large-scale interest. In Mauritius in 1973 a small-scale campaign was run on population called 'Ma Vie Demain' (My Life Tomorrow). It contained basic information on the social, economic and biological aspects of family planning and was aimed at adult and adolescent men, two vital groups largely ignored by family planning agencies. One important purpose was to reveal in the discussions the particular interests as well as the fears, prejudices and ignorance of these groups. The campaign was too short to bring about any marked change in attitudes. But the correspondence which it stimulated was enough to guide several courses on human biology, sex education, sociology and economics. Had they been offered, these would have been in direct response to a demand by large numbers for more information on particular topics. Study group campaigns can stimulate members to define what they want to learn so that future courses can become 'organised, systematised and developed "re-presentation" ... of the things about which they want to know more.' (5)

The second way to ensure participation is for study groups to be self-help affairs. All their members, usually including the group leaders, are students: there is no 'teacher' to impose or maintain an unequal relationship. The group's chairman and secretary are usually elected by the members. The leaders are taught that their role is to facilitate learning by discussion rather than to teach. This partly because they are rarely that much more knowledgable than their fellow group members, if at all. Learning has to be by sharing information brought to the group by radio or in print, and adapting it to the local situation. The groups' very existence as organisations depends largely on their members' will and skill. So in a way that can rarely be rivalled in a formal classroom, filled with the traditional authority of the teacher, a study group encourages, in fact depends on, its members' participation. The learning that takes place is their own responsibility.

Third, as we have seen in the farm forums of Canada, India and Ghana, in the campaigns of Tanzania and in the correspondence course forums of INADES in West Africa, great emphasis has been laid in many places on linking study and action. The kind of action has varied, as has the learning which led to it. But where it has worked best the group has had a chance to put learning to a practical purpose.

3 What will they learn?

One of the strengths of non-formal education is that it tackles people's immediate practical problems. If as a result they can get better jobs, or earn more money by doing their job more efficiently, or bring about other improvements in their conditions of life, education will seem worthwhile.

Since the jobs are in agriculture, so will the content often need to be predominantly agricultural. At the same time most of the students are raising families, building homes and running small-scale businesses, whether in villages or urban ghettoes. This suggests that several different practical courses at a very basic level will be needed to serve as entry points for the various groups according to their interests. The decision as to the number of basic courses to be included will obviously depend on local circumstances - the degree of economic and social variety amongst the students, and the production and organisational resources which can be mustered. The advantages of a simple core curriculum on the one hand and of flexibility and breadth of appeal on the other will always have to be weighed against each other.

But it will not be enough to provide one-off courses which offer unconnected training in particular skills. One of the great attractions of the formal system of education, and a feature common to all its varieties in the first, the second or the third world, is its sequential curriculum. Each year pupils are supposed to progress from stage to stage, to higher levels of competence and to increasing depths of understanding. In each year there is the hope of going on to more advanced stages in the following year. They can look forward to an end, whenever that is and for the few who reach it, when they will graduate with a wider knowledge of the world in which they live and work, and some ability to cope with the demands which will be made on them. Our alternative system will also need a sequential element to it.

The value of the sequential curriculum is not just that students always have an end in sight. Rather, as Bruner has argued, (6) it helps us learn to approach repeatedly familiar subject matter at deeper levels of understanding and analysis, always working from the familiar to the unfamiliar. In England pupils in some primary schools used to study English history right through from Roman times to the present day in a superficial way. They would go through the whole cycle again in greater depth in secondary school, and yet again but even more so at university, if they should chance to get there and to read history for their degree. The strength of this repetition was that it could steadily increase intellectual power. The curriculum should lead students to grasp generative concepts - concepts which enable them to solve not only the old problems in the classroom, but also the new ones met outside. As they work through a school curriculum they should find that they are increasingly working out principles for themselves and thereby increasing their ability to understand and change their own environment. A good, structured curriculum does not just enable us to memorise discrete items of information but gives us intellectual tools of general value.

In non-formal education a similar structure is needed for students, so that they can progress from a simple understanding of a particular vocational skill to a more complex and deeper study of the same thing. On the way they must have the opportunity to learn whatever related knowledge and skills are needed at the more advanced stage. The challenge is to work out a curriculum that is more than a series of instructions about better health or better agriculture - a curriculum that will be as intellectually powerful and rewarding as a good school syllabus. To do so, we need to adapt the schools' cyclical pattern of learning to non-formal education. Here are some obvious examples of how this might be done.

First is to link with the agricultural cycle. Farmers joining classes or groups, which would anyway have to be concentrated into the agricultural slack seasons, would in the first year be introduced to the most elementary scientific information that forms the basis of the agriculture they are already practising. Aims would of course include the encouragement of better agricultural practice, where there is scope for this. But, beyond that, the intention would be to lay the groundwork both for understanding the reasons behind better practice and for further learning at a deeper level in another year. The same annual cycle would be followed in succeeding years, but the skills and information would become increasingly sophisticated. Child-bearing and child-rearing with their own cycles could also be used as the basis for a curriculum of human biology. Business could lend itself to the same approach. A beginning might be made with the most straightforward activities involved in running a newly-formed co-operative through its first harvest and marketing season. The knowledge and skills for somewhat more sophisticated business management would be provided as experience grew from year to year. Or a mechanics course might start with the maintenance of the simplest machine such as a bicycle or flour mill, and progress from there to the motor bike and on to the tractor.

Thus the basic, and not-so-basic, facts of elementary science, of arithmetic and mechanics, of language, economics, commerce and civics, could all be taught through a study of the agricultural, mechanical, social and human concerns of everyday life. Essential skills such as literacy and numeracy would need to be included within such a framework both for their immediate practical value and because they enable various subjects to be studied further.

On this also we can learn from the various traditions we have been trying to bring together. The short, intensive and widely publicised courses which make up the campaigns are good at mobilising and motivating adults. If that initial stimulus is to be turned into something more long-term, the most highly motivated will have to be able to go on learning long after the campaign itself is over and before the next campaign has begun. INADES in francophone Africa and ACPO in Colombia have both shown what can be done with a carefully constructed series of courses including campaigns but in the context of a sequential curriculum.

The obvious fact is that people will never find liberation from one-off courses which teach them how and why to dig latrines. The power to alter their conditions of life in any more fundamental way depends on understanding their causes and having the skills and ability to change them.

TWO EXAMPLES

We will try to sketch two examples from very different settings. The first has been happening, in Honduras. The other is more hypothetical: set in Tanzania, where the need for radical answers to educational problems is recognised.

A real prototype - Honduras

We have already described some of the work of the radio schools programme of Acción Cultural Popular Hondureña (ACPH) in chapter 5. We stressed there the growing conviction of ACPH's leaders that education for liberation must be centred round an increase in peasant awareness of the forces which promote poverty and dependency, and the power of co-operative organisation as the only countervailing means. The normal content of education - literacy, numeracy and social and scientific knowledge - is presented in ACPH's courses in a way that promotes not only educational skills but, equally, political consciousness and economic, social and organisational skills. (7)

> Material is arranged around four main subject areas: 'work' (agriculture, use of resources, commercialisation, crafts); 'health and family' (personal and environmental hygiene, nutrition); 'communication' (written documents, letters, telegrams, means of social communication (written, spoken and mass) transport, migration, art, folklore, geography); and 'organisation' (social and civic - unions, leagues, political organisation, forms of government, national symbols, laws, workers' laws, and human rights, and social stratification). In addition 'numeracy' is developed in a functional way in conjunction with these themes.

All the subjects are included at each level and in each section of the courses. In the first stage for example, key words, such as 'plough', 'harvest', 'child', 'bathing', 'school', 'forests', are used as the basis for literacy training, as the themes of discussion of vital social and economic concerns, and as the source of numeracy exercises. In the second stage the discussions move on: under the heading WORK there is an investigation of the most important agricultural activities of village life, natural resources and how they are used, marketing of village produce and local employment. Common village illnesses, village hygiene, educational opportunities for 'campesino' families and nutrition are the topics related to HEALTH AND FAMILY. Under COMMUNICATION transport and road construction, telephone, radio and the press are discussed, and the use and construction of simple sentences are practised. At the same time, questions of population distribution, the local situation of peasant federations, the local land tenure system, and the local problems and set-up of workers' unions are raised as the ORGANISATION topic. Parallel and related NUMERACY exercises are introduced in measurement.

In a later stage a similar approach is used, but again at a

higher level of sophistication. The productive activities of the 'campesino' are analysed, and improved techniques for the cultivation of basic grains are taught as part of the WORK syllabus. More sicentific knowledge of the common diseases, details of the local health services and how to use them, and the role of the family in education, are examined under HEALTH AND THE FAMILY. The national communications system, and the use and usefulness of letters, telegrams and telephones for 'campesinos', and dialogue as a means of promoting understanding, are themes in the COMMUNICATIONS syllabus. And an analysis of the principal characteristics of Honduran society, more detailed information about peasant organisations and workers' unions and how to participate in them, the system of government and opportunities for 'campesinos' to participate, and the role of women, figure prominently under the heading of ORGANISATION. NUMERACY continues to concentrate on the development of the basic skills of arithmetic. Table 6.1 shows two examples of a week's curriculum. (8)

The government of Honduras agreed to recognise the successful completion of a four-level PEPA course as the academic equivalent of the government's own seven year primary school programme. More important than government equivalency recognition, however, was the linking of the radio schools to peasant organisations and unions, and the integration of academic content with social, economic and political concerns. ACPH's curriculum and its organisation both attempted to demonstrate in practical ways the relationships between education, development, political organisation and liberation.

Building on strong foundations - Tanzania

Two vital themes have run through Tanzania's attempts to reorganise society. The first has been the need to apply socialist principles to development in a country where more than 90 per cent of the people live in villages. This requires the diversion of resources from urban to rural areas and from industry to agriculture. In order to achieve a better balance between the quality of life in towns and villages it has been necessary to build up rural welfare facilities. To do so it has also proved necessary to persuade people to move from their traditionally scattered homesteads into much larger planned villages These are the 'ujamaa' (or socialist) villages for which Tanzania is now noted.

Only to 'ujamaa' villages is it possible to supply the schools and clinics, the piped water supplies, roads and markets on which so much of their economic and material quality of life depends. And only in village communities of a

TABLE 6.1

Level I Stage 1 Week3

LITERACY	NUMERACY	DIALOGUE
Reading and writing around the generative word CHILD ('cipote' - local slang)	Recognition and practice of numbers 1-20	1 Situation of child 2 Finality of marriage, responsibility of parents for children's education 3 Need for vaccination 4 Hygiene to maintain health

Level I Stage 2 Week 3

WORK	HEALTH AND FAMILY	COMMUNICATION	ORGANISATION	MATHS
commercialisation of production in the village, municipality etc. - main commercial centre and problems presented	analysis of education situation and possibilities it offers the 'campesino' family	situation of transport in local area. WRITTEN: use of sentences using simple consonants and dipthongs	analysis of local land tenure	how to measure

reasonable size does it make sense to talk about village government and popular political participation. The concept of education for self-reliance has been part and parcel of a general philosophy. It has in part grown from recognition of the irrelevance to Tanzanian villages of an exam-oriented system of education based on imported curricula. In contrast it stresses the potential of a reoriented system which will promote the attitudes, the relationships and the skills which are prerequisites for village socialism to succeed. The new system must also be as accessible to adults as to children. Both the change of emphasis in the curricula of schools and the creation of widespread facilities for adult education have been characteristics of education in Tanzania during the last decade. Another, the natural result of the promises inherent in the 'ujamaa' village drive, has been the demand for, and rapid moves towards, universal primary education, and the consequent recognition that for the forseeable future there will be no resources for any significant expansion of secondary and higher education. But whatever happens in the future many older people will not have been to primary school and their education rightly remains a high priority.

Tanzania has already experimented with various forms of distance teaching, as the previous chapter showed. We did not mention there two other programmes, both run by the Correspondence Education Department of the Institute of Adult Education, offering alternatives to traditional patterns of formal education. First is the production of a range of correspondence courses leading to the national public examinations for secondary schools. These courses are taken by very large numbers of young people and adults who have not been to secondary school. The syllabuses and subjects are identical to those studied in schools. The second programme is for the in-service training of tens of thousands of untrained teachers recruited in order to make possible universal primary education, as described in chapter 2.

Tanzania offers fertile ground for an alternative non-formal system. The organisational base exists as a result of these experiences. Some of her senior educational officials have recognised the need for some such alternative for the many primary school graduates in the middle 1980s for whom there will be no places in secondary schools. The following suggestions for a network of radio colleges are, however, purely ours. They are put forward only to illustrate the potential of such a system, not in any way as a prescription for Tanzania. They are an illustration of what might be done; what should actually be done must be decided by people on the spot who have far more knowledge than we do.

The prime target of such a system would be the people in

'ujamaa' villages. The base on which it would be built would be the radio study groups which have been used in the mass campaigns run periodically over the last ten years. Such campaigns would be used to focus attention on subjects of vital everyday importance, on what can be learned about them and on what can be gained from that learning. The difference from the past would be that people would be encouraged to continue to learn by the same means after the campaign was over. Continuation courses for study groups would be offered in practical skills - mechanical, craft, agricultural, social and organisational - which had been shown to be necessary during the campaigns.

Some of the students of radio colleges would be people who had never been to school, and for them functional literacy and numeracy would be to the fore. Reading and writing exercises, topics for discussion and supporting information would be backed by the usual series of radio programmes. The subjects would be political education, agriculture, health and family care, and a few essential technical skills. They would be an extension of the literacy campaigns which have already helped to reduce illiteracy.

At a second stage, when beginners would be joined by others who had finished formal primary schooling, basic COMMUNICATION SKILLS would be developed for public speaking and for letter and report writing, and attention given to some of the concepts underlying science and technology. NATIONAL POLITICAL PHILOSOPHIES covering the structure of government and basic economics would be another group of subjects. HOME AND THE FAMILY would be another, including nutrition, health education, family education and home gardening. Students would also be offered a choice of VOCATIONAL AND CRAFT courses on crop production, animal husbandry, building, bicycle and plough maintenance, and farm budgeting.

At a third stage there would be more advanced secondary school studies possibly leading to qualifications which would be at the same standard as national school examinations. POLITICS, SOCIETY and ORGANISATION would again be included, but studied at higher levels of detail and sophistication. The HOME AND FAMILY course would cover nutrition, health education and hygiene, and lead perhaps into training for rural medical aides and midwives. Sewing and knitting would lead on to clothing design and tailoring, home gardening into a study of agricultural science. Home building and repairs would at these stages cover house design, masonry, woodwork and metalwork, while budgeting and record-keeping would turn into book-keeping and basic accountancy. CULTURE AND COMMUNICATIONS would move on to more advanced public speaking, and would include reporting for local newspapers, creative writing and a study of Swahili literature. Mathematical skills would be developed through craft design and accountancy.

This curriculum would attempt to provide a framework for learning the wide variety of skills and knowledge needed, relating to social and political organisation, family life, the economy and the culture of 'ujamaa' villages. Some of the learning would be in common at all levels of educational sophistication. The aim would be to blend practical, social, political and communication skills with a measure of 'academic' learning.

It would not, of course, be totally different from the education being offered in school. Already Tanzanian schools are being encouraged to look at the village as a resource, from which knowledge and understanding of the environment can be drawn, and as a place to be served with ideas and knowledge that come from the school's work. Knowledgable peasant farmers help to teach in Tanzanian schools, while schools try to apply what they are studying in 'ujamaa' villages. A systematic development of non-formal education would help in this reconciliation, creating not two rival systems of education but two branches, each supporting the other.

THE STRENGTHS OF THE ALTERNATIVE

These two sketches (and we recognise that of course they are no more than that) of a real and a hypothetical programme seek to show how a more systematic development of non-formal education could occur. We believe it is worth trying. It could be a way of holding out hope of education to some of the many millions of people who, unless something unusual is done, are going to be deprived of it. Each of the two is set in a different national tradition. What they would have in common, however, is to our minds more significant than the differences between them. They would both be concerned to help people learn about their own lives and apply the knowledge and skills which make an improvement possible. They recognise the close relationship between education, home and work which is often missing from formal schools.

NOTES

1 International Commission on the Development of Education, 'Learning to Be'.
2 Ibid., p. 297.
3 World Bank, 'Education Sector Working Paper', p. 10.
4 Paulo Freire, 'Pedagogy of the Oppressed', p. 73.

5 Ibid., p. 83.
6 See for example Jerome Bruner, 'The Process of Education'.
7 Michael Young, 'Note on the Honduras Radio Schools', p. 21.
8 Ibid., pp. 24 and 27.

Chapter 7

TOWARDS THE BAREFOOT TECHNOLOGIST

It will no doubt be obvious from the tone adopted in this chapter where our sympathies lie - with the kind of alternative which has just been outlined. We would dearly like to see some radio colleges established in other continents than Latin America. If this were done, blending inter-continental experience in a new amalgam, distance teaching would emerge as something more than a supplement to schools. As things are, distance teaching ordinarily supports the work that is done in them, or enables people outside them to follow the same syllabus and pass the same examinations as internal students. In the absence of a radical alternative as a complement to the school, it will remain the master, and distance teaching merely one of its lesser handmaidens. But if things were turned round and the kind of alternative we have been discussing were built up, it would be done around the core of distance teaching, and made possible only by these relatively new methods. The fact that within distance teaching we have given primacy to the human element does not mean that in our new model that element could operate on its own. Radio and print are also of the essence, one so much so that it has produced the name we have chosen.

It is easy enough for us to declare our hopes in this way. What chances are there of them ever being realised in practice? The circumstances would clearly have to be very favourable for governments to be interested. They are for the most part much more likely to tread the well-trodden path and go on augmenting the formal system when any more money becomes available, in the way they have always done, with more teachers and more buildings. Well-trodden paths do not provoke questions about the direction in which people are walking, especially when trying to run gives them little time for thought.

What then should the argument be? The practical problems

for any government advanced enough to consider distance teaching are real enough. They are about its multiple uses and about the best balance to strike between them. Which to go for? If more than one, how should they fit together? Such questions cannot, of course, be decided by reference to distance teaching so much as by reference to educational principle, and always in a particular context.

If the paramount purpose of an educational system, in practice if not admitted in the rhetoric, is to produce an efficient elite for running the government, the army and the economy of a country, then there is no place for distance teaching.

Were this goal to be paramount it would be best to damp down expansion as much as politically possible, avoid the loss of quality which expansion usually entails and concentrate on the best education that can be given for a small minority at primary, secondary and tertiary levels. If all that were wanted were a well-taught and well-prepared aristocracy or meritocracy there would be no need to bother with the new-fangled armoury of broadcasting, correspondence and study groups. The image of education in an elitist society is a classroom with rows of neatly dressed children filling their exercise books with the algebra of education. The other image, which we have been calling forth in this and the last chapter, is of a group of men and women sitting in the shade of a tree or in a hut lit by a hurricane lamp and learning not only about fertilisers and nutrition but also about the means by which the poor can become less so.

The usual purpose, as expressed, is not to produce an elite. If it is accepted that all people, whatever the power or position of their parents, have an equal right to respect for what they have in them, they must have an equal right to education. If that be so, it follows that distance teaching has to be considered: it offers a means of speeding up the extension of the privilege of education from the few to the many, or, if one has got that far, from the many to the all.

YESTERDAY'S CHILDREN

The first question that has to be asked by any government so minded is how far they are prepared to put right the injustices of the past. In all the poorer countries educational expansion has left in its wake successive waves of people who have missed out on the benefits accruing to people born later in the century. There are the adults who have never been to school at all. In many countries these constitute the majority. Are they to get any consideration? There are the adults and teenagers who have been to primary school for a year or two and then dropped out. Are they to be left out because they have not been able to grasp the opportunity when it was first presented to them? Of like kind are the adults and teenagers who finished primary school but for whom there was no place in secondary. The cumulative backlog is in most countries a very large one and will remain so for generations to come.

Recognising the existence of the backlog does not settle the issue of what distance teaching should be used for. We have shown in this book that multi-media education is also multi-purpose. The combination of media can be employed for acceleration in teacher training, as we demonstrated in chapter 2; for support for teachers in the classroom, as we indicated in chapter 3; for imparting a formal education at the secondary level to people not at school, as we showed in chapter 4; or for doing the same with something much less formal, of the kind we have been talking about in the last two chapters. Distance teaching is the shadow of ordinary teaching. If its powers are not to be deployed on all educational problems at once, how is the choice of priorities to be made?

PRIORITY FOR PRIMARY SCHOOLS

It is very difficult to deny the strength of the argument for building up primary schools, and certainly we would not wish to do so. Wherever the quality of teaching allows, these schools can provide a basic education better than any alternative. Primary schools can excite some interest in further learning and produce the literacy and numeracy which are the conditions of full citizenship as well as of further learning. They are therefore the first and most indispensable element in any educational system. It follows that distance teaching should be employed to support them, and this can be done in no better way than by joining in the crucial task of training and re-training their teachers. Primary schools are unlikely to be of higher quality than the teachers in them. Distance teaching can raise that quality, and should be used to that end. Otherwise, at this level its purpose should be to provide some out-of-school equivalent for people who have never been to primary school or left it before their course was run. This would, rightly, be seen only as a stop-gap measure, even though the gap were a very wide one which might not be filled for decades.

One long-term priority should therefore be the training of teachers for primary schools. When it comes to secondary education the case for distance teaching out of school is that much stronger, because the case for 100 per cent coverage is much weaker than it is for primary schools. The two are in competition for resources, and, if primary is to have priority, the expansion of secondary cannot proceed at the same rate, especially in view of the fact that secondary is so much more expensive per head. In no developing country is it yet possible for all qualified primary leavers to enter secondary school, let alone to stay there till the end of the course; and in relatively few countries will it have come about even by the end of the century.

Despite the way schools have expanded, then, there will long be a huge backlog of adults whose life chances are limited because they were born too early to go to school or too poor to afford to stay there. Behind the generations who missed primary school march the continuing ranks of those who missed, and will miss, secondary school. Some will continue to demand formal education out of school leading to the same examinations as those taken by the more fortunate in school. Every country should offer that kind of second chance. But there is a different kind of second chance: while adolescents outside as well as in school may see the examination route as the all-important one, there is a better hope of capturing the interests of adults on topics more clearly related to what they are doing in the rest of their lives.

We have been talking of stop-gaps or second-best alternatives for those who cannot get into school. Primary equivalence would be in that category in any country which was still making progress towards the goal of universal literacy, and secondary equivalence would have that cast to it as well. But, to underline one of the crucial points in the book, it need not be so. The radio college need not remain a second best if as much imagination is embodied in the new institution as in the old. It has not been tried anywhere on the sort of scale that we would hope for, not even in Latin America; and, until it has been, no one will know how bounded ambition must be.

For our part we are, as we have shown, rather optimistic. Judged by purely academic criteria we would not expect that a radio college would compare well for most people with an ordinary secondary school. From that point of view we willingly accept the superiority of a daily seven-hour grind in a classroom. But academic criteria are not the only ones. A college not governed by the scramble for diplomas could in one way be at a great advantage. Almost everyone in an ordinary school who recognises the deadening effect of exams would also recognise that an institution not dominated by them would be in one respect enviable. It would be free to develop new curricula linked to life rather than textbooks.

The planners of radio colleges would have no choice on one matter. Their timetable and curriculum would have to be oriented to work, because that is where most of their students would be. The times set aside for study would have to be compatible with working hours, and the subjects taken up would have to be relevant to that work and such leisure as there was from it, if the interest of the students were to be maintained. As we have already argued, it follows from this, and from the fact that in developing countries the majority of people live in rural areas, that the curriculum would need to be about rural work, health, housing and leisure, though always set in the context of the broader national and international society of which each village is perforce a part. These are necessities of a rural radio college; they could as well be styled advantages.

A MIXED-AGE COLLEGE

Another necessity is that, as we said in the last chapter, the college should be open to students of different ages. This is partly because people of different ages will be keen to try themselves out as its students, especially if, as we think should happen, the distinction made in the formal system between primary and secondary is blurred instead of being perpetuated. There will be youngsters who cannot get to secondary school and older people who were not able to, who dropped out from primary school or never went. They will all be entitled to consideration. The mixing of ages has been a phenomenon in third world schools for a very long time. It is still not impossible to find a person in his twenties sitting alongside someone under ten. The segregation of people by age has not, in other words, been so marked in poorer countries as it has become in the richer. That same phenomenon would almost inevitably be present also in a radio college and could be put to advantage. The older students, some of whom could even be grandmothers and grandfathers, would have a lot to add of their own to the collective experience of the practical subjects which would be the core of the curriculum. A mixed-age college would in its basic constitution recognise that education needs to be permanent.

This is not to say that we envisage that, in the ordinary way, a radio college would contain children of primary age, though it would have adults who had not been to primary school. The first priority for any country will, as we say, remain the creation of primary schools for all young children. But beyond that we do envisage that radio colleges will serve some adolescents who cannot get to ordinary secondary schools because there are not enough places for them, and that they will mix there with people older than themselves. This happens already in the radiophonic schools of Latin America.

FROM THE REAR TO THE HEAD OF THE COLUMN

To urge all this is at the same time (despite all the manifest difficulties) to urge educators in the developing countries to do something different from what has been done so far in the other countries which have been their exemplars. Long after the colonial powers have ceased to be masters, their former subject peoples are still striving all they can to copy their educational system. It is almost as though the same gene were reproducing itself in society after society; or in other words that the education system were reproducing itself on the same template. The growth unfolds itself according to the same pattern, with primary schools being started first, teachers being painfully trained to work in them, secondary schools being gradually developed and then tertiary, with the first dribble of students at each stage being followed by great masses. As long as it is this example which is being followed it is only too easy to forecast what will happen at various points in the future, after colossal expenditure of resources. In half a century some poorer countries will be as far advanced as, say, Britain was twenty years ago; in others it will take a century to get as far as that both in quantitative and qualitative terms.

The present plight of these same countries is in itself enough to discourage too much faith in the rightness of the goal. Dore may have been somewhat harsh in his judgment on the contemporary state of affairs, but surely not so that the picture is quite unrecognisable, when he described education in developing countries in the following terms: (1)

> Primary schools which serve chiefly to give the majority of their pupils the label 'failed drop-out'; secondary schools and universities which seem designed to squeeze every ounce of curiosity and imagination out of a man before he is discharged into the bureaucracy to take responsibility for his country's destinies; growing armies of secondary and university graduates for whom no slots can be found in the bureaucracy, and - despite these growing numbers of educated unemployed - relentless and growing pressure for more secondary schools and universities in order to 'widen opportunity': such, in the developing countries of the Third World, are the consequences of using schools as the chief means of sifting each generation into those who get the

prize jobs and those who don't, and of letting that sifting function dominate - even it seems, obliterate - the schools' ancient function of providing education.

But there is no requirement of history which forces the poorer countries to follow my leader in this way. They could do something different, and if they did they might find themselves not at the rear of the long column headed by the industrial countries but at its head, moving in a different direction and themselves giving the lead to the rest of the world. Our own belief is that the radio college which embodies more of the technology of the West than of its social and educational ideas could be one of the instruments whereby this new and distinctive sort of education could be brought into existence.

The head of the column? A new excellence? Is it not a cranky bit of intellectual arrogance to suggest that we can produce something better than the English primary school, MIT or Oxbridge? Or, at best, a piece of inverse intellectual snobbery? We believe it is more than that, and we would sum up the case for the radio college by reemphasising its three advantages over a system where education in school is the only sort of education that really counts.

The first advantage comes in playing the numbers game. Tomorrow's children, like yesterday's children, will not all get to school. If it is possible, as it should be, to create a system of radio colleges more cheaply than we could create schools, then they offer the chance of redressing the dangerous imbalance between the educated haves and the uneducated have-nots. The building of schools will not solve the problem of equity in education for generations to come; a different sort of institution has a chance of doing so by providing education for adults who missed the chance of going to school when they were children.

The second advantage has to do with the diploma disease. The radio college's curriculum would be based on the concerns of its members' everyday lives, not on those of a remote and external body of examiners. Of course with any educational body there is a danger of academic drift, of seeking academic respectability at the expense of the interests of underprivileged students. But our radio colleges would have a chance of resisting the process so long as their objective remained that of educating the majority outside school rather than the minority within. The diploma disease is most serious where education becomes principally a filtering process, separating out the educated, or educable, few from the uneducated many. The radio college's vision is of a quite different sort of education.

The third advantage is that the radio college offers an

alternative method to the scholastic one in which pupils quietly sit down to learn what the teacher tells them. Forty years ago A.N. Whitehead argued that the educational tradition from classical times on (2)

> is warped by the vicious assumption that each generation will substantially live amid the conditions governing the lives of its fathers and will transmit these conditions to mould with equal force the lives of its children. We are now living in the first period of human history for which this assumption is false.

And yet, as we saw, under-equipped teachers can only teach what, and as, they were themselves taught. The methods we are advocating can short-cut, bringing to radio college or to school new resources, recently produced: education need no longer be limited to the stale facts which a teacher remembers from his own education, and from his regular annual recital of them. By changing the function of the teacher, and supporting him with resources from outside, the radio college could offer a better sort of education.

It is this set of advantages which would enable a network of radio colleges, or something like them, to offer a different kind of education - not an inadequate copy of traditional schooling but something qualitatively different.

CAN VILLAGE COMPETE WITH CITY?

One fundamental objection to any such proposal is that it runs counter to all the prevailing notions of modernity. The way modern societies are organised, anything with a rural bias is liable to be attacked just on those very grounds as inevitably second-best. Village life, so it is alleged, is inevitably thin, and a life down on the farm a thinner one. The only good life is in the cities, as witness the mass migration that has gone on and is still going on apace from the countryside to the towns. This exodus, our critics would say, could not be stemmed by a modern Virgil, let alone by lauding the virtues of a college with rural life at its heart. People are trying to escape from agriculture; if you ever suggest they should stay in it your fate will be that of all those well-intentioned colonial administrators who tried to organise schools by the plough instead of the Oxford University Press.

Harsh words, yes, but even so we doubt whether they have as much force as they once had. In rich and poor countries alike, our cities are facing problems to which we have not yet found solutions. If we can do anything to reduce the educational inequalities between town and country, there will be social as well as educational benefits. And, looking beyond our present problems, there is the new recognition of the limits placed upon further pell-mell urban expansion by the exhaustion of natural resources. Centuries of effort have gone into digging great holes in the rural areas of the world, extracting the minerals and re-fabricating them into cities; or pumping out oil from other depths for the sake of vital transport. It is not only in rich countries that people are becoming aware they cannot go on indefinitely consuming ever more scarce fossil fuels, adding more waste products to an environment whose capacity to absorb them is limited. When the oil finally runs out, it may force upon the world a reversal of the long-term trend whereby the city has gained people at the expense of the countryside. To survive, more of the world's growing population will have to grow more food from the limited land available to mankind. It is still a question whether they will be able to. If they cannot ensure that the expansion of food production keeps pace with the expansion of population there may be no long-term survival for anyone.

Seen in this light, an education which embodies the view that food production is the most vital work of all could be one of the keys to human survival. We would accept, of course, that production is not, and never will be, all that matters. The countryside needs enough food for the people who live there, and enough to export some to the city; it also needs a higher quality of life, adorned with rural industry and with many of the amenities so far exclusive to the city, if people are not only to survive but find it worthwhile doing so. Gandhi may yet come into his own.

There is another way of looking at the material presented in this book. Although there can (and of course will) be disagreements about what should be done in the future, there is less room for them on what has been happening up to date. There is not much doubt that distance teaching has been on a growth path, and also that the form it can most usefully take has become more sharply defined.

As we would now see it, many innovators have in the past put more faith in the mass media than they can bear. The mass media, and in the richer countries television in particular, have transformed the entertainment industry. They have gone some way towards transforming the home too, especially for children who cannot be dragged away from the screen. If a revolution in one sphere, why not in another? Could not education be transformed in the same way, and the best teachers the world can produce be put straight into communication with their pupils? The questions have long been obvious and pointed, and there was only one way of answering them - by practical trial.

There have now been many such trials. Some were referred to in chapter 3. The conclusion we have drawn is that the big technology of television, above all when it is used on its own, has not justified the hopes once placed in it. The early enthusiasts of television seemed to think that you could replace the teacher with the glittering screen as easily as soap opera has replaced ballads round the piano. It did not work out quite like that. Of course broadcasting can distribute information more rapidly than ever before. But practice has confirmed what theory predicted: (3) broadcasts can seldom replace the teacher, though they can change his role from one of providing information to one of helping learning. Even if we could easily distribute books, radios, radio repair shops and batteries throughout the whole world, we would still need group leaders and teachers to stimulate discussion about broadcasts, to see how they related to ordinary people's lives, and to tell the broadcasters when their programmes were on the right lines or on the wrong ones.

Technology, meaning far more the little technology of radio than the big technology of television, can be of great value, but usually only when it is used in support of live teachers interacting with other people. If you have the technology without the face-to-face groups then in educational terms nothing much may happen. If you have the groups without the technology something will happen, but it will often happen better with the support of broadcasting. For there is technical knowledge available - about better methods of agriculture, about health, about birth control - which can raise the quality of life for millions of people, and increase the control they have over their own lives, if the knowledge is made more freely available. The mass media do not have a solo part in this, but they can have a very worthwhile supporting one.

On this there has been a remarkable convergence in many different countries. It has been the experience of the Open University in Britain, and this even though it has made more use of broadcasting in conjunction with correspondence courses than almost any other of the institutions we have referred to. The lesson drawn from the developing countries has been even more emphatic. For people who are illiterate or not far from being so, the face-to-face element is even more crucial, with radio being relatively more important than print, at any rate in the early stages of any learning process. The special feature of the many institutions we have reviewed is the way in which radio is employed. That is their distinguishing mark. Hence the name we are suggesting, radio college. But this does not mean that radio has been as important as the face-to-face element. This much has been learnt from the ordinary school which we sometimes decry. The outcome has been the same in Latin America as in Africa or Asia, and as much in teacher training as in adult education.

This trend has belonged to an even more fundamental convergence. In what has been called the post-industrial society, new attitudes to technology have replaced the old. The emphasis is on humanising the machine, which means reducing its size to a human scale in education as in industry, in agriculture as in consumption. The new distance learning belongs to a worldwide movement. The barefoot technologist of education is partner to the barefoot manager and the barefoot doctor.

NOTES

1 Ronald Dore, 'The Diploma Disease', pp. ix-x.
2 A.N. Whitehead, 'Adventures of Ideas', pp. 93-4.
3 Compare Elihu Katz and Paul F. Lazarsfeld, 'Personal Influence'.

Appendix 1

A SMALL STUDY OF TEACHERS IN TRAINING IN NORTHERN NIGERIA(1)

The interviews reported here were made in 1974 when one of the authors was Visiting Professor in the Adult Education and General Extension Services Unit and the other Lecturer in the same department of Ahmadu Bello University at Zaria, Northern Nigeria. The 73 students interviewed were all teachers on study-leave taking a Bachelor of Education degree at the University. The purpose was to find out about their teacher training before arriving at the University and, more specifically, how many of them would have preferred to take their degree not through the ordinary residential institutions for upgrading but by means of distance teaching, if the University had offered it. In this book, cost and economy have been featured. But for some people distance teaching is not a second best; it would be preferred even if it were not cheaper.

The system of teacher training was the three-tiered one common to many developing countries: training colleges for children straight from primary school, where they got Grade 2 or Grade 3 Certificates (2) qualifying them to teach in primary schools; Advanced Teachers' Colleges where they could obtain a Nigerian Certificate of Education (NCE) for teaching in secondary schools; and Education Departments at this and other Universities where they could get BEd degrees or their equivalent, entitling them to teach in secondary schools or teachers' colleges. One factor of interest was the length of time they had, in the absence of in-service distance teaching, spent not teaching but away at the residential colleges, which were all that Nigeria could offer as they worked their way up through the system.

We should preface the account by customary warnings about surveys of this kind which are not accompanied by observation. We can only report what people claim to do and have done, which is not necessarily what they actually do. The questions were not only about an External Degree, even though this was the chief focus. We thought it also of interest to ask about the students' families of origin. That is the subject of the first section. The same consideration applies with more force to the second section, on their educational history before they entered university. This should clearly be taken into account before new extensions of education are planned. The third section is about the general balance between training and teaching, and the fourth about a possible External Degree for teachers. All the students have been given fictitious names in this account.

1 FAMILIES OF ORIGIN

The average age was 29, with a fairly wide spread from the youngest at 21, to the oldest at 39. These were the ages given. But several said they were not sure how old they were, since their births had not been registered. Neither Mr Tseayo, for example, nor his parents had known his birth date when the time came for him to enter school. His father had finally plumped for 1944, and picked as the 'official' birthday a month and a day pretty well at random.

More men than women students (43 out of the 48 men, 13 out of the 25 women) were married. Almost all the married people had young children.

Another difference was that the women were of higher 'status', judged by the occupations of their fathers. (3) The fathers of 16 of them were not farmers but teachers, civil servants or traders; while of the men's fathers, only 15 were in occupations other than farming. This fact about occupational origins was reflected in a further one about education. The women's fathers, other than farmers, had been to a modern school for an average of five years, the men's fathers for two and a half years. The farmers had almost invariably not been to such a school at all, so the majority of these students were the first generation in their families to have had this kind of education.

From farming families

Most of our informants had not only been brought up on farms but, girls or boys, had been little farmers themselves. Most of them seemed to remember it with pleasure.

> 'I indulged in it', said Mr Isaiah. 'I followed him to the farm at 5. I carried his hoe before I had my own. I liked farming very much from then.'

One of the first jobs for girls was carrying food and water to the fields, for boys, scaring the birds or monkeys from the crops. Near harvest time those who went to school were excused from it so that they could go to the aid of their families. As they got older, they were able to take on heavier work. This was the progression for Mr Arum.

> 'Before I could handle the hoe, I was sent to fetch water. Then I started collecting pieces of wood not needed on the farm, and taking them for the fire or for construction. When I was six I was given my own little hoe. I had my own little child's farm, and could work on it each day after I had finished what my father told me to do on his farm. The produce was mine. I also learnt basket-making for the local market.'

Farm work did not necessarily stop when the children went to school. Some did it in the evenings and holidays; some still continue in the same way even at university. Mr Gadzama said he had remained responsible for his farm through all his years of training and teaching. Out of his teacher's salary and university grant he sent money for his brother to hire labour and tractors to work on his plot. He was just about to return to his vacation job of supervising the work that his brother had to do on his behalf during term time.

In farming societies without compulsory education at least one of the sons is kept on the farm by his father, to help him and eventually take over from him. Children start school at different ages partly because some of them can not be released from the farm until later on. Mr Ajayi, for example, had to look after the animals until he was 12, when an older brother left school.

The accounts given serve as a reminder, if one is needed, of the strength of the bond with the land. The stereotype of the thriving African is of a man with only one goal - to get away from the village into the town and a well-paid white-collar job. The implication drawn for education, by Philip Foster, for instance, in his generally excellent writings, is that attempts to bring agricultural science into the schools are pretty well doomed from the start. (4) The children, and the parents, will not be interested. But the fact that so many come from farms shows that this would not necessarily be true if the curriculum of the schools, and thence of teacher training, was related to the previous and continuing experience of pupils from farming communities. This may be one reason the first training colleges no longer operating in that form - the Grade 1 colleges centred on rural education - are sometimes spoken of as just about the most successful training colleges Nigeria has ever had. We certainly got from these university students hardly a derogatory word about farming.

Rather, like the first-generation of people who have left the land elsewhere, they were nostalgic about it. Most of them kept a direct, continuing interest in their home-villages and home-farms.

The same may well apply to many of the inhabitants even of a city like Kano. There is a great deal of backwards and forwards migration between city and country. This would add to the case for a combined rural-urban focus for schools in both towns and villages. And where children have their own little plots, it would seem more sensible to encourage them from the school to improve these, and to bring their observations to the classroom, rather than trying to set up a special school farm.

2 THEIR EDUCATIONAL HISTORY

We asked a series of questions about the stages through which people had gone in order to become teachers, and then proceed to the university. 'How old were you when you decided to try for University?' 'At what age did you decide to become a teacher?' and so on.

The stock answer to this last question was, 'I did not decide it - it was decided for me.' That 'decision' was, in other words, very much like the earlier one, to go to school at all, which had not been the child's to make. The missionaries had decided, or the father, or an elder brother.

> 'In the beginning my father was asked to bring one of his children to school. I was the youngest, and so eventually I was brought. I'm the only one in my family who has benefited from education. They associate the school with religion. They thought anyone who goes to school will be associated with Fulani and become a Muslim, and so be won away from their traditional religion.'

The fear that the schools as they were at that time would convert not pagans to Islam, but Muslims to Christianity, was more common. Our sample did not contain many more Christians than Muslims.

Another related question made more sense than the one about decisions. It was about the job which, at the time people left primary school, they looked forward to having. Only 22 had hoped to become teachers, 28 something else, while the remaining 23 did not have any specific job in mind.

Those in the first group who claimed longstanding keenness for teaching were mostly influenced by one particular person in the school they attended.

'I liked the way my Principal conducted himself around.'

Others were just impressed by teachers, in the plural:

'In my area teachers seemed to be the most important persons in the society.'

For the man who said he just wanted any 'Mature job', teaching was the most obvious one to aspire after.

The 28 who had other ambitions were more specific - 10 women had wanted to become nurses, one a doctor and one a stenographer. Almost all mentioned the uniform as one of the attractions.

'The uniforms the white lady nurses wore in a hospital made me feel like becoming a nurse.'

'I was fascinated by their uniform and their cap.'

One man picked the same feature of his chosen profession.

'I liked the academic gown. I saw a photograph of a neighbour in his gown. We looked up to him like a God.'

Others were similarly attracted to the Army. Mr Bajoma said,

'I was a Scout member, and liked the way Armies marched, especially on Empire Day. I liked their bright uniforms.'

He still wanted to go into the Army after graduation, but 'as an intellectual'.

The family was the more usual influence. One man wanted to be a motor mechanic like his father; another a driver, another a carpenter like his senior brother ('I was enticed by the way he was enjoying his profession'); and for several it was a case of 'Those who can, farm; those who can't, teach.'

'I always wanted to be a farmer. I helped my father whenever I could. If I had the chance I'd still get a piece of land and farm. I didn't think any job better than farming. It was just that I was trained for teaching.'

To the training college

The turning point was being sent to a training college rather than a secondary school when they left primary school. Altogether 58 went to a training college - all but three of the men and 12 of the women. Once again choice hardly entered into it. The missionaries decided. Or their fathers could not afford to pay the secondary school fees. Or it was the practice of the primary school head to pick for training college children who were physically bigger, and the smaller and younger for the more prestigious secondary school. When children are uncertain about their true ages, their physical development may be the best criterion from the point of view of the training colleges. They are more likely to seem like adults when they start teaching five years later. If ages could be relied on, there would be more pressure to treat children of like age alike, and to make examination performance the criterion for selection. Then the teacher's colleges would be more likely to come off second best, whereas selection by height may mean that the colleges get at least their share, and perhaps more, of 'ability'.

The method by which Mr Hassan was chosen applied to quite a few others:

> 'We were patterned by the Headmaster. Some filled the forms for secondary school, some for training colleges, some for craft schools. It went by size. If you are very small, they did not like to admit you to the training college.'

Mr Hassan was so upset by the consequence of his size that at one point, after a holiday, he rebelled and refused to go back unless to a secondary school. The Local Education Authority brought such pressure on him that after a month he gave in and went back to the college he disliked so much.

So with little choice about it, most of the students went to training colleges, mostly to five-year Grade 2 colleges. Thirteen went to Grade 3 colleges for three years before continuing at a Grade 2 college for the final two, but these were older people who had left their primary schools when Grade 3 colleges, as separate institutions, were still common.

At this period of their lives some people were already thinking far ahead. The ambition might be just for a lengthy period of education.

> 'As a child I used to say I would go to a school for a very long time - 12 years.'

In fact Mr Asimin has done much better than that. At that stage, the goal might even be, specifically, a university. Mr Rufa'i said,

> 'I wanted to be the first person in our household to have a degree. I would be able to help my older brothers with their work as traders, by writing letters and planning their businesses for them.'

But the great majority saw before them only the prospect of becoming teachers.

> 'At training college', said Mr Gadzama, 'our highest hopes then were the Grade 2'.

Mr Gora was one of many who were quite satisfied with that.

> 'When you're a teacher you're a big man in society. I had no idea about the University. I would be quite a big enough man as a teacher.'

At their colleges, none of the staff at that time had university degrees.

When they left college, all of them having gained the Grade 2 instead of being like so many of their fellow-students 'Grade 2 Referrals', (5) almost all did some teaching, even if only for a short time. The average period spent as a teacher, in the type of school (primary) for which they had been specifically trained, was two years. Several did so only because the Grade 2 exams were at the end of the calendar year, with the results not out till the following June, and they had to fill in for nine months before they could go on to the next stage.

Advanced Teachers' Colleges

By the time they left their first training college, even if they were not yet aiming for university, they were thinking about the next stage in their own advancement. Advanced Teachers' Colleges (ATCs) would remove them from the primary schools, and prepare them for teaching in secondary schools. One man was not so much dissatisfied with primary schools as with all schools. He said,

'I didn't want to teach, therefore I went to the ATC'.

But he was in a minority. The others continued to think of themselves as teaching, but hoped, by continuing their training, to do so with higher status and more reward. Only three of the students, those with Higher School Certificate, did not go to an ATC. Mr Ali said that while there,

'I thought the ATC was the end of the road.'

But, like others, he changed his view. Ambitions escalated just through being at the ATC. The students illustrated a general rule, that aspirations rise to match opportunities; and the opportunity, or at any rate the possibility, of university now began to be a real one. By the date they left ATC, most had made up their minds to move on to university, which meant that any time spent after graduation in the kinds of schools they were now trained for (secondary) was wasted. The important thing was to move on as fast as possible into tertiary education. The average period spent teaching after ATC and before university was one and three-quarter years.

Those who had not already come to this conclusion were brought to it by their experience in the schools they joined, by the way graduates were treated compared to themselves. In their own opinion, Nigerian Certificate of Education holders were at least as good teachers as their graduate colleagues, and, having been expressly trained for it, often better. Their pupils knew this perfectly well. But they were paid less than graduates. They had worse houses. They never got preference for in-service courses. Their allowances were inferior. Whereas before the rise of universities they could have become education officers, now this rank was reserved for graduates, and the best they could become to start with was an assistant education officer. All communications from ministries came to them second, after the graduates had received them. Their promotion prospects were less good. Their prestige was less. As Mr Nuhu said,

> 'It's unfortunate in our society, whatever you are doing in education, if you don't have a degree, you are not regarded as a capable somebody.'

It can in some settings be a kind of reverse Gresham's Law in education that the higher drives out the lower.

Mr Abubakar summed it up:

> 'I came to university because of the pressure in my secondary school. I thought I was doing as much as a person with a university degree, but I was not paid as much. More than salary, I was discriminated against just because of the colour of my certificate. I was told I was not entitled to a quarter, to free medical care and other things. But with the boys I was working with, they understood how much I could do. There was no discrimination by the boys, only by the Ministry.'

3 THE PERIOD OF TRAINING

These students nearly all had lengthy periods of training, first at teacher training college, second at Advanced Teachers' College, last at university. By the time they have completed their BEd, they will have spent 11 years being trained as teachers, five at the first college, three at the second, and three at the university. Against that, they had spent an average of three and three-quarter years teaching.

Mr Aboki had done this same bit of simple arithmetic about his own career:

> 'I recently calculated the number of years I have been in training and the number of years' service I have given. It did not seem to balance.'

The contrast was all the sharper because everyone realised how much their services were needed in the schools. In the interim between ATC and Ahmadu Bello University, 32 people taught in a secondary school, 31 in a Grade 2 training college, eight did not teach at all and two taught in primary schools. All but four of the first 32 said there were unfilled posts in the school during the period they were there; and all but eight of the 31 from Grade 2 colleges, mostly in maths, English and sciences.

This shortage was itself one of the causes of the high turnover. When there were so many vacancies, teachers in one school could always apply to another, and ministry officials were under great pressure to permit the change. So there was constant movement away from schools with inferior housing, or very little water, or few if any textbooks, or poor discipline, and above all from the rural to better staffed schools in more congenial urban areas. Any move might have to be compensated for by ministries transferring someone else to fill the vacancy. Whenever a new school was opened, some experienced staff had to man it, and that meant further transfers to fill the holes in the older schools. The consequent high turnover meant that many children could have several teachers for a particular subject within the span of a year. For months at a time they could be without any teacher at all.

Should the training be shortened?

One conclusion from this seemed to be that the total length of training should be cut down, so that schools would not be without the services of teachers for quite so long. For this particular group of BEd students it centred on a question about the duration of the NCE and BEd courses when considered together. Was six years for the two of them too long?

Part of the case for thinking so was straightforward enough: 63 students said that in the 1973-4 session at ABU they had repeated to a greater or lesser extent courses they had already taken before, the more so because most opted for the same subjects they had already studied at the ATC, and before that at the teacher training college. Indeed, Mr Angulu had one fear when he was told he had been accepted for the BEd:

> 'I was confused. I said don't let them give me a subject I had not taken before at the ATC.'

Mr Nwana was very sweeping:

> 'It's practically all the same as the ATC for the first year. It's mostly the same textbooks. I haven't had to do any extra work.'

Mr Ajahi agreed:

> 'The first year of the degree course comes in easy for people who've been at ATC. It's only revision.'

Most were more specific, referring to particular examples of repetition in educational theory and methods, in the philosophy, history and administration of education, in developmental psychology and in physical education. A few people mentioned biology, chemistry, needlework and English, though adding that at the University they had been 'going deeper into it'.

The obvious conclusion was that, if the repetition could be cut out by joint planning of ATC and Faculty courses, the length of the whole could be reduced. This is the conclusion that was generally drawn. Of the 73 students, 61 considered that the combined course should be cut from six to five years, and a further seven that the period should be only four years. Many arguments were presented in favour of such a change. It did not make sense for Nigeria to have a longer period of teacher training than almost anywhere else. Nor should Ahmadu Bello University's combined course take longer than at the University of Lagos. Higher School Certificate students cover in two years much the same ground as the ATC in three, and Schools of Basic Studies in even less. Many said that if the load of work could not be substantially reduced, then let the teaching at least continue into a fourth term, in the long vacation. Several of them, without jobs to go to and with little enough money to spend, said they looked forward only with dread to the vacation.

> 'Why a Long Vacation at all? It should be the Short Vacation.'

Three extra terms would, as they saw it, enable the whole to be reduced to two years.

Appreciation of the BEd course

Whatever particular criticisms there may have been, the students were generally very appreciative: 57 were happy to be doing the BEd, although very few had given it as their choice when they applied for admission to the University, since at that time most did not know it existed. The main reason for liking the course was its professionalism. Most felt it was closely related to their future work. As Mr Agana said

> 'There are so many things that are good. It's planned to the needs of the country.'

Mr Ogbole expressed a similar appreciation.

> 'It's a good move towards having a better foundation for children. In the old days the standard was much higher in writing and speaking English. Now children pass out who can hardly write their names. If a child failed in the old system they were kept back to repeat the class. Now they just push them through whether they know it or not. This course will help to improve things.'

It is significant, too, that almost all the students looked forward to becoming teachers again after their graduation.

4 POSSIBLE EXTERNAL DEGREE

We expected that the reaction to the question of an External Degree would depend to a large extent upon whether students could get financial support from their states for an Internal

Degree. If they could, then presumably fewer of them would be interested in an External Degree. But if they would have to pay, in whole or part, out of their own pockets (or their relatives') to maintain themselves as full-time students, we expected many more to favour an External Degree. It did not exercise the imagination of the students with generous support to conceive what it would be like without it. The differences in standard of living were very marked. Some, with car and other allowances from their states as well as their full salaries, drove up to the Faculty in the same cars they had as teachers; others could not afford even a bicycle and had to walk. Some had their families with them in Zaria; some could not afford even to visit them except in vacations, even if they had reports (as one put it) that their children were starving, and they said they themselves often had to attend lectures on an empty stomach for want of money for food. Some had allowances for the purchase of textbooks; others none, and had therefore bought no books at all. Such differences depended in part upon which state the students came from, and will presumably continue to do so until a uniform system of grants is introduced, either by the federal government or by the northern States acting in concert.

The relevant question was not easy to phrase. This was not just because it was hypothetical. It was rather that the extent of financial aid could vary so much. People might get their salaries maintained, and on top of that a range of allowances; they might get the allowances without salaries; they might get just their tuition fees paid; they might get nothing at all. The attitude to an External Degree might depend upon precisely which of these various levels of support was provided for an Internal Degree.

What we did was to put the question in a general form, lumping various forms of support together, asking the students if they would have preferred an External to an Internal Degree under two sets of circumstances: first, if there had been financial sponsorship for an Internal Degree, and second, if there had been no such sponsorship. The answers were of three kinds - they would have preferred an External Degree under all circumstances, they would have preferred it only if there were no financial sponsorship for an Internal Degree or they would not have preferred an External Degree whatever the financial circumstances. The division between the three was as shown in Table A1.1.

For the biggest group, the one in the middle, the result was as expected. If financial support were withdrawn from the Internal Degree, a large number of people would obviously consider an External Degree rather than none at all. What was of more interest was the number who would prefer an

TABLE A1.1

Prefer External Degree with or without sponsorship	Prefer External Degree if no sponsorship	Would not prefer External Degree, with or without sponsorship
14 students	34 students	25 students

External Degree whether or not there was support for an Internal one. These represent the people who would apply for an External Degree without any change whatsoever in the provision of financial support from the states.

The amount of state support that people were getting did influence their decision, but not as much as the size of the financial burden they were carrying anyway. Even those from the most generous states would still have been better off, with more allowances, if they had remained as teachers or administrators instead of coming to ABU. So all were losing something, and this was the more crucial to people the more they had to squeeze every Kobo (6) they could get for their families.

It is worth giving some examples from the 14 partisans for an External Degree. The first three had children to support, and little or no help in doing so from their relatives. Mr Goro had seven children by his two wives. Before he came to ABU he had established his older wife as a petty trader. But she had not succeeded. He had transferred his hopes to his younger wife. She stood a chance of bringing in more money to the husband than she could by ordinary trading if she was accepted for a course in Home Economics, which would entitle her to a grant. But even if this happened, he was worried about his children, and would have preferred to remain in his job, studying at the same time.

Mrs Tukur had five children and had brought the three youngest (four, two and six months) with her to live in Samaru with her widowed mother to help look after them. But it was expensive maintaining two households, and she did not like being separated for three years from her husband, her son and her proper home. An External Degree would have allowed her to maintain her family life intact.

The motive was the same for Mr Aruwa.

> 'I would have liked an External Degree because I would have been with my family. I had them with me when I was at the ATC because I then had the allowances. In my first year I've only been able to see them once, at Christmas. I could not go home in the Easter Vacation. I could not afford the six Naira for the journey.'

The other four examples are all of people who were struggling not so much to support their families by marriage as their extended families. Mr Khalil used some of his grant for paying the school fees for his younger brother and sister as well as his own children. He also had to keep a house in his original village for them to live in. Mr Ali had to pay ₦80 a year for one brother at a mission school, and ₦24 each for two others also at secondary school. Mr Sawa used to have his two younger sisters living with him Bauchi. But he had had to move out of his own large house there and rent a small house for his own wife and children, while also giving enough to his sisters for them to go on living elsewhere.

Mr Abu, the fourth, unlike many of the other students who had jumped at the chance of entering university as soon as it offered itself, had prudently put it off until members of his extended family were better able to take the strain. For five years he kept at his job because he had to pay school fees for several siblings - his father's children by his first wife. Luckily his father had not married his second younger wife the moment Mr Abu's mother had stopped bearing. There was a gap. This meant that when the first batch had left secondary school, and were reaching towards the higher education for which the taxpayers in general rather than Mr Abu in particular would pay, the second batch was still at primary school. By the time they reached secondary, Mr Abu would be back at his post, and, as a graduate, earning a higher salary to support the further half-brothers and sisters who might yet be born. Despite all this fine strategic planning, Mr Abu would have chosen an External Degree. Since coming to Zaria, he had nothing at all to spare, as he had before, for his own aged mother and his aged if still active father.

These are all examples of people who would have preferred an External Degree in any event. They are unlikely to be unique in the Northern States. The families which constrain them surely do so for others as well. We only interviewed people already at ABU, not the people who were not there owing to family circumstances, who could not contemplate a degree at their stage of life. To find out about these possible external students one would have to go outside ABU to sample those who might, if the institution changed, become students in the future.

But whatever scope there might be for an External Degree, there would be many for whom it would not be appropriate. This was made clear by the third category of people who would not have preferred such a Degree whether with or without financial sponsorship. They were mostly not sufficiently confident in their powers to master a degree at the same time as teaching. Moreover, those majoring in physical education or creative arts said they did not see how it could be done by correspondence. Mothers who had left children behind wondered how they could have managed to keep up with the lectures and reading at all if they had not. Some said they would have been willing to try an External Degree if all the courses had been within the Faculty at ABU. Yet others thought that the great education of ABU was more in the complexity of campus life than in the Faculty, and for external students that would be lost. 'The environment of the campus is the lesson.' The reasons seemed just as sound as those motivating the people who favoured the External Degree.

CONCLUSION

So what, if any, general conclusion can be drawn? The students we interviewed would, when they graduated, have spent a considerable time being trained as teachers, and relatively little time putting that training into practice. Most of them favoured cutting down the length of the period spent at ATC and university, involving a joint replanning or rephasing of the courses at the two institutions. The provisions of an External Degree, and for that matter an External NCE as well, though not an alternative to the shortening of the internal courses, would have achieved the same objective, that of allowing teachers to spend relatively longer in the schools which are so short of staff. It looked as though there were quite sizeable numbers of people who would opt for an External Degree, and so help to achieve this objective, without any changes being made by the states in the support they gave to internal students. These conclusions should apply as much to lower levels as to university education. For such reasons it is heartening that since this little survey was made, steps in this direction have been taken at ABU and, much more decisively, at the University of Lagos and in the planning of the National Teachers' Institute at Kaduna. An incidental finding of the survey was that these teachers had nearly all been 'farmers' at some point in their lives, and are much less hostile to it than some accounts would imply teachers generally are. That could be one of the growing points of the 'new education'.

NOTES

1 This appendix is by Michael and Sasha Young.
2 Grade 3 teachers used to enter training immediately from primary school. Teachers are no longer trained to this

level. For Grade 2 status, they may enter training after primary, after some secondary or after full secondary. All these routes, varying in length, lead to the same Grade 2 exam. The Nigerian Certificate of Education is a further three year course, requiring school certificate for entry.

3 This is in line with other findings based on much larger samples than ours. See P.A. Beckett and J. O'Connell, Social Characteristics of an Elite-in-Formation.

4 See for example Philip Foster, 'Education and Social Change in Ghana', pp. 293-5.

5 These are teachers who completed the Grade 2 course and sat the examinations but failed in one or two subjects.

6 Nigerian currency is 100 Kobo = 1 Naira (₦). In 1975, ₦0.67 = $1.00.

Appendix 2

NOTE ON RADIO SCHOOLS IN COLOMBIA[1] (ACPO-Acción Cultural Popular)

This is a note on ACPO written after a brief visit to Colombia in April 1977. The intention was not to give anything in the nature of a complete account of the organisation, which would in view of its size and complexity take a book, so much as to pick out some of its features which might be of special interest to people engaged in multi-media education in Africa and elsewhere. The interpretation is of course a purely personal one, and not that of ACPO itself. Rather than embarking right away on any sketch as seen from the head office in Bogotá, it starts in section 1 at the other end, with one 'radio school'. Each family or other group, or even an individual studying on his own, is counted an 'escuela radiofónica'. The succeeding sections are as follows:

2 Some organisers in training
3 Growth of ACPO
4 The multi-media approach
5 The changes of 1976
6 Financial problems.

1 'CAMPESINO' MOUNTAIN FAMILY

It was half an hour's walk up a steep hill before we came to a primary school perched on a small parcel of flat land. The altitude was about 8500 feet, not high by the standards of the Andes. Then down again for another half hour, past tiny houses made up of mud bricks with thatched roofs and men ploughing on 45° slopes. Each had a team of two oxen, the lower ox on the slope pushing at an angle to hold the other one up, and the peasant farmer (i.e. 'campesino') leaning with all his weight against the wooden shaft to keep the ploughshare from slipping downways. There were no terraces such as used to exist, according to some accounts. The radio school we were making for was sited in a homestead that looked like many of the others. Two small huts - one thatched, one with corrugated iron - with earthen floors, built on rock platforms, again to prop the buildings up against the slope. A smoke-blackened space at one end of the larger hut for the hearth, the cooking pots and a pile of cane baskets in various stages of construction. One and a half hectares of land. Two pigs. Two rabbits. Some very lively hens.

We were not expected. The mother who greeted us when we branched off the main path wore a blue cracked hat, a whitish shirt and yellow trousers. It turned out she was the 'auxiliar' (or monitor) for that particular radio school. The radio lying on the ground near the baskets was the only product of modern industry to be seen, apart from a poster issued by the Misión Biblica Catolica and another advertising we did not know what. A chair and a stool - the only ones? - were brought out from the house for us to sit on; and we were told a little about the school.

Its meeting place was the ground in front of the house. The members were the other members of the family, who attended as they could: her father and mother, her two brothers who worked in a village some ten miles away and her sister, together with young children from other families who came to get a good grounding before they entered the primary school. How often and in what numbers they settled around the radio depended on the demands of work. On that day they were not going to listen at the usual evening hour of 5.30 because it was a day for basket-making. An Indian woman under a much broader black hat was squatting on the ground busily splicing canes for the mother and daughter to dye and fabricate. She was an employee to do this particular job.

The mother said they had learnt from the radio school to make a latrine at a distance from the house; to grow vegetables that they had not before; to organise a basketball team which played against others on the pitch at the primary school; to have catechism classes on Sundays and to discuss the Bible. There were 25 other 'auxiliars' in her 'vereda', the neighbourhood made up of similar homesteads grouped along a particular network of mountain paths. They had no regular 'líder' (see below) of their own, but had recently been visited by one who was going to arrange a day's course for them on a Sunday in May. Since it was one of her busy days, and darkness was near, we did not stay for long before returning down the (literally) breathtaking hillside to the van. A dog barking and snapping at the moving wheels seemed to fall off the road, and disappeared.

There is probably no typical radio school, neither this nor any other. But the visit to it - if 'it' is the right word -

made at least one point very clearly, about the influence of geography. People in Colombia on other mountains are often even more sparse on the ground than they are here, although not so sparse as in Australia, with its outback radio schools. Landowners have taken most of the best land in the valleys, and forced the 'campesinos' to snatch a precarious foothold and a precarious living on the marginal slopes above. In many districts there are no villages nor ordinary schools within scores of miles of each other. In some places the nearest neighbours may be a day's walk. Meeting together is difficult and, when the rains have turned the paths into mud, impossible. Roads are bad. In the western half of a country with over 20 000 000 people the ubiquitous radio is the only regular means of communication with the world beyond the homestead. The radio is the obvious teaching instrument, and the family the obvious educational unit.

2 SOME ORGANISERS IN TRAINING

This radio school was close to Sutatenza, where ACPO was started by Father Salcedo in 1947, and which has provided the name by which ACPO is often known, Radio Sutatenza, and the site of the training school for field organisers at various levels. Since the students there with whom we spent a good part of the day represented different levels, we should say something about them, starting with those who do not come to Sutatenza at all for training.

The woman in the yellow trousers belonged to this, the most numerous set, that of 'auxiliar', or to give the full name, 'auxiliar inmediato'. They do not have any formal courses, being trained informally by the people at the next level up, the 'dirigentes'. These are unpaid, and even have to find their own money for travelling over what can be a large educational domain. But they do get a four-month training at Sutatenza paid for by ACPO, although the communities they serve have to put together the money for their fares to get there. At the next level up again in the career structure are 'líderes' (or leaders) who have an additional four-month course. Some of them are paid a small 'scholarship' which enables them to give their whole time to organising the 'dirigentes' and classes for the 'auxiliares'. Others continue to work voluntarily. About 40 per cent of the 'líderes' over the whole country are women, though some more remote areas are represented exclusively by men. A few 'líderes' go on to a further 10 month training and become 'supervisores', responsible for one area of one of the seven zones into which the country is divided for administrative purposes.

The courses have some common themes, treated at different depths, loosely related to the five central 'notions' of ACPO, literacy, numeracy, health, work and religion. According to the students we saw, a good deal of the day-to-day instruction and discussion was devoted to relating knowledge to action that could be taken by 'campesinos' to improve their own lives. Agricultural improvement was therefore very much to the fore - introduction to fruit trees and new and hardy vegetables, better cattle-rearing practices, care of pigs and chickens, means of building and getting the most out of compost heaps, new methods of planting out seedlings so as to get a coffee crop after two instead of three years, how to bargain to get better prices for cash crops. Better health is also featured. They are taught not just how to grow but also how to cook vegetables so as to preserve as much as possible of their nourishment, and how to make latrines of the sort our 'auxiliar' had made. Then there are crafts like basket-making and carpentry, and a lot of emphasis on sports like football and basketball, also chess on which ACPO has regular courses. It is good, they say, for people to have to think as well as act.

So to the seven students we saw. We were assured they were not untypical, although obviously they were, like others, chosen to attend the course because of their keenness. They had volunteered to see us. First Rosmira, a 22-year-old girl who had reached fifth grade at primary school, that is finished it. Four years later she became interested in radio schools and went to her local priest to find out about them. She became an 'auxiliar' for a school which started with members of her own family and then grew continuously for a year until it eventually had 25 people in it, including several children between 7 and 16 who had no opportunity to go to ordinary school. She was chosen by her community to come to Sutatenza for the 'dirigente' course. Her brother carried on as 'auxiliar' while she was away. She had later attended the four month 'líder' course and was now in training to be a supervisor. Maria, a 23-year-old, had also gone through primary school. She was encouraged by her local priest not to become an 'auxiliar' but secretary of a young people's group, one of whose purposes was to promote radio schools and raise money to send people to Sutatenza. She was on the 'dirigente' course.

Ramiro was not at primary school, although of age. His mother said to his father that something must be done about his education, and that they must therefore buy a radio. His mother could read and write, having been at primary school up to the second grade, and she was the 'auxiliar' for himself and his four brothers and sisters. Then a primary school was built in the district, and he entered at the second grade and continued till the fifth. Like all the other students who had been at both, he preferred the radio to the primary school. In the latter the teachers beat them and discipline was generally harsh, whereas radio teachers cannot beat their pupils. In the primary school all the teaching was theoretical so that there was no motive to learn, while in the radio schools most of the teaching was practical, related to the everyday needs of 'campesino' life. In the primary school the purpose seemed to be just learning to read and write, regardless of what reading and writing were for. Radio schools prepare people to live in rural communities as members of groups; primary schools prepare them for individual advancement and to get out of rural areas into urban. If his mother had not had to work so hard herself it would for such reasons have been better for Ramiro to stay at the non-formal school. When he had finished the fifth grade he formed a radio school and became an 'auxiliar' for eight men, none of whom were from his own family. When he came to Sutatenza at his present age of 18, his mother took his place.

Jose's mother was also the prime mover ('men are interested in work, women in education'). She had once been a nurse and had saved some money, and she bought one of the special ACPO radios which at that time cost 75 pesos. (2) They are robust, and as well as the ordinary medium wave are fixed with a crystal which tunes them in to receive the radio school programmes on short wave. Amongst other things this enables the programmes to be repeated more frequently. People can buy the radio in instalments from the Agrarian Bank - which has the advantage for the Bank that it brings them more clients. Anyway, Jose's mother was too busy to be an 'auxiliar' herself but she found another family with someone in it who did have the time and competence. Seven people went from Jose's family and joined with nine others, children and adults. It was generally recognised that adults were easier to teach because they were more motivated, and because the radio school programmes were designed specifically for them. The school was never continuous. There were always breaks when field work demanded it. He took about two years of intermittent work to cover much of what ACPO had to offer. He never went to primary school and has never regretted it until his present age of 23.

Luis was at primary school, and after a long illness he started a miniature radio school mainly for his mother who was illiterate. She took it seriously. His father listened now and then when the programmes were about agriculture. His mother learnt dressmaking from it and now earns a living from her new-found work.

Ellsi (29) had been at primary school for two years when, as the eldest girl, she had to leave in order to look after the younger children. Her mother was the 'auxiliar' for herself and the other children. There had been a family radio school before that, and they had made many changes over the years in their practices to do with agriculture and health.

Francisco (25) went to primary school and then left because he disliked it so much. One day boys went to school, another day girls. A two-shift system is also common. He much preferred the radio school even though for a long time it was not really a radio one at all. They could not afford a radio, and he and his sister learnt from the books alone.

We clearly cannot draw any general conclusions from these seven potted accounts. But they do illustrate one particular feature of the ACPO system which is worth drawing attention to. This is its apparent flexibility. There can be radio schools, fed, as we shall see soon, from the same diet of broadcasts and books, but always guided by an informal teacher, for adults alone, for children alone or for both together. The routine can be broken, as the lockstep of school can seldom be, when people have more pressing calls on their time, and then taken up again. There can also be a flexible relationship with the formal system. Children can start at radio school and then, with credit for what they have gained, enter at an appropriate stage of the primary. Children can start at primary school and then leave to continue at a radio school, either as members or as 'auxiliars'.

The two systems, the formal and non-formal, can evidently live together, although it is worth stressing again that, for these people at any rate, the radio schools were markedly superior in most important respects, and above all in the relevance of their teaching to the everyday problems of peasant families. By giving their ages we have stressed that they were all young and mostly unmarried, though there were some much older people on one or other of the courses, for 'dirigentes' or 'líderes'. Most of the field organisers are, however, young, at the period of life before they have set up families of their own, when they have most time and most enthusiasm for work of this sort. The policy is to have a fairly rapid turnover. The training is not wasted even though one generation of 'dirigentes' and 'líderes' gives way to another. Yet another point, to which we will turn in a moment, is the role of the parish priest.

3 GROWTH OF ACPO

We must now move from the particular to the somewhat more general, in order to place those seven young men and women in perspective. We have said ACPO was started by Father Salcedo, and it has retained a link with the Catholic Church ever since. This has been an undoubted source of strength to it in the Andean regions, although sometimes the opposite in coastal areas where anti-clericalism is common. 'Campesinos' who, partly because of the terrain, are not easily organised into collective groups, usually do have a relationship with their parish priest, who is therefore a point of contact for ACPO wherever he is favourable rather than unfavourable to it. He is often the adviser to the young 'líderes' on what to do next and who to get in touch with. The 'líderes' on their journeyings stay with him; there is nowhere else. The institute at Sutatenza has something of the air of a seminary, and the 'dirigentes' and 'líderes' some of the sense of dedication of lay brothers. Religion is a prominent feature in all the teaching. Without this large supporting institution behind it, it is unlikely that ACPO would have flourished as it has. This is not to say the Church as a whole has been uniformly positive. Many of the more conservative bishops and clergy have been against. Some priests, we were told, use 'campesinos' to work their Church land, and are no different in their attitudes from other landowners. Others, though accepting the notion of planned parenthood, oppose the use of contraceptives and make ACPO's promotion of family planning a reason not to lend support, or even for active opposition.

If in the main the Church has been supportive, the opposite has applied to the landowners. The descendants, as far as power goes, of the 'conquistadores' who were granted land by the Spanish crown have amassed most of the best land into their 'latifundios', or large estates. INCORA (the Colombian Institute of Agrarian Reform) was set up in 1961 to bring about a more just allocation of land. But in the face of landowner opposition it has been able to do very little about existing holdings, and has turned instead to colonisation of the vast Amazonian and 'llanos' regions. The wet tropical conditions there have not lent themselves well to cultivation by peasant family labour. The landed class has remained much as it was, and rarely have its members been favourable to ACPO. Unaware peasants dependent upon their patronage suit them much better. They have sometimes smashed the precious radios, and will manufacture tasks which have to be performed by the peasants they employ at times when they could be listening to the broadcasts.

This being so, the survival and growth of ACPO is all the more remarkable. It is not as if it has had steady support from the government. By its own efforts it has held together, even through the long period (known as 'La Violencia') from 1948 to 1958, when the country was plunged into what was almost civil war between the adherents - landowners, officials, peasants - of the two poly-class parties, the Conservatives and the Liberals. The growth of ACPO has been well chronicled. (3) Today it is the main educational organisation for rural people. Radio Sutatenza, with its transmitters throughout the country, is the best-known radio system in the country, more so than the commercial chains. There are some 1000 people on the payroll in all the divisions, including the local 'líderes'.

Also very much to its credit is the fact that it has inspired similar developments throughout the continent. Many priests and others have come to Colombia and returned home to teach by some variant of the same model. ACPH (4) is just one of many which in its case has gone for 'primary equivalence' but without a formal primary curriculum. There is now an association, ALER, linking about 30 similar projects. (5) Though none of them is an exact copy, they all have the same concern with primarily illiterate adults, and thence with literacy and basic practical education; they all work through schools which are in effect small listening groups under the guidance of a volunteer; they all employ field organisers, or 'animateurs' as they would be called in francophone Africa; and they all use multi-media methods. Which brings us to our next subject, the instructional materials.

4 THE MULTI-MEDIA APPROACH

The fact that ACPO has applied to itself, and become known under, the general classification of radio school could be misleading. The work is not done by the daily radio programmes alone, vital though these are. The part played by the 'auxiliars' has already been noted. In addition, there is a range of other aids, chief amongst them being the booklets and supporting books. The booklets are constantly referred to by page number in the broadcasts. They are for the eyes while radio is for the ears, the like messages reinforcing each other. There is one booklet for Basic Education in literacy and numeracy, covering the groundwork which has to be mastered before full advantage can be taken of the other five booklets on the five main 'notions' of literacy, numeracy, health, economy and work and spirituality. These booklets ('cartillas') are distributed free to 'campesino' learning groups either by the 'líderes' or through the 'representante parroquial', an additional person in the field organisation who is not involved with instruction, but serves an organisational purpose as distributor of materials - especially important if there is no 'dirigente' or 'líder' in the area. Nor is there any registration fee. Editorial Andes, the publishing division which works with its own large printing works, is also responsible for a series of books incorporated in the Biblioteca del Campesino. These are sold at 5 pesos each (US 14 cents). They are on more specialised subjects such as dressmaking (now the best-seller), vegetable growing, pig keeping, fishing, coffee growing, maize, chickens, sex and marriage, and basic health care.

That is not the end of it. The basic course is reproduced on records for people who cannot listen regularly to the programmes or want to proceed at their own pace. Correspondence is encouraged from 'líderes', 'auxiliars' and families. In 1976, according to Bulletin no. 22 of the ACPO Data Bank, some 47 000 letters were received, which was less than in previous years. Then there is a well-produced weekly newspaper, 'El Campesino', which has the largest circulation of any paper in rural areas. Weekly sales in 1976 were 41 522, again a drop on previous years possibly caused in part by the rise in price from 2 to 3 pesos. The newspaper is distributed through local representatives, some of whom also stock the booklets and books. The paper contains news, education and entertainment written in such a way as to interest peasants, and prints the radio programmes for that week. It features from time to time within the overall educational programme particular 'campaigns' on soil conservation, nutrition, housing and the like. Altogether, it amounts to a formidable array of resources for learning.

5 THE CHANGES OF 1976

An important set of changes were introduced in 1976. Up till that time there were three main courses. The first, on basic education, has already been mentioned. It is the one which survives intact. The material is sequential: students must start at the beginning and continue through to the end. Each course on the radio lasts four months and then is repeated. The programmes that go with it are from 5.30 to 6 a.m. and from 5.30 to 6 p.m. each day. In the week we were there the radio was covering pages 58 to 62 in the textbook.

Before 1976 there were two other courses, the first being called progressive. The aim was, and generally still is, 'fundamental integral education'. The programme content was not strictly sequential. It could be begun at any time. The other was called the complementary course, and was introduced in 1970 in response to audience requests. The object was to prepare primary school drop-outs for the primary leaving exam and the government diploma. It took three years and was sequential.

From 1976 the complementary course was dropped completely, and the progressive course altered, the name being dropped but the broad subject areas within it being maintained and expanded in reorganised form. Up till 1976 different subjects like health, or within the broad heading of agriculture, like pig keeping, were kept running throughout the year. From 1976 the timetabling was revised around three broad subject areas: health and work, numeracy and communication, and 'our community'. Within these areas subjects were divided into short courses so that one subject was covered at a time before moving on to another - e.g. pig keeping, coffee growing. There is a progressive element within each 'cursillo' (short course), but rarely between courses unless 'cursillos' are being specifically designed in a series. The booklets are not organised in this way, or will not be until they are again rewritten (they have been on five different occasions in the 30 years of ACPO's existence). But it does not matter much. The radio tutor can refer people to page 18 and then immediately afterwards to page 57. They are in any case not intended as books to be read through from cover to cover. Another change was that for financial reasons the time given to each chunk of instruction was reduced to five minutes or so from 15 minutes before the musical interlude in which students are meant to look at the books or discuss. The duration of the 'year' has not changed. For ACPO it starts in February and runs till December. January is traditionally the holiday period in Colombia.

At the same period the amount of air time devoted to education was reduced, presumably due to the financial squeeze referred to later and, more particularly, the need to broadcast more programmes which would attract commercial advertising. At the time of our visit there were five hours of educational broadcasting each day. An indication of the content of the daily programmes is given in the announcements in 'El Campesino'.

Why were the changes made?

Colombia has been changing a great deal since ACPO was created, and continues to do so. Urbanisation has been proceeding apace, here as elsewhere. In 1950, soon after Radio

Sutatenza went on the air, the population of Bogotá, for example, was half a million. Today it is four and a half millions. The country has jumped, as Dr Bernal of ACPO put it, from the donkey to the jumbo jet. Bus services are improved. People are much less conservative, less under the influence of the Church, more cosmopolitan, more individualistic, more critical. And, more directly to the point, migration has become much more common. People have gone where there was seasonal work available on the land, or to towns and cities for a spell in search of work. As a result, fewer radio schools are able to keep going continuously with a stable membership throughout the year. If the basic unit of study is a subject, a person who leaves his homestead will not in those circumstances lose the thread so easily. When he returns home he can start up again on another subject. Broadcasting 'cursillos' instead of the more tightly controlled and more sequential longer-term programmes is in recognition of the extent of ACPO's 'open' audience. Because of geographical and economic factors, it is impossible for all listeners to be organised into the formal learning groups to which programmes were initially aimed. The 'cursillos' take into account that the time free for study is limited and unconsecutive, both from day to day and season to season. Another reason is that people can choose the subjects they are interested in and miss the others. What use (it was put to us) is it for a 'campesino' who is not in a coffee-growing district to hear about how to do it? Regional and local differences have all along been a problem for ACPO, as they always are for any radio education which has central programming, as it usually does. Also it will be easier to programme courses to 'campesino' requests, and to change them from year to year according to changing needs, than the previous system, in which information was split up and programmed over the whole year. By focussing attention on one topic at a time, over a span of days or weeks instead of years, it is hoped that action will be more forthcoming from the knowledge generated.

Another of the changes - the dropping of the complementary course - was apparently less in tune with the times. Colombia has not been free from the 'diploma disease', although perhaps less afflicted by it than most African countries. People, including even some of the students at Sutatenza, want certificates to enable them to get jobs outside agriculture. But ACPO has resisted this trend. Certificates of a kind, of attendance, may be given to people who persist with their course over a lengthy period, but they are not designed to be equivalent to anything which is recognised in business and industry, as are the certificates awarded by the very large

Colombian organisation for technical education, SENA. (6) Certificates of the ordinary kind will take people away from the rural areas, whose uplift is the concern of ACPO. For people who think like this, the introduction of the complementary course was an aberration.

6 FINANCIAL PROBLEMS

We have said that ACPO has grown greatly. Is it still growing? Apparently not. The numbers of students claimed - now in the 40 000s - are less than figures for the past. But they may never have meant very much. There cannot be exact figures in this sort of non-formal education, where people may join for a time and then miss out before rejoining and perhaps being counted again, if counted at all. The people are not there on every hillside to count the numbers as they can in formal schools. More reliable are the figures for publications distributed and, particularly, sold. The Data Bank we have already referred to shows not just that the sales of 'El Campesino' have been falling: so have the numbers of letters received, the number of 'líderes' and the number of 'dirigentes' and 'líderes' in training.

All this is a reflection of financial pressure. The world-wide inflation has hit Colombia hard in recent years. This is particularly serious for an organisation which cannot sell its services to 'campesinos' who have no money to pay for books, and which anyway cannot in the nature of things pay for the radio programmes they receive. But costs rise inescapably all the time. More and more effort must therefore go into raising money in an attempt to keep pace with costs. Fortunately for ACPO, some 75 per cent or so of its income comes from its commercial services. Advertising time is sold on the air. Editorial Andes produces books beyond those mentioned, for a commercial market. Gramophone discs are pressed in its own workshop. The printing business is a large, and largely commercial, one. The recording studios are hired out. Its farm sells its products. There is some rent from buildings. The difference, after all commercial sales have been taken into account, has in the past been met by income from government contracts and from overseas grants, largely from Catholic aid organisations in Germany and other countries. These have by no means kept up with inflation. The going is tough and will remain so. There will be hard decisions still to make.

NOTES

1 By Michael Young.
2 At the time of this visit 37 pesos = $1.00.
3 See the directory of distance teaching projects, pp. 174-5.
4 See chapters 5 and 6.
5 The Association of Latin American radio schools. See also Emile McAnany, Radio Schools in Nonformal Education.
6 SENA has used trucks as mobile workshops to take training to technical apprentices and others in remote areas. It is now considering a variation of the ACPO model for training in areas too remote to be served in this way. SENA stands for Servicio Nacional de Aprendizaje.

AN ANNOTATED DIRECTORY OF DISTANCE TEACHING PROJECTS

This directory has three sections:

Section 1 A list of distance teaching institutions and projects in developing countries, excluding those operating at degree level only. With each of these entries there is a brief survey of the institution or project's activities, and a selected list of references, with a note on what each covers.

Section 2 A list of distance teaching institutions in developing countries operating at degree level only, with references. This section is not annotated.

Section 3 A list of projects and institutions in Europe, North America, Japan, the USSR and Australasia. Only those projects mentioned elsewhere in the book are included. Major references only are quoted. This section is not annotated.

In each section countries are arranged in alphabetical order, with institutions or projects within each country arranged in chronological order of starting operations.

Entries in section 1 start with a brief outline of the nature of the project and its history. Where projects are well documented a selection of references has been made to include one or two comprehensive case studies and reports that deal with particularly unusual or interesting aspects of the project. Sometimes two or three similar case studies, perhaps by the same author, are included, in case one is more readily available than another. We have tried to make section 1 comprehensive, but there are inevitably omissions. First, there are omissions which come from simply not knowing about an institution. Second, commercial correspondence schools operating in developing countries have been omitted as of little interest to readers of this book. Third, some have been omitted from lack of information. For example there are about thirty radio schools operating in Latin America. Not all these have been included in the directory. Finally, we have included documentation on the use of broadcasting in schools where this has been significant in changing the role of the teacher. It is sometimes difficult to decide when schools broadcasting is merely enrichment to support the teacher, and where it plays more of a distance teaching role. Some innovative ventures in this area may therefore have been omitted in error.

In using this directory it will become clear that different forms of distance teaching predominate in each continent. In Latin America, for example, there are many radio schools for adult education, while correspondence colleges are numerous in Africa.

We have found great differences in the range of information available on projects. In some cases 20 or more documents and reports of interest are available on an institution; in other cases, particularly of Asian projects (with some exceptions), documentation is thin on the ground. Although there are several institutions with which the authors have close personal contact, the majority of the brief outlines of projects are based purely on the sources quoted. We have therefore not made judgments in this directory on the quality of the projects. Clearly a chaotic and unsuccessful project may appear in a report written by an interested party or an imperceptive outsider as a valuable piece of work, or a valuable project as chaotic. The directory will give you a general idea of a project's aims; but we leave qualitative assessment to your personal investigation. Our own judgments are bound to be misleading in some of those cases where we have sparse or second-hand information.

But one general point relating to quality is worth mentioning. The directory entries give each different project roughly the same space. But of course projects vary a great deal in scale and significance. For example, Botswana Extension College's activities are wide ranging, affect a large proportion of the country's adult population and go a long way towards developing an integrated non-formal adult education system within the country. In contrast, the 'Pila' project in Guatemala was a tiny experiment, interesting for its unusual technique, potentially of some significance for future efforts, but equally possibly a technique that will only ever be of use on a small scale for small jobs. There needs to be some awareness of differences in impact, in scale of operation, in the integration (or lack of it) of various different elements, in the length of time a project is likely to keep going relative to the organisational effort put into it and the educational impact it has. In particular a number of projects quoted are experiments. Sometimes experiments are started with the intention of carrying them on or replicating them through the country, like the non-formal education programme in Ecuador; others, like the Uganda television projects in the 1960s, seem to lead to a permanent or temporary dead end; yet others may finally find an appropriate format but are not yet clearly going in a particular direction, and one should be wary of accepting them as viable models for replication - an example here is the Project Impact in the Philippines.

One interesting result of listing the projects together, as we have done here, is the feeling that sometimes the right hand does not know what the left is doing (or has done). For several countries, a number of institutions and projects are mentioned. In some countries we know that they work together. For example, the two institutions mentioned for Tanzania have worked together in developing the radio-campaign approach. But in other countries, institutions seem to work separately, perhaps unaware of what others are doing. We quote for example, three Guatemalan projects, all concerned with rural adults; there is no indication that these have shared experience. There are, moreover, some other privately run small radio schools in Guatemala, not documented.

We hope therefore that this directory, besides offering information, will lead to an opening up of communication channels amongst educators both within and between countries.

SECTION 1 DISTANCE TEACHING INSTITUTIONS AND PROJECTS IN DEVELOPING COUNTRIES

Afghanistan

Assistance to rural broadcasting

Started in 1976 in four provinces to improve information and support services for farmers. The presentation of an existing farmers' radio programme was improved, while cassettes and sometimes filmstrips used to circulate information on topics of local seasonal interest. Extension agents encourage interest in the broadcasts and tapes, and collect questions and comments from farmers.

References

CLEARINGHOUSE FOR DEVELOPMENT COMMUNICATION, Assistance to Rural Broadcasting, Afghanistan, 'Project Profiles', Washington, CDC, April 1978. Contains a description of the project, results of the first phase, and lists six notable features.

Algeria

Centre national d'enseignement généralisé (CNEG)

Since 1963 CNEG has been teaching adults at a distance. Ventures have included teacher training and secondary-level correspondence courses for adults, published in newspapers and with radio support. By the late 1960s demand for these was flagging, and a new programme of more basic work-related courses started for adults in 1969. Courses in arithmetic or functional French were distributed in factories to interested workers. Lessons were simply written, some to fit the specific requirements of each workplace. Tutorial help was available in the factories. Courses of varying difficulty in the same subject were available to suit the needs of different individuals. The first year was an experiment, but so successful that the courses were subsequently re-offered.

References

BERKA, MIROSLAV, Professional Education of Workers by Correspondence Teaching, 'Convergence', vol. 5, no. 3, 1972, pp. 58-69. Also, same author, same title, in Ponsoien, A. (ed.), 'Educational Innovations in Africa: Policies and Administration', The Hague, Institute of Social Studies, 1972, pp. 200-11. These two articles cover much the same ground, mainly on the courses for workers.
LYLE, JACK, Two Uses of Mass Media for In-service Teacher Training in Algeria, in Schramm, Wilbur (ed.), 'New Media in Action: Case Studies for Planners', vol. 2, International Institute for Educational Planning, Paris, Unesco 1967, pp. 157-77. This covers the early distance teaching activities in Algeria, showing a creative and determined approach.
DE BIEVRE, G., BAUVRY, M. and GREGOIRE, R., 'Algérie: activités du centre national d'enseignement généralisé', Paris, Unesco, February 1972. A consultants' report with a brief history up to 1971 and suggestions for future directions.

Argentina

Instituto de Cultura Popular (INCUPO)

This radio school serves a rural area in the north of Argentina. In 1972 INCUPO estimated they had 400 000 listeners daily, while 30 000 copies of a monthly news bulletin were distributed. There are three modes of operation: first, 'open' broadcasts to encourage people to take part in educational activities; second, organised groups with local leaders who use radio and printed materials to learn basic literacy and numeracy, health and nutrition, and Christian education. Special themes are incorporated in the exercise booklets and in the monthly news bulletin. Third, such groups may move into an area of practical action for development; in this case they are given support by INCUPO staff, although this sometimes has to be limited owing to lack of resources.

References

INCUPO, paper presented to the Dartington workshop on distance teaching and rural development, International Extension College, 1977.

NARDELLO, P., ENRIQUE, ANTONIO, Que es INCUPO?, in Oficina de servicios para América Latina, 'Las Escuelas Radiofónicas En América Latina', Sutatenza, Colombia, 1972, Primera Parte, pp. 23-30. A paper giving a clear outline of the organisational structure, the aims of INCUPO and some data on students.

Benin

Rural Radio Clubs

Started in 1968, for village groups. About 600 clubs existed in 1972 with 12 000-15 000 members altogether. One 30-minute radio programme is broadcast weekly for most of the year in 10 languages, to stimulate agricultural and community development. Groups have local leaders and the support of a village-level agricultural worker. The leaders send monthly reports to the Rural Radio.

References

MCANANY, EMILE, Rural Radio in Dahomey, Institute of Communication Research reprints, University of Stanford, September 1972. A description which covers also the problems of expansion and the need for inter-departmental co-operation.

Bolivia

Escuelas Radiofónicas de Bolivia (ERBOL)

ERBOL is the nonprofitmaking association to which Bolivian radio schools belong. In 1972 three schools were members. Radio courses have printed support materials, and village groups study with the help of trained local leaders.

1 Escuelas radiofónicas San Gabriel This school operates in seven provinces with a mainly Aymara-speaking population. Of the 15 members of the organising committee 12 are farmers. In 1972 there were 443 study groups with 6167 members. The schools are partly self-financing, with members paying 60 per cent of costs.

2 Radio 'San Rafael' (ERSAR) This school's broadcasts reach

over 300 000 people, about half the population of nine provinces. In 1972 about 1000 students were organised in listening groups. Courses are organised to fit with the agricultural cycle.

3 Acción Cultural Loyola (ACLO) In the south-west, reaching both urban and rural people speaking Spanish, Quechua and Guarani. It started work in 1967. In 1972 nearly 2000 people were following literacy programmes. ACLO also runs short courses and publishes a monthly periodical, 'En Marcha'.

References

BARRIENTOS DE UGARTE, JOSE, Escuelas Radiofónicas de Bolivia, ERBOL.

BARRIENTOS DE UGARTE, JOSE, Camcos - Centre Aymarista de Medios de Communicación Social: Radio San Gabriel; Escuelas radiofónicas San Gabriel, periodico el Gabrielito: centro de Peliculas de promoción para el campesino - Bolivia.

GODOY, MARIO E., 'Radio San Rafael' Cochabamba - Bolivia. Informe Breve de las Actua Actividades de ERSAR 1970-1972.

TRIAS, P. JORGE, Acción Cultural Loyola - Sucre - Bolivia.

A series of brief case studies, all in Oficina de Servicios para América Latina, 'Las Escuelas Radiofónicas en América Latina', Sutatenza, Colombia, 1972, pp. 31-64.

ERBOL/ACLO, Educación Radiofónica en Bolivia, Sucre, Bolivia, 1977. An extensive evaluation of the achievement of Bolivian radio schools, published to celebrate 10 years of the association. The report also considers the future direction such education should take in Bolivia.

Botswana

Francistown Teacher Training College

A project run from 1968 to 1973, to train about 600 unqualified primary school teachers. The trainees studied for three years by correspondence linked with residential courses and radio programmes. Trainees were also occasionally visited in their schools.

References

EL-BUSHRA, JUDY, 'Correspondence Institutions in the Commonwealth, 1976', London, Commonwealth Secretariat, 1976.

KINYANJUI, PETER, 'Training Teachers by Correspondence', Cambridge, International Extension College, 1974.

Both of these reports contain very brief case studies of this project.

WHITE, C.J.B., Training teachers through correspondence education in Botswana, in Ponsoien, A. (ed.), 'Educational Innovations in Africa: Policies and Administration', The Hague, Institute of Social Studies, 1972, pp. 184-91. A slightly longer report, written while the project was in full swing.

HILL, E.D., 'Final Report on the Francistown Teacher Training Project', Botswana, Francistown Teacher Training College, 1972, mimeo. This report contains an analysis of teachers' progress and performance.

Botswana radio campaigns

In 1971 a small radio campaign was piloted by the University Department of Extra-Mural studies (DEMS) on the five year plan, 1970-5. Twenty-four groups listened to 12 radio programmes under the guidance of group leaders and with the aid of a simplified bilingual English/Setswana version of the plan. Questions were answered over the air by government ministers. This was followed by a national campaign in 1973 on the new five year plan, on the same model. 1432 groups participated this time.

In 1976 a third campaign took place, this time with the Botswana Extension College working with DEMS. It aimed to open up for public discussion the new Tribal Grazing Land Policy. About one in six of the country's adults participated, in over 3000 groups.

References

COLCLOUGH, MARY and CROWLEY, DAVID, 'Setshaba le Togamaano: The People and the Plan', vol. 1, UBLS/DEMS, 1974. About the pilot campaign and the preparations for the 1973 campaign. Contains much discussion of the campaign technique, especially useful on the training of group leaders and practical problems in group organisation.

CROWLEY, DAVID and KIDD, ROSS, 'Radio Learning Group Campaigns in Botswana', paper presented to the Dartington workshop on distance teaching and rural development, Cambridge, International Extension College, September 1977. This paper discusses the 1976 campaign in particular. It also discusses the campaign approach in relation to other non-formal educational provision.

MINISTRY OF LOCAL GOVERNMENT AND LANDS, 'Lefatshe la Rona - Our Land', Gaborone, Republic of Botswana, September 1977. A very full, illustrated evaluation report on the 1976 campaign. A number of progress reports or technical notes are also available, from the ministry or from Botswana Extension College.

Botswana Extension College (BEC)

Started in 1973, the College provides correspondence courses with radio support for adults and young people needing school qualifications; it helps existing organisations with training, information or other problems, using distance teaching. It provides non-formal distance education for adults, with special emphasis on rural development. Projects have ranged from a correspondence course on map reading for agricultural demonstrators to a pilot adult literacy project.

References

PERRATON, HILARY, 'Starting the Botswana Extension College', Cambridge, International Extension College, 1977. A comprehensive account of setting up the College and the first two years' activity.

INQUAI, SOLOMON, 'Non-formal Education and Rural Development: A Botswana Experience', paper presented to the Dartington workshop on distance teaching and rural development, International Extension College, September 1977. Discusses the Village Home Affairs leadership project and the development of the functional literacy project.

KIDD, R. and BYRAM, M., 'Laedza Batanani: Folk Media and Development', Gaborone, Botswana Extension College, 1976. An account of experiments with popular theatre for rural education.

ETHERINGTON, ALAN, 'Radio Programmes for 4B Clubs: The Results of a Small Survey', Gaborone, Botswana Extension College, 1976. Interesting insights into the potential for the use of radio by village groups, and their attitudes to the medium.

BEC EVALUATION UNIT, 'Go Bala ke Tswelelopele', Gaborone, Botswana Extension College, May 1978. A report of the pilot functional literacy campaign.

BEC EVALUATION UNIT, 'Report on the Radio Programme "Re Botseng"', Gaborone, Botswana Extension College, June 1978. Evaluation of a radio question-and-answer programme.

See also: Botswana radio campaigns.

Brazil

Movimento de Educação de Base (MEB)

MEB started in 1961, providing radio schools for rural adults. There were over 7000 groups with a total of 400 000 members at the time of the military coup in 1964. Subsequently, membership declined in areas of political tension. By 1972 there were only 80 000 students. Literacy and basic education is taught by radio, texts and monitors. The 'conscientisation' method is used and the curriculum linked with the agricultural cycle. The work is co-ordinated nationally, with regional 'systems' of radio production teams, peasants, monitors. From 1973 the schools have been using MOBRAL materials.

References

DE KADT, EMANUEL, 'Catholic Radicals in Brazil', Oxford University Press, 1970. Chapters in this book relate the early development of MEB, analysing the problems that arose as the emphasis on community development increased and describing the political repression after the coup.

LOPES CORREA, ARLINDO, 'Permanent Education and Adult Education in Brazil', Brazil, Ministério da Educação e Cultura, 1973. A chapter in this report, written by the executive secretary of MOBRAL, describes the recent work of MEB and its relationship with adult education in Brazil generally.

CORTEZ ROMERO, CARLOS, Movimiento de Educación de Base, in Oficina de Servicios para América Latina, 'Las Escuelas Radiofónicas en América Latina', Sutatenza, 1972, pp. 73-98. A detailed account of MEB's curriculum and approach with a short history of activities.

Fundação Educacional Padre Landell de Moura (FEPLAM)

An organisation founded in 1965 to develop the use of mass media for education. It has a small central staff and many local volunteer helpers. The work of FEPLAM has been varied and often experimental. Most of its work has been with adults. Its first television series, recorded and then transmitted by commercial stations, in 1966-7, was on car mechanics and understanding electricity, using domestic appliances to explain the content. Several similar series have subsequently been produced.

On radio, the College of the Air was started as an experiment in 1966-7. From a small start, it continues today to provide courses for students for the 'madureza', a primary-equivalence exam for out-of-school adults. College of the Air also provides some special programmes, such as two series for people on the move because of government resettlement, one for adults and one for children.

In addition FEPLAM has done important literacy work, including a 1970 experimental comparison of literacy work with and without radio. The radio group was considerably more tenacious and successful, and this finding influenced MOBRAL to move towards greater use of radio. Since 1974 FEPLAM has been responsible for the implementation of project MINERVA in one province, a national distance teaching course for the 'madureza' exam. It has also pioneered school equivalency courses for workers.

References

FEPLAM, 'Estrutivia e organização da FEPLAM', Porto Alegre, Brazil, January 1976. An account of the history, organisation, aims and activities of FEPLAM.

COMPARSI, ANGELICA, Fundación Educacional Padre Landell de Moura, Porto Alegre, Brazil, in Oficina de Servicios para América Latina, 'Las Escuelas Radiofónicas en América Latina', Sutatenza, 1972, pp. 65-71. A brief account of FEPLAM's various activities up to the early 1970s.

OLIVEIRA, J.B. and ORIVEL, FRANÇOIS, The Minerva Project in Brazil, in Perraton, Hilary (ed.), 'Alternative Routes to Formal Education: Distance Teaching For School Equivalency', Washington, DC, World Bank, forthcoming. Includes an account of the Minerva Project, with which FEPLAM has been closely involved.

Educational Radio Broadcasting Institute (IRDEB), Bahia State

Set up in 1969, IRDEB has been involved in a number of distance teaching programmes. The largest of these has been courses for the state 'madureza' exam, equivalent to primary leaving standard but for out-of-school adults. In 1977 enrolments were around 8000 students. Students follow daily broadcasts and texts at home or in one of over 200 listening centres under the guidance of monitors. The state chose to run a 'madureza' programme independently of the federal MINERVA project (see FEPLAM), but at present the system does not look economically viable.

References

OLIVEIRA, J.B. and ORIVEL, FRANCOIS, A 'Madureza' Project in Bahia Brazil, in Perraton, Hilary (ed.), 'Alternative Routes to Formal Education: Distance Teaching For School Equivalency', Washington, DC, World Bank, forthcoming. A thorough case study.

Movimento Braziliero de Alfabeticação (MOBRAL)

Started in 1970. By the end of 1973 over 5 000 000 of an estimated total of 18 million adult illiterates had learnt to read. Policy is decided centrally but there is municipal control at local level. The main instruction is in classes with a variety of printed materials but radio is used to train instructors in groups, and experiments have recently been conducted on literacy teaching by radio and radio education for new literates.

References

UNESCO REGIONAL OFFICE FOR EDUCATION IN LATIN AMERICA AND THE CARIBBEAN, 'MOBRAL - The Brazilian Adult Literacy Experiment', Unesco, Educational Studies and documents, no. 15, 1975. A thorough case study.

CAIRNS, JOHN, MOBRAL - The Brazilian Literacy Movement; a First Hand Account, 'Convergence', vol. VIII, no. 2, 1975, pp. 12-21. A brief but comprehensive description.

LOPES CORRẼA, ARLINDO, 'Permanent Education and Adult Education in Brazil', Brazil, Ministério da Educação e Cultura, 1973. A survey of provision for adult education in Brazil, and the part MOBRAL intends to play co-ordinating this work.

La Fundação Maranhense de Televisão Educativa (FMTVE)

Since 1970 up to 15 000 students a year in 300 classes have been taught by television in the region of São Luis de Maranhão. These are children who would not otherwise have found room in school. Each class is organised into groups; this structure saves a great deal in expenditure on teachers since mutual peer-teaching within groups is encouraged. Classes are supervised by 'orientators' whose function is to guide the class and help those with special problems. They are often highly qualified in specific subjects but do not teach in the traditional way. Drop-out from classes is very low, usually under 10 per cent per year, and annual exam pass rates are over 90 per cent. The system is also considerably cheaper than conventional schools.

References

AGENCE DE COOPERATION CULTURELLE ET TECHNIQUE, Brazil: un géant de la télévision éducative, 'Direct', 1, 1976, pp. 17-44. A thorough case study.

ARENA, EDUARDO, JAMISON, DEAN, OLIVEIRA, JOÃO B. and ORIVEL, FRANÇOIS, 'Economic Analysis of Educational Television in Maranhão, Brazil', Paris, Unesco, 1977. Explains the project and analyses its costs against the background economic picture of that state of Brazil.

'João da Silva'

A course started in 1970 for primary-school drop-outs in cities, mainly young people, with most of the teaching done by television. Over 10 000 a year enrolled at viewing centres in first years; some programmes had an audience of over 300 000. Five half hour programmes were broadcast weekly for 25 weeks in a soap opera format. Students followed the course with a tutor in viewing centres, at home with a weekly session with counsellors, or at home alone. Each programme was broadcast three times daily at different times.

References

D'ARINOS SILVA, LUIZ VICTOR, João da Silva: a Telenovela Course, 'Educational Broadcasting International', March 1975, pp. 29-31. A description of the project, giving information on programme content and on students' performance.

Canary Islands

Radio Emisora Cultural de Canarias (Radio ECCA)

This radio school for adults began in 1965. It offers courses at primary level, and higher-level courses in, for example, business studies. In the first ten years over 100 000 students were enrolled, about 20 000 being active at any one time. Students are of all ages, though from 1976 no student aged 14 or under was admitted, on the grounds that they should be in school. Radio programmes and workbooks mirror and reinforce each other, and participants attend weekly at one of 455 learning centres. Some Latin American radio schools have based their approach on Radio ECCA, notably Radio Santa Maria (see Dominican Republic).

References

RADIO ECCA, 'Radio ECCA, Centro Docente', Las Palmas, 1976.

A history and description of the school, lavishly illustrated. CLEARINGHOUSE FOR DEVELOPMENT COMMUNICATION, Radio ECCA, Canary Islands, 'Project Profiles', Washington, CDC, January 1978. A brief description and analysis of results.

Chile

Fundación Radioescuela para el Desarrollo Rural (FREDER)

FREDER's main means of communication is Radio la Voz de la Costa, a private radio station serving a small isolated rural area with poor communications. Radio school broadcasts started in 1968 and include literacy classes and programmes for school equivalency; these latter are often followed by individuals rather than groups because of the difficulty of terrain and weather. In addition the radio organises a successful annual 'campesino' festival.

By 1972 the drop-out rate in the primary course had risen to 50 per cent. The main problem was seen to be an inappropriate curriculum. Since then short courses have been broadcast, while a new integrated basic curriculum is being developed.

Recent developments have been 'radiovision' courses on agriculture, using sets of slides tied in with radio programmes; and the creation of a 'campesino' library of easy-to-read books.

References

SANCHES, P. MANUEL, Escuelas radiofónicas Santa Clara, Radio la Voz de la Costa, Osorno, Chile, in Oficina de Servicios para América Latina, 'Las Escuelas Radiofónicas en América Latina', Sutatenza, 1972, pp. 117-25. A detailed account of the structure and activities of the schools.

FREDER, 'Radio "La Voz de la Costa", Osorno', Chile, FREDER, 1974. A similar but longer and more recent outline of activities.

FREDER, 'Qué Somos, Qué Hacemos, A Dondé Vamos', Osorno, Chile, FREDER, 1975. Includes a description of the radiovision project, the new library, and a report on the difficulties of devising a new curriculum for basic education.

FREDER, 'Una Experiencia en Teleducación dirigida al Sector Rural', Osorno, Chile, FREDER, n.d. (1972?). An account of how the radio-school system was set up, focussing particularly on the training of the radio teachers and the monitors.

China

Distance education

Distance education has been important in China since the 1950s. A number of university-level and teacher-training opportunities became available by correspondence, often with radio or television support from this time.

In non-formal education the media have been used consistently and imaginatively. For example, in the late 1950s there was a large-scale literacy campaign. While most teaching was face-to-face, radio, lantern lectures, exhibitions, films, plays and wall posters were also used. There is a flexible approach to educational needs, using any method appropriate to meet them. Barefoot doctors, for example, take health education to villages assisted by radio and low-cost teaching aids such as pictures, filmstrips and exhibitions.

References

PRICE, R.F., 'Education in Communist China', London, Routledge & Kegan Paul, 1970. This includes an account of literacy campaigns and information on correspondence courses.

LEE, H.P., Education and Rural Development in China Today, in Foster, Philip and Sheffield, James (eds), 'World Year Book of Education 1974', London, Evans Brothers, 1973, pp. 209-33.

RICHMAN, BARRY M., 'Industrial Society in Communist China', Random House, 1969. You can glean some information on urban/workplace adult education from this book.

CHOU LI-FANG, Correspondence Schools in China, 'Peking Review', 1963. Shows the extent of correspondence education in the 1950s and early 1960s, but unfortunately rather out of date now.

HOWSE, HUGH, The Use of Radio in China, 'China Quarterly', no. 2, April/June 1960. Interesting account of development of radio facilities in the 1950s.

Colombia

Acción Cultural Popular (ACPO)

Started in 1947. Radio schools for peasants, adults and young people, with current enrolments at over 40 000. Courses in literacy and basic education lead to the primary school leaving exam. Campaigns are linked with the courses. Small groups, often based on a family, work with a monitor supported by local and regional leaders. Members learn from the radio and special texts. ACPO also publishes readers for new literates, and a weekly 16-page newspaper, 'El Campesino'. Over 700 young people each year also attend courses in leadership for community development at 'campesino' institutes. These range between four and ten months.

References

BRUMBERG, Stephen F., Colombia: A Multi-Media Rural Education Programme, in Ahmed, Manzoor and Coombs, Philip (eds), 'Education for Rural Development', Praeger, 1975, pp. 1-60. A thorough case study of the history and present position of ACPO.

MUSTO, STEFAN, 'Los Medios de Communicación social al servicio del desarrollo rural', Bogotá, Editorial Andes, 1971. An evaluation of ACPO's achievements.

BELTRAN, LUIS RAMIRO, Social Structure and Rural Development Communication in Latin America: The Radiophonic Schools of Colombia, in Chu, Godwin, Rahim, Syed and Kincaid, D. Lawrence (eds), 'Communication for Group Transformation for Development', University of Hawaii, East-West Centre, September 1976, pp. 217-49. A description of ACPO's activities which also addresses the question of the relationship between the educational objectives of ACPO and the political development of Colombian 'campesinos'.

BRAUN, JUAN, 'Communicación, educación no formal y desarrollo nacional: las radio escuelas colombianas', ACPO, 1976. A study of five small Colombian communities with active radio schools, looking at the variables which affect participation in radio schools and the factors which affect the diffusion of innovations.

BERNAL ALARCON, HERNANDO, 'Educacion fundamental integral: teoría y aplicación en el caso de ACPO', Bogotá, Editorial Andes, 1978. A major book on ACPO and its philosophy. The first part is a collection of recent articles on ACPO's history and achievements. The second part is a detailed analysis of the theory and practice involved in creating an integrated fundamental curriculum, drawing closely on ACPO's achievements.

<ins>Schools television project</ins>

Started in 1964, this project was originally meant to bring quality into deprived schools; in the event television lessons with guides for teachers were provided in problem subjects - social studies, music and new maths - and were used in a large number of schools, but predominantly ones with reasonably good facilities to start with. All the same the programmes provided a gradual improvement in the children's performance and helped the teachers improve their teaching. But even the better qualified teachers found it a strain to use the programmes well and needed support.

References

LYLE, JACK, Colombia's National Programme for Primary-level Television Instruction, Schramm, Wilbur (ed.), 'New Educational Media in Action: Case Studies for Planners', vol. 2, Paris, Unesco International Institute for Educational Planning, 1967, pp. 49-75. Discusses the organisation and impact of the scheme in its early stages, and its future.

COMSTOCK, G., 'The Peace Corps Volunteer and Achieving Educational Change with New Media', Rand Corporation, Santa Monica, August 1969. An interesting report on this project, making clear how important support systems are for implementing new projects.

Universidad Abierta de Javeriana (JOUP)

This is an open university programme for rural primary school teachers. It has been running since 1974 serving about 2000 teachers. Courses consist of printed lessons, two weekly television lessons, group sessions with monitors and a postal question and answer service. The programme is run by an independent Catholic universtiy and does not offer certification. Future plans are for courses for other educational agents, especially in the health area.

References

PENA,BORRERO, LUIS BERNARDO, 'Colombia: Open University Program for Rural Primary School Teachers', paper presented to the Dartington workshop on distance teaching and rural development, Cambridge, International Extension College, 1977. This paper outlines the programme and discusses its structure and objectives in some depth.

PENA BORRERO, LUIS BERNARDO,'Tecnología intermedia en teleducación', paper presented to international seminar on transfer of technology in distance teaching projects, São Luiz-Maranhão, Brazil, February 1978. A description of the project which also includes an analysis of the University's experience with group learning.

Costa Rica

Centro de Orientación Familiar (COF)

Founded in 1968 to promote 'integrated sexual education', its programme now includes health and community education. COF uses a variety of media in its activities, including face-to-face training courses, booklets, correspondence courses, radio programmes. Two particularly interesting activities are, first, the 'health and happiness' weeks, informal festivals in slums with a variety of events and classes, special radio programmes and written materials; and, second, a daily radio programme, 'Dialogo', with a listenership estimated in 1973 as a quarter of the country's population. Each week's programmes are on a special theme. Thousands of letters are received and answered; the content of letters is also studied systematically as a guide to future programme content.

References
EL BUSHRA, JUDY and PERL, SUSAN, 'Family Planning Education in Action: Some Community Centred Approaches', Cambridge and London, International Extension College/International Planned Parenthood Federation, 1976. This book contains a case study of COF and references for further information. The project is compared with other similar ones.
RISOPATRON, FELIPE and SPAIN, PETER L., 'An Evaluation of Dialogo: Human Sexuality Education through Radio in Costa Rica', University of Stanford, Institute for Communication Research, July 1979.

Cuba

Broadcasting for distance teaching

Since the Cuban revolution mass media have been an important factor in equalising educational opportunity in Cuba. Television instruction has been widely used in secondary schools. Educational television with printed support materials has been consistently used in primary and secondary schools since 1959. From 1968, 60 programmes weekly were broadcast for students nearing the end of high school, with written lesson-guides. It appears that in 1970-1 these programmes were made available on video. Since 1967 television has been particularly important in providing part of the instruction in schools in the countryside.

Broadcasting is also widely used for formal courses for adults. In 1974, for example, 150 000 followed daily Russian lessons on the radio, with printed lessons published in a weekly magazine. In 1962, after the literacy campaign, continuation classes were set up for all those over 14 with less than three years' primary schooling. The majority of these classes were taught by television.

Non-formal courses are also run using broadcasting. The Popular Technical Institute, for example, started in 1966. Weekly programmes on agricultural production were supported by newspaper articles and seminars. Questionnaires provided feedback.

These developments were possible because of well-developed television coverage left by the previous regime. The emphasis has deliberately been on improving opportunities at primary and secondary level. Detailed evaluations of the work are not available.

References
WERTHEIM, JORGE, 'Educational Television and the Use of Mass Media for Education in Cuba', University of Stanford, 1975. The author has gathered as much information as possible for

this article, and made the best of disappointingly patchy documentation.

Dominican Republic

Radio Santa Maria (RSM)

Started in 1964, for rural people. Enrolments over 20 000 each year. Courses cover the whole primary-school curriculum, adapted so that it is relevant to rural people and organised round a central theme each week. RSM also broadcasts programmes to stimulate action for community development. On weekdays, students listen to the radio and complete worksheets in their homes. On Saturdays they attend a group session with monitors, who also distribute materials, collect fees, and feed back comments to the central office.

References

WHITE, ROBERT A., 'An Alternative Pattern of Basic Education: Radio Santa Maria', Experiments and innovations in education 30, Paris, Unesco, 1976.

WHITE, ROBERT A., 'The Use of Radio in Primary and Secondary Formal Education: The Radio Santa Maria Model in the Dominican Republic, in Spain, Peter L., Jamison, Dean T. and McAnany, Emile (eds), 'Radio for Education and Development: Case Studies', vol. 1, Washington, World Bank, May 1977, pp. 172-98. Two versions of the most comprehensive case study of this project, the latter being rather briefer.

CABEZAS ESTEBAN, ANTONIO, 'Documento informativo sobre Radio Santa Maria', paper presented at a seminar at Santo Domingo, 3-12 April 1975. A brief description by the director of RSM.

RADIO SANTA MARIA, 'Educational Methodology and Administrative System of Radio Santa Maria', paper presented at the IEC workshop on distance teaching and rural development at Dartington Hall, September 1977. This paper mentions some recent modifications to RSM's system.

Interview with FATHER ANTONIO CABEZAS, 'Development Communication Report', July 1978, pp. 12-13. This transcript contains a number of interesting details which do not appear in the lengthier reports.

Radio School for Family Education

This was set up under the auspices of the Dominican family-planning association in 1972. Daily broadcasts on commercial stations reach out particularly to rural areas. Family planning is integrated with child care and health education. Posters, leaflets and booklets are used as back-up materials, and listening groups encouraged. Letters from listeners are used to determine programme themes, and inform outreach workers who liaise between the PPA and local groups and clinics.

The programme is expanding to include volunteers recruited at village level and a wider variety of activities.

References

EL BUSHRA, JUDY and PERL, SUSAN, 'Family Planning Education in Action: Some Community Centred Approaches', Cambridge and London, International Extension College/International Planned Parenthood Federation, 1976. A short case study, including references for further reading.

Ecuador

Escuelas Radiofónicas Populares

The school offers a variety of courses using radio, print, group meetings and seminars, for country and urban people, including training courses for group leaders. Besides a periodical for 'campesinos', local wall-newspapers are encouraged. A major aim is the encouragement of mutual aid. The schools work closely with co-operatives, trade unions and other similar organisations, encouraging membership and development. Two smaller radio school organisations also operate in Ecuador, Escuelas radiofónicas de Pichincha (Radio Mensaje - see also 'nonschool rural education in Ecuador'), which serves a small area and has experimented with group use of tape recorders for 'campesino'-made programmes; and Radio Federación Sucua, providing functional education for children and adults in Spanish and the local Indian language. It also broadcasts general cultural programmes of local interest.

References

VELOZ, P. RUBEN, Escuelas Radiofónicas Populares, Ecuador; BARRIGA, P. ISAIAS, Escuelas Radiofónicas de Pichincha - Radio Mensaje, Ecuador; SHUTKA, P. JUAN, Radio Federación Sucua, Ecuador. Short case studies, all in Oficina de Servicios para América Latina, 'Las Escuelas Radiofónicas en América Latina', Sutatenza, 1972, pp. 127-44.

GUNTER, J. and THEROUX, J., Open Broadcast Educational Radio: Three Paradigms, in Spain, Peter L., Jamison, Dean T. and McAnany, Emile (eds), 'Radio for Education and Development', vol. 2, Washington, World Bank, 1977, pp. 338-59. An account of Radio Mensaje's use of tape recorders.

BRAUN, JUAN, 'Las Escuelas radiofónicas de Pichincha - Ecuador', Chile, Centro de Documentación en Comunicación Educativa, 1976. A study of some communities where radio schools operate, showing that conditions of life make it difficult for 'campesinos' to follow extended courses and implement new ideas.

Nonschool rural education

Started in 1972, the project aims to develop a variety of cheap, easily reproduced materials that stimulate learning and action amongst rural people. The project has a 'cafeteria approach' - groups or agencies select, try out and develop whatever appeals to them. Village 'facilitators' are central in promoting the materials and supporting learning groups. Materials include fluency games (e.g. dice or cards with letters or numbers); simulation games (e.g. 'hacienda', a board game on the social and economic structure of an Andean village); media-based materials (e.g. 'fotonovelas', comic books for easy reading with photos); expressive materials (e.g. puppets and community newspapers to encourage the expression of ideas). A local radio school, Radio Mensaje, also uses tape recordings made entirely by villagers to stimulate action and discussion (see also Ecuador: Escuelas radiofónicas de Pichincha). The plan is that use of the materials will multiply gradually to create a stable non-formal education system.

References

EVANS, DAVID R., An Approach to Nonschool Rural Education in Ecuador, in Labelle, Thomas (ed.), 'Educational Alternatives in Latin America: Social Change and Social Stratification', Los Angeles, UCLA, 1975, pp. 169-84. A general account of the project's activities.

ECUADOR PROJECT STAFF, 'An Approach to Nonformal Education: Nonformal Education in Ecuador 1971-75', Amherst, University of Massachusetts, July 1975, revised edition January 1976. This is a thorough general account of the project. The Centre for International Education at the University of Massachusetts has also published 13 technical notes on different aspects of the work.

HOXENG, JAMES, 'Let Jorge Do It', Amherst, University of Massachusetts, 1973. An earlier account of the project which discusses the philosophy of the approach.

GUNTER, J. and THEROUX, J., Open Broadcast Educational Radio: Three Paradigms, in Spain, Peter L., Jamison, Dean T., and McAnany, Emile (eds), 'Radio for Education and Development', vol. 2, Washington, World Bank, 1977, pp. 338-59. An account of Radio Mensaje and the use of tape recorders.

ROTHKEGEL ORTUZAN, EDGARDO, The Ecuador Nonformal Education Project, in Niehoff, Richard O. and Neff, Kenneth L. (eds), 'Nonformal Education and the Rural Poor', East Lansing, Michigan State University, 1977, pp. 111-20. Some critical and retrospective reflexions on the project.

<u>Advertising technique mass media campaign</u>

A campaign over 15 months (1974-5) in two provinces of Ecuador. Five nutrition messages, intended to inform and lead to action, were prepared on varied selected topics. These were recorded as one-minute dramas, and broadcast on the radio 10 to 15 times a day at the height of the campaign.

Also, 50 000 reinforcing posters were distributed. Surveys were conducted before, during and at the end of the campaign. Though a high level of adoption of new practices was recorded half-way through the campaign, this fell off towards the end. It was felt that face-to-face support was needed in addition to the radio to encourage action. Some of the messages chosen involved actions that were difficult - boiling all drinking water was hard for poor people because of fuel costs, for example - and these messages resulted in less changes in practice.

References

LESLIE, JOANNE, Five Nutrition Projects That Use Mass Media, 'Development Communication Report', no. 20, September 1977, pp. 4-6. This article summarises several projects and looks critically at evaluation methods.

GUNTER, JONATHAN and THEROUX, JAMES, Open Broadcast Educational Radio: Three Paradigms, in Spain, Peter L., Jamison, Dean T. and McAnany, Emile (eds), 'Radio for Education and Development: Case Studies', vol. 2, Washington, World Bank, 1977, pp. 338-59. Outlines this project and suggests the technique could be used for more ambitious objectives.

El Salvador

Escuelas Radiofónicas de El Salvador

The radio schools operate in a particularly oppressive political situation, where humanitarian development work tends to be labelled subversive. However, they carry out basic educational work thanks to the firm support of the archbishop. The schools depend greatly on volunteers as local leaders and the support of parish priests.

References

RUTILIO SANCHES, P. JOSE, Escuelas radiofónicas de El Salvador, in Oficina de Servicios para América Latina, 'Las Escuelas radiofónicas en América Latina', Sutatenza, 1972, pp. 145-9. Covers the organisation, content and financing of the schools, and discusses the implications of the political situation in which they work.

Television and Educational Reform

In 1969, after several years planning, television was used to teach the seventh grade of school. This was part of a general reform of education. By 1971 television was used to teach classes up to ninth grade, and thereafter primary grades. The plan was to use television in all schools. A new curriculum was introduced, television classes were supported by student workbooks, and teachers were given up to one year's retraining for their new role in supporting television lessons.

References
HORNIK, ROBERT C., INGLE, HENRY T., MAYO, JOHN K., MCANANY, EMILE and SCHRAMM, WILBUR, 'Television and Educational Reform in El Salvador: Final Report', AID Studies in Educational Technology, Washington, Academy for Educational Development, August 1973. A summary report on all aspects of the reform.
SCHRAMM, WILBUR, 'Instructional Television in the Educational Reform of El Salvador', AID Studies in Educational Technology, Washington, Academy for Educational Development, March 1973. Covers much of the same material as the final report, but rather briefer.
INGLE, HENRY T., with VELASCO, JOSE R. and ZELADA, VICTOR M., 'Television and Educational Reform in El Salvador: Follow-up Study on the First Group of Ninth Grade Graduates', research report no. 12, Academy for Educational Development, June 1973. Detailed study of the progress and attitudes of a group of students nine months after graduation.
INGLE, HENRY T., INGLE, YOLANDA R., HORNIK, ROBERT C., MAYO, JOHN K., MCANANY, EMILE and SCHRAMM, WILBUR, 'Television and Educational Reform in El Salvador: Report on the Fourth Year of Research', AID Studies in Educational Technology, Washington, Academy for Educational Development, May 1973. This report contains an account of an observational study of two classrooms.
MAYO, JOHN K. and JUDITH A., 'An Administrative History of El Salvador's Educational Reform', research report no. 8, Academy for Educational Development, November 1971. A careful and detailed report on one of the least documented but most crucial aspects of this type of project.
SCHRAMM, WILBUR, 'The Use of TV in the El Salvador Program of Educational Reform: Differences between This Project and Some Others', AID Studies in Educational Technology, Washington, Academy for Educational Development, April 1969. A brief but useful comparative document.
INGLE, HENRY, Reconsidering the Use of Television for Educational Reform in El Salvador, in Arnove, Robert F. (ed.), 'Educational Television', New York, Praeger, 1976. A retrospective critical analysis of the reform.

Ethiopia

Agri-service Ethiopia (ASE)

Started in 1969, the organisation aimed to provide INADES-style courses adapted for use in Ethiopia (see entry under Ivory Coast). The project had a slow start, due to difficulties in working out its relationship to other agencies, problems in adapting materials, and a shortage of money.

By 1976 the situation had improved. Over 2000 students were registered, with probably many more unregistered participating in groups. Courses in agriculture, hygiene, home science and socio-economics were in operation or production.

References

UNITED NATIONS ECONOMIC COMMISSION FOR AFRICA, 'Evaluation of the Agri-service Ethiopia Programme', Addis Ababa, 1976. An account mainly of problems encountered, with some findings during the pretesting of materials.

CLEARINGHOUSE FOR DEVELOPMENT COMMUNICATION, Agri-service Ethiopia, 'Project Profiles', Washington, CDC, October 1977. A description of the development of the project.

Work-oriented Adult Literacy Project (WOALP)

A project begun in 1969 for members of co-operatives. A two-year curriculum is supervised by local instructors trained for two weeks. Materials available are primers, readers, posters, cassette lessons and radio talks. All farm inputs are available to learners through their local co-operative societies. The project seems to be leading to increased membership and involvement in co-operatives, and widespread adoption of new practices by farmers.

References

TYAGI, S.S., Principles, Methods, Materials and Organization of Co-operative Functional Literacy, in International Co-operative Alliance, 'Functional Literacy and Co-operatives', report of ICA seminar at Ibadan, London, ICA, 1975, pp. 25-35. A brief description of activities.

Fiji

The University of the South Pacific, Diploma of Education

A scheme to provide in-service training at a distance for unqualified teachers over ten countries in a vast region of scattered islands. Correspondence teaching started in 1971, with supporting radio programmes. Trainees spend their final year of study full-time at the University after completing the equivalent of two years' training by correspondence.

References

KINYANJUI, PETER, 'Training Teachers by Correspondence', Cambridge, International Extension College, 1974. A short case study.

Ghana

Rural radio forums

Started 1964, as an incentive to group action for farming

people. Weekly forum programme contains reports from forums, questions for discussion after the programme and a drama or discussion presenting the theme for the week. No printed materials are provided to the groups. Forums are formed after a request from a village to the Rural Broadcasting Unit.

References

COLEMAN, W.F., OPOKU, A.A. and ABELL, H.C., 'An African Experiment in Radio Forums for Rural Development, Ghana 1964-5', reports and papers on mass communications no. 51, Paris, Unesco, 1968. A detailed case study of the early years.

University of Ghana, Institute of Adult Education Correspondence Course Unit

A correspondence-course programme for secondary-level education for adults started in 1970. Initially some face-to-face sessions were included but these were dropped in 1974; there is as yet no radio component. Course production has been very slow, with still only a handful of courses available. Students are drawn from those unable to get places in secondary schools, secondary school drop-outs and adults, so that many students are very young.

In its first years the unit had about 20 000 students, but from 1974 to 1976 it closed temporarily, and is only now rebuilding its reputation. Current numbers are around 6000.

References

AGGOR, REUBEN and BARNOR, JOHN, Ghana Case Study, unpublished paper presented at 1977 course on distance teaching in developing countries, London, International Extension College/ Institute of Education. A comprehensive study.

KABWASA, A. and KAUNDA, M. (eds), 'Correspondence Education in Africa', London, Routledge & Kegan Paul, 1973. Includes a factual outline of the Institute.

Guatemala

The radio association La Voz de Atitlan

In 1969 a radio-school literacy programme was started for the 35 000 indigenous people speaking Tzutzuhil-Maya, who live around the volcanic lake Atitlan. The radio service is now locally and co-operatively run. At present the 'school' programme is being completely revised; literacy in this minority language with no literature is of no practical use on its own. In future the association will provide an integrated programme covering all major areas of importance: agriculture, health, women's needs and co-operatives, linked with literacy as appropriate. Local volunteer monitors are being trained. Though tiny, the system is interesting for its local control and for its imaginative use of radio for instruction where print is of little use.

References

CHERRITT, IAIN, 'The Radio Association "La Voz de Atitlan"', paper presented to the Dartington workshop on distance teaching and rural development, Cambridge, International Extension College, 1977.

Basic Village Education Project (BVEP)

A five-year experiment in communication with rural farmers, 1973-8. Different communication methods are being compared as to effectiveness in increasing production and relative costs. The project was in two pilot areas, one Spanish-speaking and the other Indian. Four approaches using different combinations of radio, cassette recorders, visual aids, monitors and agricultural experts have been tried in different places.

References

MOSHA, LADISLAUS and MATTE, TERESA, 'Audience Groups in Mass Communication for Development', Institute for Communication Research, Stanford University, 1969 (mimeo).

NESMAN, EDGAR G., RICH, THOMAS A. and RIVERS, SARA G., The Basic Village Education Project, 'Development Communication Report', no. 22, April 1978, pp. 6-7. Some major findings of the project, and an account of an informal tour to assess the impact of the radio programmes.

The 'Pila' Project

Thirty-minute programmes of health and nutrition messages interwoven with entertainment items were recorded on audio-cassette. A teenage girl from a village was taught to handle a portable recorder. Each day for three weeks in 1975 she took a tape to the 'pila', the village communal wash place, and played it four or five times during the day. Village women come here regularly, and were able to get on with their washing while they listened. The women apparently enjoyed the programmes, and also tried out some of the recommended ideas. Long-term evaluation had to be abandoned because of the 1976 earthquake.

References

EDITORS, The Pila Project: Cassettes Reach Rural Women, 'Development Communication Report', no. 18, April 1977, pp. 1-3. A brief case study.

FERNANDEZ, SUSANA,and COLLE, ROYAL D., 'Communication at the Pila', New York, Cycle, n.d. (1976?). An impressionistic account with plenty of photographs.

FERNANDEZ, SUSANA and COLLE, ROYAL D., 'The Communication Factor in Health and Nutrition Programs', Geneva, World Health Organisation, n.d. (1977?). Meant as a training unit, this paper gives interesting information on the background and content of the project.

A large number of short items on the project have appeared in various bulletins, 1977-8.

Haiti

'Radio Docteur'

Started in 1967, this radio series teaches the adult population about health. Twice a day, six days a week, there is a lively 10-minute dialogue between two popular presenters in Creole. The programmes deal with a different health area each day, and have national coverage and a large audience. The impact of the programmes, judging by their popularity, is great, but is reinforced by the firm collaboration of the health services. Cassettes repeating the programmes' messages are played in clinics, interspersed with music. The Centre d'Hygiène Familiale, which plans the programmes, also produces other health education materials, and there is a health education radio series for schools with an annual competition. The Centre works with the ministries of health and education, and their activites are strongly influenced by feedback from listeners.

References

HOLLANT, EDITH, On the Air, 'Salubritas', vol, 2, no. 2, pp. 1-3. A clear information article, illustrated with photographs and a sample of a quiz for schoolchildren.

Honduras

Acción Cultural Popular Hondureña (ACPH)

Started 1960, for peasants. Number of students annually uncertain at present, owing to political difficulties, but 16 000 started the primary equivalence programme in 1976. Started offering basic education relevant to peasants, but during the 1970s has developed both the full primary equivalence programme (PEPA) and a special agricultural programme (PPA). Both programmes are followed in community study groups, listening to a daily broadcast and following study notes, with the help of a monitor. PPA encourages co-operative farming. ACPH has always modified its programmes as needs changed and political contingencies demanded.

References

WHITE, ROBERT A., 'Mass Communications and the Popular Promotion Strategy of Rural Development in Honduras', Institute for Communication Research, Stanford University, July 1976. This is the most substantial study of ACPH. A briefer version by the same author and under the same title is also available in Spain, Peter L., Jamison, Dean T. and McAnany, Emile (eds), 'Radio for Education and Development', vol. 2, Washington, World Bank, May 1977, pp. 200-59.

LYLE, JACK, The Radio Schools of Honduras, in Schramm, Wilbur

(ed.), 'New Educational Media in Action: Case Studies for Planners', vol. 3, Paris, Unesco/International Institute for Educational Planning, 1967, pp. 95-110. This earlier account gives an interesting perspective on the subsequent changes of direction of ACPH.
YOUNG, MICHAEL, 'Note on the Honduras Radio Schools (ACPH - Acción Cultural Popular Hondureña)', paper presented to the Dartington workshop on distance teaching and rural development, Cambridge, International Extension College, 1977.

India

Radio rural forums

After a pilot in the Poona region in 1956, the permanent programme started in 1959. At present 22 500 forums registered, some active, many defunct. Half-hour radio programmes broadcast twice weekly to groups of 15 to 20 farmers, dealing mainly with agricultural matters. Group convenors keep records and also send comments or questions arising from group discussion to radio stations; those are then broadcast.

Despite little organisational support in recent years, in some states forums are functioning well.

References

NEURATH, PAUL, 'Radio Farm Forum in India', Delhi, Government of India Press, 1960. The most thorough report on the pilot stage.
SCHRAMM, WILBUR, Radio Rural Forums in India, in Schramm, Wilbur (ed.), 'New Educational Media in Action: Case Studies for Planners', vol. 1, Paris, Unesco, International Institute for Educational Planning, 1967, pp. 105-34. Contains a shorter report of the pilot and a description and analysis of the problems of implementing the forums on a national scale.
KHAN, ABDUL W., 'All India Radio's Non-formal Education Broadcasts for Rural Development', paper presented at Dartington workshop on distance teaching and rural development, Cambridge, International Extension College, September 1977. Describes the present state of the forums, together with other rural radio programmes in India.

Farmers' training and functional literacy programme

Started 1967-8 to help the country become self-sufficient in food. There are now over 48 000 'Charcha Mandals' (farmers' discussion groups). The ministry of agriculture provides farmers' training facilities, the ministry of education is responsible for functional literacy, with manuals designed to suit local farming needs, and the Farm and Home Unit of All-India Radio provides publicity and programmes that relate to the manuals and encourage discussion and action. There are also programmes answering questions sent in: groups send in up to 50 000 letters a month. Each district organises supervision, one full-time person working with 30 groups or a part-time one working with ten. Local instructors are either teachers or farmers.

References

DIRECTORATE OF ADULT EDUCATION, Farmers Functional Literacy Programme, folder 1, New Delhi, ministry of education and social welfare, n.d. Describes the aims of the programme, its methods and the problems to be solved. Dates from the early 1970s.

DIRECTORATE OF ADULT EDUCATION, 'Farmers Functional Literacy Programme: Preparation of Problem Oriented Learning Materials: Experimental Project in Jaipur district', New Delhi, ministry of education and social welfare, 1974. A case study in syllabus and curriculum presentation.

KHAN, ABDUL W., 'All-India Radio's Non-formal Education Broadcasts for Rural Development', paper presented at the Dartington workshop on distance teaching and rural development, Cambridge, International Extension College, September 1977. Describes the role of radio in the programme, including the different kinds of groups that are organised.

Mass communications nutrition campaigns

A number of experimental campaigns have taken place in recent years, using advertising techniques to reach large numbers of people with information on better nutrition.

In 1972 a 10-week campaign in two states publicised selected messages about diet in pregnancy, weaning and general nutrition. Radio spots, film shows, and various printed materials - largely highly pictorial - were used, reaching 250 000 people. An evaluation of a sample showed a big increase in knowledge amongst all reached, rural or urban, and whatever their age, sex, income or caste. A negative 'shock' approach had more impact than a positive one. Although the mothers clearly needed face-to-face encouragement from extension agents to change their habits, they had few reservations about the new ideas after the campaign.

A campaign of one year in Maharashtra state, reported in 1976, aimed at middle-income mothers, to get them to give their children more protein. Cinema and press advertisements and posters were used, and a free booklet on offer. Over 2 500 000 people (53 per cent of the adult population) knew of the campaign; about a quarter of these modified their diets, and a quarter sought advice from others on change.

In 1977-8 a campaign aiming at 40 000 slum women in South India gave a different perspective. Forty-eight local women were trained as demonstrators of nutrition and family planning; they were trained to use flip charts and other visual aids, and radio, films, and comics publicised the campaign. But these poorer women were less able to respond than those in the second campaign, because of poor living conditions and lack of control over their lives, as women.

References

PARLATO, MARGARET BURNS, 'Breaking the Communications Barrier', India, CARE, 1973.

PARLATO, RONALD, Advertising and Mass Communications: A Model for Rural Nutrition Information Programs, 'PAG Bulletin', vol. IV, no. 1, 1974, pp. 17-18.

These are two accounts of the 1972 campaign.

PAG SECRETARIAT, A Pilot Study on the Feasibility of Using Mass Media for Imparting Nutrition Education in Maharashtra, India, 'PAG Bulletin', vol. VI, no. 1, 1976, pp. 37-41. Covers objectives, strategy, costs and research results.

MOSS, MANORAMA S., What Extension Educators and the Mass Media Can and Can't Do - A Nutrition Education Project in India, 'Development Communication Report', no. 23, July 1978, p. 11. The 1977-8 campaign. Less detail on operation than on the other two, but a thoughtful analysis of shortcomings of the approach.

Farm School-on-the-Air

Started by All India Radio in 1975, this is a new strategy for broadcasting to farmers. Courses are broadcast in weekly half-hour lessons. Students send in by post answers to questions at the end of the programmes. At the end of the year students receive a certificate. The project so far reaches small numbers of better educated farmers.

References

CLEARINGHOUSE FOR DEVELOPMENT COMMUNICATION, School-on-the-Air, India, 'Project Profiles', Washington, CDC, June 1977. Description and results of the first two years of the project.

KHAN, ABDUL W., 'All India Radio's Non-Formal Education Broadcasts for Rural Development', paper presented at the Dartington workshop on distance teaching and rural development, Cambridge, International Extension College, 1977. Describes this project along with several others, showing how each serves different but complementary needs.

Satellite Instructional Television Experiment (SITE)

A one-year experiment from August 1975 to 1976, to see what use could be made of satellite television in underdeveloped areas. Used in 2400 villages in six states, morning programmes for primary schools, and evening ones seven nights a week, for adults. Also 2400 primary teachers given some training, with a 12-day course followed by television, radio and print support. Evaluation awaited.

References

AGARWAL, ANIL, Who Watches India's Schoolroom in the Sky?, 'New Scientist', 24 June 1976.

DINSDALE, J., India's Satellite Broadcasting - Interim Report, 'Wireless World', September 1976.
Both brief descriptive articles, giving some evaluation findings.
CHANDER, RAMESH and KARNIK, KIRAN, 'Planning for Satellite Broadcasting: the Indian Instructional Television Experiment', reports and papers in mass communication, no. 78, Paris, Unesco, 1976. Covers the project planning, including the results of programme pretesting.
MODY, BELLA, Planning Development-communication Software: Lessons from SITE, 'Development Communication Report', July 1978, p. 6. A brief but perceptive article by a member of the evaluation team.

Indonesia

Proyek Pamong

See Philippines, Project Impact

Iran

The Free University of Iran

Established in 1973, the first intake of students was in 1977. It aims to provide opportunities for higher education and lifelong learning amongst the general population. Its courses are mainly print-based correspondence courses, with some broadcast support and a network of local study centres with tutorial and audio-visual facilities, libraries, laboratories and computer terminals. Initial priorities are for teacher education, paramedical training, general education and rural development.

References

BEARDSLEY, JOHN R., The Free University of Iran, in MacKenzie, Norman, Postgate, Richmond and Scupham, John (eds), 'Open Learning', Paris, Unesco, 1975, pp. 183-208. A comprehensive account of plans, with some indications of problems foreseen.
NAFICY, HAMID, The Free University of Iran: Research and Evaluation of TV and Radio Programmes, 'Educational Broadcasting International', vol. 9, no. 3, September 1976, pp. 130-3. Includes a general account of the University's aims as well as an account of the thinking behind broadcasting plans.

Israel

Everyman's University

A distance-teaching university to provide in-service teacher training, secondary and tertiary courses for adults, and general adult education, especially for immigrants. Courses are multi-media with limited use of television. Local study centres are also provided. The first student intake was in 1976, limited to 2200 students, while the fourth biennial intake was 6200. Most students so far have enrolled on degree courses. Other courses produced have included one for electronic technicians, with home study kits; preparatory courses for degree-level work; and general-interest courses in Arabic and environmental studies

References

NELSON, FRED A., Everyman's University, Israel, in MacKenzie, Norman, Postgate, Richmond and Scupham, John (eds), 'Open Learning', Paris, Unesco, 1975, pp. 209-30. An account of the plans for the University.

MELMED, A.S., ELLENBOGEN, B., JAMISON, DEAN T. and TURNIANSKY, U., Everyman University in Israel: The First Two Years, in Perraton, Hilary (ed.), 'Alternative Routes to Formal Education: Distance Teaching for School Equivalency', Washington, World Bank, forthcoming. An account containing an analysis of the costs of the University.

TWITE, ROBIN, The First Three Years of an Open University, 'Educational Broadcasting International', vol. 11, no. 1, March 1978, pp. 40-3. An interesting personal account of the founding of the University and problems encountered.

Ivory Coast

Institut Africain pour le développement économique et social (INADES)

Started 1962, to revitalise village communities. Runs three correspondence courses: 'Cadre-service Afrique', for middle-level rural workers, studying as individuals; 'Service féminin', for 'animatrices rurales', women who work with groups of village women; and 'Agri-Service Afrique' for groups of village farmers, or occasionally individuals. The latter course is in simple French, and those following it work through its recommendations on a group plot of land. Each group has a literate leader, supported by local animators. The courses are used, with regional modifications, in 20 countries in Africa.

References

INADES, 'What is INADES?', Abidjan, 1972. A brief introduction.

DODDS, TONY, INADES - A Case Study, in Kabwasa, Antoine and Kaunda, Martin (eds), 'Correspondence Education in Africa', London, Routledge & Kegan Paul, 1973, pp. 13-30. A briefer case study by the same author is in 'Multi-media Approaches to Rural Education', IEC, 1972.

CHANDON-MOET, 'Les groupes INADES - ASA dans le pays Bwa du Mali', INADES, 1972. A detailed study of the performance of 22 farmers' groups in one region.

The Television Project

After some years of planning, teaching by television started for 447 primary classes in 1971. The ministry of education aims to teach by television all primary classes, and ultimately also secondary children and adults. Adult programmes started in 1973, while by the end of 1975 over 5000 classes in five primary grades were using television. The programmes have introduced a new curriculum, and television with some radio and printed materials is used to provide continuous support for the teachers.

References

AGENCE DE COOPERATION CULTURELLE ET TECHNIQUE, Côte-d'Ivoire: la rénovation d'un système, 'Direct', October 1975, pp. 15-42. A full account of all aspects of the project.

KAYE, ANTHONY, The Ivory Coast Educational Television Project, in Arnove, Robert F. (ed.), 'Educational Television', New York, Praeger, 1976, pp. 140-79. An account of the first years of the project, including an assessment of the problems encountered.

MINISTERE DE L'EDUCATION NATIONALE, 'Programme d'éducation télévisuelle', Ivory Coast Republic, 1968. Eleven volumes of planning documents and background research. Volume I describes the initial aims and proposed methodologies for the project.

EICHER, JEAN-CLAUDE and ORIVEL, FRANCOIS, 'Cost Analysis of the Primary Instructional Television Program in the Ivory Coast', Washington, Academy for Educational Development, n.d. (1976?). Analyses present and future costs in detail, and suggests that budgetary constraints will force some proposed developments to be delayed.

LENGLET, FRANS, 'The Impact of 25 Television Programs on "water", Produced and Broadcast by the Ivorian Out-of-School Education Project', Washington, Academy for Educational Development, 1976. Detailed research of the effects of some programmes for adult groups, and suggestions of how the project could be improved.

Jamaica

Ministry of education correspondence course section

This unit grew out of demand from young teachers. In 1959 correspondence courses were provided to help these teachers acquire higher qualifications. They were run until 1971, and replaced in 1973 by a new scheme. Since 1964 correspondence courses in school certificate subjects have been available, and are mostly used in schools with staffing problems. Activities in liaison with other educational bodies are planned.

References

EL BUSHRA, JUDY, 'Correspondence Institutions in the Commonwealth', London, Commonwealth Secretariat, 1976. A brief factual account.

The Jamaican Movement for the advancement of literacy (JAMAL)

The Jamaican government has actively supported adult literacy work since the 1950s. In 1966 an initial experiment with literacy teaching employing closed-circuit radio and television led to the widespread use of the two media in adult literacy work. At present JAMAL runs a successful adult literacy programme, but is concerned to extend its work so that people have more chance of gaining paid employment. Chances of jobs for those with minimal education are painfully small; JAMAL is therefore investigating new approaches for these people, including distance teaching.

References

THE LITERACY SECTION, SOCIAL DEVELOPMENT COMMISSION, Literacy through Radio and Television in Jamaica, 'Educational Television International', vol. 4, no. 1, March 1970, pp. 50-4. An account and evaluation of the use of radio and television for literacy teaching for adults in the late 1960s.

JAMAL, 'Operations with Special Reference to the Use of Media', paper presented to the Dartington workshop on distance teaching and rural development, Cambridge, International Extension College, 1977. Describes the objectives and achievements of JAMAL and explains how media are currently used in conjunction with face-to-face teaching.

'Have a Heart'

Started in 1975, this was a campaign run by the National Family Planning Board. While previous education projects had stressed the benefit to individuals of planned parenthood, this campaign linked personal responsibility with national development. Five-minute radio programmes are backed up with full-page newspaper advertisements. Results have included thousands of requests for information, and an increase in sales of contraceptives. An Advice Bureau has now been established, and deals with letters, phone calls and visits.

References

CLEARINGHOUSE FOR DEVELOPMENT COMMUNICATION, The 'Have a Heart' Family Planning Campaign, Jamaica, 'Project Profiles', Washington, CDC, June 1977. A brief factual account.

Kenya

Correspondence Course Unit (CCU)

Started in 1967, the Unit produces correspondence courses for the Kenya Junior Certificate of Secondary Education (KJSE), for private candidates and for unqualified teachers who were to be upgraded on passing the certificate. This latter programme has now been suspended. By early 1972 over 6000 had enrolled on the teachers' programme and about 2250 for KJSE. Students receive individual tuition by post. The Unit has an allocation of five hours' radio time per week.

References

KINYANJUI, PETER E., In-service Training of Teachers through Radio and Correspondence in Kenya, in Spain, Peter L., Jamison, Dean T. and McAnany, Emile (eds), 'Radio for Education and Development: Case Studies', vol. 1, Washington, World Bank, May 1977, pp. 152-71.

KINYANJUI, PETER E., Kenya: The Use of Radio and Correspondence Education for the Improvement of Teaching, in MacKenzie, Norman, Postgate, Richmond and Scupham, John (eds), 'Open Learning', Paris, Unesco, 1975, pp. 253-72.

KINYANJUI, PETER E., 'Training Teachers by Correspondence', Cambridge, International Extension College, 1974.

All these cover much the same ground.

TREYDTE, KLAUS-PETER, 'Radio/Correspondence Instruction and Development in Kenya: The CCU Case; from the Evaluation Point of View', Friedrich Ebert Stiftung, April 1973. Includes an interesting comparison of the performance of students on each of the two programmes.

SIELE, JOHN ARAP and HACKER, GERRY, 'Teaching Science at a Distance', Cambridge, International Extension College, 1977. Includes a section on the CCU's experiments and experiences with science teaching at a distance.

HAWKRIDGE, DAVID, KINYANJUI, PETER, NKINYANGI, JOHN and ORIVEL, FRANCOIS, In-service Teacher Education in Kenya, in Perraton, Hilary (ed.), 'Alternative Routes to Formal Education: Distance Teaching for School Equivalency', Washington, World Bank, forthcoming. A case study with particular emphasis on the costs of the project.

Kipsigis Homesteads Cattle-Dip Management Program

See under Tanzania, Arusha Appropriate Technology Project

'Zaa Na Uwatunze'
The title of this radio series means 'giving birth and caring for your children'. Fifteen-minute programmes are broadcast each week at a popular listening time. Each programme has a theme, but the script is improvised by three top radio comics. After the first year a survey of listening and learning was made. With listenership estimated at about 3 000 000, those in the survey who had heard some programmes had a high recall of topics.
References
HOSTETLER, SUSAN, Health Messages through Humor, 'ICIT Report', no. 15, July 1976, pp. 1-2.

Lebanon

The UNRWA/Unesco Institute of Education, Beirut
Started in 1964 to train teachers working in schools in Palestinian refugee camps. By 1974, 3983 elementary school teachers (80 per cent of the total) had been upgraded, and 1048 students were following a variety of courses. Courses are now also available for lower-secondary teachers, head teachers and school supervisors, as well as some specialist and refresher courses. Students study correspondence lessons and attend weekly or fortnightly seminars with a field teacher who has access to visual aids, and there are also compulsory summer schools. Post and radio are not used, as the scheme crosses four national boundaries.
References
PIRES, EDWARD A. with BARTRAM, BERNARD, Teachers for Refugees: The UNRWA/Unesco Institute of Education, Beirut, Lebanon, in MacKenzie, Norman, Postgate, Richmond and Scupham, John (eds), 'Open Learning', Paris, Unesco, 1975, pp. 273-94. A full and up-to-date case study.
LYLE, JACK, In-service Training Programme for UNRWA/Unesco Teachers, in Schramm, Wilbur (ed.), 'New Educational Media in Action: Case Studies for Planners', vol. 2, Paris, Unesco/International Institute for Educational Planning, pp. 179-208. Describes the planning of the scheme and methods used.

Lesotho

The Lesotho Distance Teaching Centre (LDTC)
Started in 1974, to expand the use made of distance teaching in the country, both in formal and non-formal education. The Centre acts as a service agency, designing and producing educational materials for other agencies. It also runs corres-

pondence courses for Junior Certificate and GCE exams, with weekend courses and radio support. Since January 1978, 400 unqualified teachers have been enrolled on a training project run jointly by LDTC and the National Teacher Training College. For rural adults, booklets are produced on practical topics. These are on sale for individual reading, or are used in learning groups, and sales of individual titles have been as high as 35 000. The Centre is also developing literacy and numeracy materials for out-of-school youth.

References

Lesotho Distance Teaching Centre Reports are produced every six months, available from PO Box MS 781, Maseru. Each report summarises previous work as well as documenting new developments. The centre has also published over 30 research reports - list available from the same address.

COURRIER, KATHLEEN, Close-up on Distance Teaching in Lesotho, 'Development Communication Report', no. 21, January 1978. A brief survey of LDTC's work.

SIELE, JOHN ARAP and HACKER, GERRY, 'Teaching Science at a Distance', Cambridge, International Extension College, 1977. Includes an account of LDTC's correspondence course in agricultural science.

Malawi

Malawi Correspondence College

The college was established in 1964, to offer courses to primary school-leavers who could not get into secondary school. Courses for the in-service training of primary-school teachers are also provided. Radio lessons are provided as well as print, while face-to-face teaching is available at over 60 correspondence college centres and 24 night secondary schools. Enrolments are limited to about 3500 students per year.

References

EL-BUSHRA, JUDY, 'Correspondence Institutions in the Commonwealth 1976', London, Commonwealth Secretariat, 1976. A brief factual case study.

WHITE, C.J.B., 'Correspondence Education in Central Africa, Report on a visit to Zambia, Malawi and Rhodesia', Gaborone, ministry of development planning, n.d. A short analysis focussing particularly on organisation and administration.

KABWASA, A. and KAUNDA, M. (eds), 'Correspondence Education in Africa', London, Routledge & Kegan Paul, 1973. Includes a factual outline of the College.

WOLFF, LAURENCE and FUTAGAMI, SHIGENARI, The Malawi Correspondence College, in Perraton, Hilary (ed.), 'Alternative Routes to Formal Education: Distance Teaching for School Equivalency', Washington, World Bank, forthcoming. The history and progress of the College and an analysis of costs.

Radio Listening Groups and Extension Aids Service

Groups of farmers listened to the radio with an extension staff member to lead discussion. Half-hour weekly programmes started in 1966. In June 1967 it was estimated that 6000-7000 farmers sought the advice of extension workers as a result of the programmes. Soon after the groups started it was suggested that other educational extension aids - mobile film units, booklets and other printed materials - should be revised so that an integrated system of agricultural extension education could be developed. This suggestion has been implemented.

References

KLONGLAN, GERALD E., 'Radio Listening Groups in Malawi, Africa', Iowa State University, Department of Sociology and Anthropology, rural sociology report, no. 70, October 1967. An outsider's evaluation report, describing the first year of the groups and making suggestions for future development.

MACDONALD, I.S., 'A Practical Guide to Extension Organisation', Malawi, Extension Aids Service, 1970. A handbook for extension supervisors which indicates the policy for integration of farmers' education services.

DODDS, TONY, 'Multi-media Approaches to Rural Education', Cambridge, International Extension College, 1972. Contains a brief item on Malawi Extension Aids Service.

WARR, DAVID, Evaluating Media in Malawi, 'Educational Broadcasting International', vol. 11, no. 3, September 1978, pp. 121-3. An account of the approach used by the Evaluation and Action Research Unit (EAR) of the Extension Aids Branch. A recent development, EAR helps the media producers design more effective materials.

Mali

Functional literacy programme

After several years of preparatory work a Unesco-sponsored programme really got going in 1970. Villages are encouraged to set up their own literacy centre and select a literate person as local organiser. A variety of printed materials have been produced in several local languages. Vans stocked with audio-visual aids tour villages and provide practical demonstrations and opportunities for discussion which encourage people to take an interest in becoming literate. Radio is also used to support the programme, and a newspaper, 'Kibaru', has been provided for new literates since 1972. Starting from a situation of near-universal illiteracy in rural areas with very poor transport facilities the project appears to be making an impact.

References

DUMONT, BERNARD, 'Functional Literacy in Mali: Training for Development', Paris, Unesco, 1973. Basic information on the literacy campaign.

AGENCE DE COOPERATION CULTURELLE ET TECHNIQUE, La radio rurale au Mali: pour les milieux ruraux, la place qu'ils méritent, 'Direct', nos 10-11, 1977, pp. 120-5. This article describes the successful range of programmes provided for rural people. These include a 10-minute programme five nights a week, to help rouse interest in literacy, and an extremely popular magazine programme running most of the day on Fridays (rest day), which includes half an hour given over to letters from 'Kibaru' readers.

BLAUG, MARK, COLCLOUGH, CHRISTOPHER and JOLLY, RICHARD, 'Case Studies of Reforms: Ethiopia, Algeria, Botswana, Mali, Egypt, Zambia and Kenya', paper presented to conference on new trends in African education, Brighton, Institute of Development Studies, May 1977. The section on Mali comments on the educational and economic success of the functional literacy programme.

Mauritius

The Mauritius College of the Air (MCA)

The College was founded in 1972. The first courses were to help improve secondary education, using television, radio and correspondence materials for children to work on in class under the supervision of their teachers. Enrolments were held low in the first years, though 12 120 students were enrolled in five subjects by 1974. People can also enrol on these courses as individuals. MCA's nonformal work has been slower to start, but study centres for young people are currently being established and a range of courses will be developed.

References

DODDS, TONY, 'The Mauritius College of the Air: The First Two Years', Cambridge, International Extension College, 1975.

DODDS, TONY and ETHERINGTON, ALAN, Modern Media and Rural Education: Two Case Studies from Mauritius, 'Rural Africana', spring 1975. Two projects for out-of-school young people described.

DODDS, TONY, Vocational Education at a Distance, 'Convergence', vol. 6, nos 3 and 4, 1973, pp. 19-31. This article describes two post-secondary courses, one in modern maths for primary school teachers, and the other in office management for employees of the Development Works Corporation. It also mentions briefly in-school secondary courses, and plans for expansion.

SIELE, JOHN ARAP and HACKER, GERRY, 'Teaching Science at a Distance', Cambridge, International Extension College, 1977. Includes a study of MCA's science courses for schools.

DODDS, TONY, The Mauritius College of the Air, in Perraton, Hilary (ed.), 'Alternative Routes to Formal Education: Distance Teaching for School Equivalency', Washington, World Bank, forthcoming. Covers the first five years of the College and analyses costs.

Mexico

Radio schools of Tarahumara

Started in 1957, to provide teaching by radio for the first four grades of primary schooling to young people in a remote area where nearly half the population is Indian. By 1971, 46 schools were using the scheme, each with one or two 'auxiliaries', supervisors with only primary education themselves. Radio lessons were supplemented by work on the official primary education texts. The curriculum was inappropriate to rural children, particularly the Indian population whose first language was not Spanish. In 1974 the programme was temporarily stopped for reassessment. A conflict had arisen between those who felt the priority was community education for all and those who wanted to continue providing the basis of a primary education for children.

References

SCHMELKES DE SOTELO, SYLVIA, The Radio Schools of the Tarahumara, Mexico: an evaluation, in Spain, Peter L., Jamison, Dean T. and McAnany, Emile (eds), 'Radio for Education and Development: Case Studies', vol. 1, Washington, World Bank, 1977, pp. 33-68. An evaluation report, which also assesses the problems of developing the schools' work.

LLAGUNO, P. JOSE A., Informe sobre las Escuelas Radiofónicas de la Tarahumara, Mexico, in Oficina de Servicios para América Latina, 'Las Escuelas Radiofónicas en América Latina', Sutatenza, 1972, pp. 167-87. A less recent account by the director of the schools.

Sistéma Educative Radiofónico

An association formed in 1964 concerned with offering basic education by radio to marginal indigenous communities. It has been particularly difficult to develop programme content that suits the diverse needs and languages of these peoples. In 1972 there were 80 centres with about 2000 group members.

References

MEZA CASAS, ROSA MARIA, Informe de sistéma educativo radiofónico de Mexico, A.C. Escuelas de Radio Huayacocotla, in Oficina de Servicios para América Latina, 'Las Escuelas Radiofónicas en América Latina', Sutatenza, 1972, pp. 151-65. A case study giving detailed information on the background and environment of some indigenous communities.

Telesecundaria

Started in 1966, to provide alternative secondary schools, particularly in rural areas, for children who had no access to ordinary schools. By 1976, 50 000 had graduated with over 60 000 enrolled. Children are taught by televised lectures supported by workbooks. Each class has a co-ordinator, a primary teacher who attends a brief training course, followed by in-service training by television and printed support materials. In 1973 a new secondary curriculum was introduced.

References

MAYO, JOHN K., MCANANY, EMILE and KLEES, STEVEN J., 'The Mexican Telesecundaria: A Cost-effectiveness Analysis', AID Studies in Educational Technology, Washington, March 1973. Though concentrating on the issue of costs, this is an extensive case study.

NOGUEZ, ANTONIO, The Mexican Telesecundaria: A Review, 'Educational Broadcasting International', March 1976, pp. 43-6.

HOOPER, RICHARD, Some Recent Mexican Educational Developments, 'Educational Broadcasting International', September 1976, pp. 124-9. Two later and sometimes critical viewpoints.

NOGUEZ, ANTONIO, How Evaluation and Research Have Helped the Mexican Telesecundaria, in Bates, Tony and Robinson, John (eds), 'Evaluating Educational Television and Radio', Milton Keynes, The Open University Press, 1977, pp. 46-50. Relates how the 1972 evaluation, reported in the first entry on this list, led to important changes; some states have now incorporated Telesecundaria in their educational systems, and the co-ordinators are now given added status and training.

Radioprimaria

Started 1970, using radio lessons to provide classes for the fourth, fifth and sixth grades of primary education in 'incomplete' schools. The pilot area was in and around the city of San Luis Potosi. In 1970-1, 49 schools used the scheme, dropping to 37 in 1972-3. The scheme has not since expanded. Each of the three grades has one and a half hours' radio programmes each day, listening and working on the official primary textbooks and special exercise sheets in turn. One teacher supervises all three grades, helped by a news-sheet of information.

References

SPAIN, PETER L., The Mexican Radioprimaria Project, in Spain, Peter L., Jamison, Dean T. and McAnany, Emile (eds), 'Radio for Education and Development: Case Studies', vol. 1, Washington, World Bank, 1977, pp. 69-113.

Open learning systems

The early 1970s saw a fashion for open learning projects in Mexico. A number of schemes started at university level (see section 2) and below. Among the latter are CEMPAT (1973), running courses preparatory to university entrance, an open primary and an open secondary school (both started 1975), and another open preparatory school (1976). These mostly use television and print, with little counselling or tuition, though there are some study centres. Each of these projects has several thousand students. They are successful, in the sense that people obtain certificates to move on to the next stage, but the quality of the materials is questionable and there is much duplication of effort between schemes.

References

HOOPER, RICHARD, Some Recent Mexican Educational Developments, 'Educational Broadcasting International', September 1976, pp. 43-6. A report of an educational study tour, covering also university level open learning and the Telesecundaria.

Nicaragua

Radio Católica/Escuelas Radiofónicas

Radio Católica started in 1961, and began promoting radio schools in 1966. The number of organised groups is apparently small, but at the time of the report efforts were being made to train large numbers of local leaders. Printed materials are loaned free to the group leaders, and only 2 per cent have been lost. Each community is responsible for the provision of school space and equipment.

References

ECHARRI, P. BONIFACIO, Radio Católica - Escuelas radiofónicas, Managua, Nicaragua, in Oficina de Servicios para América Latina, 'Las Escuelas Radiofónicas en América Latina', Sutatenza, 1972, pp. 189-90. A sketchy case study.

Mass media nutrition-advertising campaign

A campaign from 1975 to 1976 to assess how great an impact radio advertising alone could have on behaviour. The target audience consisted of mothers of children of five or under, teaching them how to make and use a lemon drink for their children with diarrhoea. Six one-minute messages, carefully researched, were recorded and broadcast regularly for a year. Mothers were interviewed before, during and after the campaign, but there was no control group. At the end a quarter of the mothers claimed to be using the lemon drink for diarrhoea treatment, where only 2 per cent had done so before. But only about half had learnt all the correct ingredients or the correct dosage. A major problem was the failure of the lemon harvest that year.

References

MANOFF, RICHARD K., COOKE, THOMAS M. and ROMWEBOR, SUSAN M., 'Radio Nutrition Education - Using the Advertising Technique to Reach Rural Families: Philippines and Nicaragua', Washington, Manoff International, 1977. The final report on the project. A number of brief items have appeared in journals in 1977-8.

Radio Mathematics Project

Started in 1975, as an experiment in using limited and low-cost resources for maths teaching in primary schools, the radio programmes are used in all the schools near the capital. The curriculum is carefully structured for radio presentation. Radio does all the teaching, requiring the children to make numerous active responses during the programmes. Exercises afterwards are supervised by the class teachers.

References

SEARLE, BARBARA, SUPPES, PATRICK and FRIEND, JAMESINE, The Nicaraguan Radio Mathematics Project, in Spain, Peter L., Jamison, Dean T. and McAnany, Emile (eds), 'Radio for Education and Development: Case Studies', vol. 1, Washington, World Bank, May 1977, pp. 2-32. A detailed case study explaining the curriculum and giving an example of a worksheet.

SEARLE, BARBARA and SUPPES, PATRICK, The Nicaragua Radio Mathematics Project, 'Educational Broadcasting International', September 1975, pp. 117-20. A briefer article covering the same material.

JAMISON, DEAN T., 'Radio Education and Student Repetition in Nicaragua', Washington, World Bank, 1977. This paper shows that the radio project reduces repetition rates, and the costs per graduate are therefore less than by traditional teaching.

SUPPES, PATRICK, SEARLE, BARBARA and FRIEND, JAMESINE (eds), 'The Radio Mathematics Project; Nicaragua 1976-1977', Stanford, Institute for Mathematical Studies in the Social Sciences, Stanford University, 1978. A detailed report of over 300 pages.

Niger

Radio clubs

Started in 1962, to promote action for national development among villagers. The number of clubs is kept small, 28 in

1972, but also 50 listening centres with unpaid 'animateurs'. Themes of programmes are chosen in advance by representatives of clubs. Each club conducts a survey on a suggested theme and tape-records its findings. A radio programme is made up from the tapes and written reports received and discussed by the club. The leader has reference materials to help guide the discussion. Each club then takes decisions for action, and the leader sends in a report. Radio programmes are therefore largely made up of contributions from the groups. A weekly programme of 30 to 45 minutes is broadcast from November to June of each year in two local languages.

References

RONDEAU, ROGER, 'Un exemple d'éducation permanente par les mass-média: l'expérience des radio-clubs du Niger', Paris, Université René Descartes, 1973 (unpublished thesis). This is the most comprehensive report, though compiled mainly from analysis of literature.

LEFRANC, ROBERT, Radio Clubs in Niger, in Schramm, Wilbur (ed.), 'New Educational Media in Action: Case Studies for Planners', vol. 3, Paris, Unesco/International Institute for Educational Planning, 1967, pp. 59-78.

MCANANY, EMILE, 'Radio Clubs in Niger', Institute for Communications Research reprints, Stanford University, 1972. Two briefer case studies of the project.

Télé-Niger

Started in 1964 with the aim of increasing the number of children with access to primary school by television teaching. Expansion was limited; by 1975 only 214 classes containing only 10 per cent of primary age children were using television. In 1972 some evening programmes for adults were introduced.

Television provides the main core of teaching. A new curriculum introduced with the television encourages children to learn by discovery. Class teachers are replaced by monitors, young primary school graduates given training and support by special television programmes and manuals. The whole curriculum is taught in French. Educationally, the project is very successful, but it met with much local resistance and is very expensive.

References

SILVERMAN, THERESA, 'TéléNiger: Adapting an Electronic Medium to a Rural African Context', information bulletin no. 8, Washington, Clearinghouse on Development Communications, 1976. An up-to-date summary report in English.

EGLY, MAX, The End of a Period for Télé-Niger (1964-71): Some Observations for Future Projects, in Schramm, Wilbur (ed.), 'Quality in Instructional Television', Honolulu, University Press of Hawaii, 1972, pp. 23-39. An assessment by the former director of the project.

AGENCE DE COOPERATION CULTURELLE ET TECHNIQUE, Niger: Télévision Scolaire en Marge, 'Direct', September 1975, pp. 15-49. A comprehensive summary report in French.
MINISTERE DE LA COOPERATION, 'La Télévision Scolaire du Niger 1964-71', 11 vols, Paris, 1974. These are the detailed research and evaluation reports from which most of the information in summary case studies are taken. Very readable, but in French.
LEFRANC, ROBERT, Educational Television in Niger, in Schramm, Wilbur (ed.), 'New Educational Media in Action: Case Studies for Planners', vol. 2, Unesco, International Institute for Educational Planning, Paris, 1967, pp. 11-48. The background of the project and how it looked shortly after starting.
MINISTERE DE L'EDUCATION NATIONALE, 'Programme d'éducation télévisuelle 1968-80', vol. III, Republique de Côte d'Ivoire. A follow-up to Lefranc's study, examining the project as a background to planning educational television in the Ivory Coast.

Nigeria

My Brother's Children

An unusual family planning venture which took place in 1971. 'My Brother's Children' is a film in the Yoruba language, acted by a famous group of Yoruba actors in the form of a traditional-style play. The aim of it was to change attitudes in favour of planning families by presenting ideas in a familiar way. This imaginative and attractive approach had little effect. Among the reasons suggested are that the film needed to be backed up more substantially - comic books were available retelling the story, but discussion groups were little used; and that messages of the film were too many and complex, sometimes contradicting accepted customs.

References

EL-BUSHRA, JUDY and PERL, SUSAN, 'Family Planning Education in Action: Some Community-centred Approaches', Cambridge/London, International Extension College/International Planned Parenthood Federation, 1976. Covers the development, implementation and evaluation of the project, and draws conclusions from the results.
OKEDIJI, F. and OGIONWO, W., 'Experiment in Population Education and Attitude Change: An Evaluation of the Film "My Brother's Children" in Two Rural Nigerian Communities', Ibadan, IPPF Africa Regional Council and Family Planning Council of Nigeria, 1973. A detailed evaluation report.
FUGLESANG, ANDREAS, A Family Planning Campaign, in Fuglesang, Andreas (ed.), 'The Story of a Seminar in Applied Communica-

tion', Uppsala, Dag Hammarskjöld Foundation, 1973, pp. 107-13. A brief account of the research and making of the film, with illustrations of posters and comic books.

The National Teachers Institute (NTI)

With the advent of universal primary education many primary school-leavers were recruited as teachers, given simply an induction course, while others started teaching after only a fraction of their college training. NTI's first job is therefore to assist in training these under-qualified teachers at a distance. The first intake of 15 000 students was due in autumn 1977. The course texts are carefully planned, but the problems of starting off a project on such a large scale are immense, particularly in areas where individual states are asked to share responsibility for organising the infrastructure of the programme.

References

ROBINSON, AJAYI, 'The National Teachers' Institute of Nigeria', paper presented to the 1977 course on distance teaching in developing countries, London, International Extension College/Institute of Education. Covers the objectives, structure and administration of NTI. The Institute publishes regular progress reports.

Pacific Islands

A nutrition campaign in the Yap district

Started in 1975, this was a project on a tiny scale, involving one full-time nutrition worker, a very small budget, and a mixture of appropriate media. The 17 islands of the Yap district had a population of 7500, mainly on one island. The diet was largely dependent on food imported from the USA. This was not only very expensive, but people also selected unsuitable foods. The campaign tackled two areas, sugar intake and infant diet. To reduce sugar eating, people were encouraged to drink coconut milk in place of imported soft drinks. The organiser used comic books, posters and newspaper advertisements, and also persuaded shopkeepers to store more chilled coconuts. Two spontaneous reactions within the community were a political newspaper cartoon, with a coconut and a canned drink as the chief characters, and a coconut-gathering service organised by local boys. After two years, imports of soft drinks were about a quarter the previous level. To encourage breastfeeding and wholesome supplementary infant foods videotapes were made showing local personalities and used with booklets and a mother's calendar in clinics. After the campaign 25 per cent more women were seen to be breastfeeding in clinics instead of using bottles.

References
RODY, NANCY, Things Go Better with Coconuts - Program Strategies in Micronesia, 'Journal of Nutrition Education', vol. 10, no. 1, January-March 1978, pp. 19-22. This account is illustrated with a cartoon and a sample of a comic strip.

Pakistan

Allama Iqbal Open University (AIOU)

Founded in 1974, the University uses printed materials, television and radio to provide professional and vocational courses, general academic education and courses for rural development. It started work with teacher training at a distance. Study centres are being established. The range of activities of AIOU is still rapidly expanding.

References
KHAN, ANSAR ALI, People's Open University in Pakistan, 'Educational Development International', vol. 2, no. 4, October 1974, pp. 176-9. Describes the objectives, establishment and initial organisation of the university.

Panama

Radio Educativa de Veraguas

Started in 1969 as part of the work of CEPAS (Centro de Estudios Promoción y Asistencia Social, a church organisation). The aims are to contribute to the development of poor rural people. Work is in groups, giving basic education by radio and booklets, with emphasis on the development of co-operatives. In 1972 59 new groups were formed, with numbers gradually increasing over the years. Plans included developing post-literacy education and a stronger bias towards technical and practical education.

References
BATISTA, LUIS, Radio Educativa de Veraguas Panama C.A., in Oficina de Servicios para América Latina, 'Las Escuelas Radiofónicas in América Latina', Sutatenza, 1972, pp. 191-5. A brief but dense case study.

Paraguay

Rural Radio Education Project

Begun in 1976, this is a government-sponsored scheme to assist rural children and adults to complete their primary schooling. In 1978 there were over 700 students in a pilot area, with full-scale expansion imminent. The curriculum covers the third to sixth grades of primary school and there is a qualifying exam for entry. Radio programmes provide the bulk of the teaching, with supporting workbooks. Learning centres have been set up for group meetings with monitors.

In 1979 an evaluation was to take place.

References

CLEARINGHOUSE FOR DEVELOPMENT COMMUNICATION, Rural Radio Education Project, Paraguay, 'Project Profiles', Washington, CDC, July 1978. Describes the projects and some formative evaluation findings.

Peru

La Telescuela Popular Americana (TEPA)

Started in 1962 in the city of Arequipa to give primary-level teaching to out-of-school youth, mainly domestic servants. Several hundred enrolled in the first year. They watched a daily 40-minute television programme at home and attended Saturday afternoon group meetings. Students were achieving an exam pass rate of 85 per cent.

TEPA planned other projects, including literacy for adults. No later information on these has been located.

References

LYLE, JACK, La Telescuela Popular Americana of Arequipa, Peru, in Schramm, Wilbur (ed.), 'New Educational Media in Action: Case Studies for Planners', vol. 2, Paris, Unesco/International Institute for Educational Planning, 1967, pp. 77-98. Covers the background, organisation, costs and impact of the project.

In-service teacher training by correspondence

As part of Peru's educational reform, all teachers are to be retrained by 1980. To assist in this, correspondence courses have been in use since 1972, prepared by the National Institute of Research and Development of Education (INIDE) distance education department. A first year's enrolment of 3000 teachers has been followed by annual enrolments of over 20 000. The programme is beset with difficulties of size, terrain and language, and is trying to call in other resources besides print. Little detailed information is known.

References

RUIZ, RUIZ, TERESA, 'Correspondence Courses for "in-service" training of teachers in Peru', Lima, Instituto Nacional de Investigación y desarrollo de la educación, n.d. (1975?). A sketchy outline of the programme.

Philippines

Project Impact (Instruction Managed by Parents, Community and Teachers)

An unusual recent approach to the problem of providing primary education for all with a shortage of teachers. The curriculum content for the fourth to sixth grades has been reproduced in easy-to-read books. This major job has been in progress since 1973, and the scheme is still experimental. Children study the booklets individually and work together in peer groups. The system is flexible, and children's performance in tests is already slightly surpassing that of children in conventional schools. If successful, it means that a school with 10 teachers can be replaced by a school with two instructional supervisors, one rural co-ordinator and one aide.

The same scheme is being tried out simultaneously in Indonesia under the name 'Proyek Pamong'.

References

SANGER, CLYDE, 'Project Impact: An Experiment in Mass Primary Education', Ottawa, IDRC, 1977. A detailed progress report, thoroughly illustrated with colour photographs which say as much about the project and its success as the text. Despite its title, this report covers both the Philippines and Indonesian schemes.

SANGER, CLYDE, Less Schooling, More Learning, 'The IDRC Reports', vol. 6, no. 2, 1977, pp. 3-5. A more concise account.

Agricultural analogy approach to family planning

Started in 1974, this project aims to introduce family planning to rural people without using unfamiliar technical terms. Discussion at interviews and meetings is supplemented by 16-page comic books, issued monthly, and colourful flipcharts. These use analogies from plants, animals, household articles and local beliefs to explain contraceptive methods and human reproduction. There has been a decline in the birthrate amongst women involved in the project.

References

CLEARINGHOUSE FOR DEVELOPMENT COMMUNICATION, Agricultural Analogy Approach to Family Planning, Philippines, 'Project Profiles', Washington, CDC, June 1977. A clear summary.

MAGLALANG, D.M., 'Agricultural Approach to Family Planning', Manila, Communication Foundation for Asia, 1976. A detailed report on the project, including numerous illustrations of materials, and evaluation of pre-tests.

Mass media nutrition - advertising campaign

This campaign from 1975 to 1976 was an experiment to assess how great an impact radio advertising alone could have on behaviour. The topic chosen was the infant's supplement to breast milk: mothers were to be taught to enrich the diet, and some traditional misplaced beliefs about food were to be challenged. After preliminary research, six one-minute messages in drama form were recorded and these were broadcast twice daily for a year. Back-up information was circulated to health centres and available on request from radio stations, but no further effort was made to encourage health workers to work with the campaign. A year after the start, a quarter of mothers interviewed now used some oil to enrich their babies' diets. Costs appear high.

References

MANOFF, RICHARD K., COOKE, THOMAS M. and ROMWEBER, SUSAN M., 'Radio Nutrition Education - Using the Advertising Technique to Reach Rural Families: Philippines and Nicaragua', Washington, Manoff International, 1977. This is the final report on the project. A number of short items have appeared in journals in 1977-8.

Educational Radio Technical Assistance Project

This is a three-year pilot project to discover appropriate ways of extending the use of radio for education in the Philippines. Broadcasts started in 1978. The project is concerned with in-school primary education and agricultural improvement. Primary school teachers are receiving radio lessons in five basic subjects, supported by printed materials and occasional group meetings. Over the three-year pilot period 12 000 teachers will try out the scheme. In addition, lessons in Filipino language will be broadcast daily to classes of each of three school years. The sixth grade programmes will also include social studies topics. Both students and teachers will also have notes, and 2500 classes will take part in the pilot.

For agricultural education, radio is being used to complement training and support for extension workers and local leaders. It is used in conjunction with pamphlets and other printed visual aids. Radio campaigns on other topics of importance for rural development will also be aired.

References

FUTAGAMI, SHIGENARI S. and JAMISON, DEAN T., 'Philippines Educational Radio Technical Assistance Project: Review Mission Report', Washington, World Bank, November 1977.

Rwanda

L'Université Radiophonique de Giterama (URG)

Started in 1964, to improve the primary school curriculum content and make it more appropriate for an agricultural environment.

URG has a network of audio-visual centres where children are shown sets of slides. These are locally made and cover the core of the curriculum. Teachers are provided with a commentary or in some cases with notes on lesson preparation. For some subjects, such as French and environmental studies, packages of exercises and ideas for activities are provided. Tape recordings are also used for teaching French. Parents are encouraged to come to occasional slide shows designed for them.

In addition URG runs a rural trade training centre for young people.

References

'L'Université Radiophonique de Giterama', Rwanda, November 1974. Describes the background and methods, including some data on producing the slides and costs of the project.

AGENCE DE COOPERATION CULTURELLE ET TECHNIQUE, Rwanda: techniques audiovisuelles au service de l'extrascolaire, 'Direct', no. 7, 1976, pp. 26-8. Describes the organisation of URG and its programme for school children, as well as a complementary project for out-of-school agricultural training for young people. This was started by URG in 1968 in response to pressure from parents of schoolchildren using the audio visual centres.

Samoa

The Samoan Television Project

Started in 1964, to improve the quality of teaching throughout the school system. The entire 12-year curriculum was taught almost immediately by television. 6000 programmes were being broadcast live annually. Every class had a television set, and teachers had centrally produced notes. In the early 1970s the programme shifted from American to Samoan control, and with this change came a change in the position of television. Teachers felt they wanted more control of the classroom, and since 1974 the programmes have become optional classroom-enrichment materials.

References

SCHRAMM, WILBUR, 'ITV in American Samoa - After 9 Years', AID reports, Washington, AID, 1973. A summary report of the period of American involvement.

AGENCE DE COOPERATION CULTURELLE ET TECHNIQUE, Samoa: échec à la mesure des espoirs, 'Direct', no. 3, 1976, pp. 19-35. Covers all aspects of the project, but in particular looks at the problems encountered and documents its decline.

MASLAND, LYNNE with MASLAND, GRANT, Some Cross-cultural Implications of Educational Television: The Samoan ETV Project, in

Arnove, Robert F. (ed.), 'Educational Television: A Policy Critique and Guide for Developing Countries', New York, Praeger, 1976, pp. 180-202. Looks into the effects of external decision-making and control on the project.

Senegal

Television clubs
A Unesco pilot project with CCTV in Dakar from 1965 to 1968. In the first two years bi-weekly programmes were broadcast to up to 500 women in teleclubs, 10 in the first year and 14 in the second. Programmes were in the Wolof language and dealt with health and nutrition. Discussions took place after the programmes, and the women learnt a great deal. A one-and-a-half-hour magazine programme was also shown to mixed groups on Friday evenings. The discussions here worked less well. An attempt was also made to use television to help with literacy, and to provide young people with programmes, but neither of these made much impact before the project ended.
References
CASSIRER, HENRY, 'Mass Media in an African Context: An Evaluation of Senegal's Pilot Project', reports and papers in mass communication, no. 69, Paris, Unesco, 1974. This also covers the radio project.
FOUGEYROLLAS, PIERRE, 'Television and the Social Education of Women', reports and papers in mass communication, no. 50, Paris, Unesco, 1967. This describes the project and analyses in detail the effects of the programmes on the knowledge and attitudes of viewers.
Radio Educative Rurale (RER)
Started in 1968 as part of a Unesco experiment in mass communications but continues to flourish. It started in one region with 57 groups, and is now available in three more regions, with an increase in individual as well as group listening. In 1974 RER received 350 letters a month from listeners. Programmes are broadcast three nights a week and contain information on themes listeners have defined as important, generally agricultural or political. Seventy per cent of each programme is recorded outside the studio.
References
CASSIRER, HENRY, 'Mass Media in an African Context: An Evaluation of Senegal's Pilot Project', reports and papers in mass communication, no. 69, Paris, Unesco, 1974. An account of both the television projects and the start of RER.
CASSIRER, HENRY, Radio in an African Context: A Description of Senegal's Pilot Project, in Spain, Peter L., Jamison, Dean T. and McAnany, Emile (eds), 'Radio for Education and Develop-

ment', vol. 2, Washington, World Bank, May 1977, pp. 300-37. An updated account of RER only.
CASSIRER, HENRY, Listening/Viewing groups - Challenge and Obstacles, in 'Educational Broadcasting International', March 1971. A briefer article by the same author.
MCANANY, EMILE, African Rural Development and Communication: Five Radio Based Projects, in 'Rural Africana', spring 1975. An article comparing the achievements and methods of RER with some other projects.
CLERC, JEAN-PIERRE, Rural Educational Broadcasting in Senegal, 'Prospects', vol. IV, no. 4, winter 1974. An article which suggests that radio has been more effective in Senegal than other methods of promoting development.
SOCK, BOUBACAR, 'Senegalese Experience in Using Radio Broadcasting for Animating and Educating Basic Communities with a View to Development', paper presented to the Dartington workshop on distance teaching and rural development, Cambridge, International Extension College, September 1977. An up-to-date account.

Schools television

A pilot project with television teaching for primary schools. It is hoped that the television will increase access to schools, keep down costs of expansion and assist in training teachers. In 1974-6 the whole of the core of the primary school curriculum was taught by closed-circuit television to 10 classes only.

References

AGENCE DE COOPÉRATION CULTURELLE ET TECHNIQUE, La télévision scolaire au Sénégal: des coûts mesurés et une éducation rénovée, 'Direct', nos 10-11, 1977, pp. 111-19. An extensive illustrated account of the project.

Somalia

Radio for adult education and literacy

In 1974 an estimated 1 250 000 Somali adults learnt to read during a campaign. Distance teaching is now being introduced on a large scale for follow-up activities, with particular attention being paid to the education of the 50 000 nomads who were resettled from 1973-6. From 1976 up to 15 quarter-hour radio programmes a week have been broadcast to help with Somali language skills and general knowledge. So far there have been no integrated support materials or feedback facilities, but a major new programme designed for group use was to start in 1978.

References

HASHI, FADUMA OMAR, 'The Elimination of Illiteracy', paper to

the international meeting to continue the work of the world congress for International Women's Year, Berlin, 1977. An account of the 1974 campaign.
MARTIN, DANIEL P., 'Radio for Adult Education and Literacy (Somalia)', Paris, Unesco, 1977. Outlines the proposed follow-up activities to the campaign.

South Korea

Mothers' Clubs
This project had no elements of distance teaching initially, but media have been gradually introduced to increase its impact.

A network of women's clubs has existed in South Korea for 25 years. These were discussion groups, particularly concerned with the economic advancement of women. In 1968 the Planned Parenthood Federation of Korea offered new support to these groups as Mothers' Clubs. There now exist 28 000 of them. Discussions frequently lead to club projects. The clubs are supported by co-ordinators who oversee several thousand clubs each. A monthly magazine, with a circulation of 60 000, provides material to inspire the group discussions. While use of media to date is limited, radio programmes are to be introduced shortly.
References
EL-BUSHRA, JUDY and PERL, SUSAN, 'Family Planning Education in Action: Some Community-centred Approaches', Cambridge/London, International Extension College/International Planned Parenthood Federation, 1976. Describes the clubs and outlines planned future developments.
ROGERS, EVERETT M., PARK, HYUNG JONG, CHUNG, KYUNG-KYOON, LEE, SEA-BAICK, PUPPA, WILLIAM S. and DOE, BRENDA A., Network Analysis of the Diffusions of Family Planning Innovations Over Time in Korean Villages: The Role of Mothers' Clubs, in Chu, G.C., Rahim, S.A. and Kincaid, D.L., 'Communication for Group Transformation in Development', Hawaii, East-West Center, 1976, pp. 253-76. An analysis of the relationship between social networks and the activities of Mothers' Clubs.
Nutrition Campaign
A nation-wide campaign throughout 1970, teaching about balanced diets. Short daily radio spots, posters, comic books and calendars were used. Evaluation was limited.
References
HIGGINS, MARGOT and MONTAGUE, JOEL, Nutrition Education through the Mass Media in Korea, 'Journal of Nutrition Education', vol. 4, no. 2, spring 1972, pp. 58-62. Covers planning, organisation and evaluation of the project and includes a sample page from a comic book.

LESLIE, JOANNE, Five Nutrition Projects that Use Mass Media, 'Development Communication Report', no. 20, September 1977, pp. 4-6. An outline of the programme and evaluation methods, comparing it with other projects.

The Air Correspondence High School

Set up in 1974 by the Korean Educational Development Institute (KEDI) to provide high-school level courses for young people and adults out of school. Courses use correspondence texts, radio and fortnightly face-to-face sessions on Sundays. By 1977 nearly 10 000 students had enrolled for the first of three grades. Students follow up to 14 subjects. All three aspects of the course are compulsory. The students are highly motivated; nearly half of those enrolled in 1974 graduated in 1977 despite a very heavy study schedule. The recurrent costs per student are about one-fifth the cost of a regular high school student.

References

LEE, KYE-WOO, FUTAGAMI, SHIGENARI and BRAITHWAITE, BERNARD, The Korean Air Correspondence High School, in Perraton, Hilary (ed.), 'Alternative Routes to Formal Education: Distance Teaching for School Equivalency', Washington, World Bank, forthcoming. A description of the project and analysis of cost effectiveness.

Sri Lanka

Correspondence Teacher Education Unit

This unit started operating in 1972, to increase the rate at which the country's 40 000 untrained teachers were receiving in-service training. Three courses are available; one for teachers with a full secondary education, who take three years to complete the equivalent of a two-year college course; another course is for graduate untrained teachers who study for two years to complete the equivalent of a one-year college course. In the first four years over 5000 teachers enrolled. The third is a course for school principals. There are some radio discussion sessions provided and annual one-week vacation seminars.

References

EL-BUSHRA, JUDY, 'Correspondence Institutions in the Commonwealth 1976', London Commonwealth Secretariat, 1976. A brief account.

Swaziland

William Pitcher Teacher Training College

Started in 1973 as a five-year programme to train 600 unqualified but experienced primary teachers, but now extended to include a further 500. New students, 50 at a time, start their training with a six-week residential course. After this, they study by correspondence, supported by two 15-minute radio programmes a week, occasional one-day subject seminars (open to any teacher) and visits by field staff. Each year students return to college for another short residential course and an examination. Only about 20 students had dropped out by 1977.

References

NZIBANDZE, M.J. and GREEN, CLIFFORD, In-service Teacher Training in Swaziland, in 'Prospects', vol. VIII, no. 1, 1978, pp. 110-16. Although brief this article contains much detail on the organisation and effectiveness of the scheme.

YOUNG, MICHAEL, 'Multi-media Education in Swaziland', Cambridge, International Extension College, July 1973, mimeo. This paper includes an account of a visit to one of the residential courses.

Swaziland International Education Centre (SIEC)

From 1974 SIEC has been issuing correspondence courses for adult Junior Certificate and 'O' Level students. Study centres and residential courses are provided for face-to-face support. Courses are developed slowly and carefully and dropout rates so far are low, while exam pass rates are high.

References

SWAZILAND INTERNATIONAL EDUCATION CENTRE, 'Annual Reports' and 'Newsletters'. These are available from SIEC at PO Box 547, Mbabane, and give a useful account of progress. The newsletters are sent to students so give a flavour of the college's style as well as information.

'Botswana Lesotho Swaziland Correspondence Committee Newsletter'. Published about twice a year; there are regular reports from SIEC included.

Tanzania

Cooperative Education Centre, Moshi (CEC)

Since 1965 the College has been running correspondence courses of three kinds: training for co-operative staff and officials as a prerequisite for acceptance on in-college courses; courses in member and committee education; and courses to help improve the standard of living of members. There are nearly 10 000 students, most studying in groups. From 1967 onwards CEC experimented with radio programmes directed at groups. This work, together with that of the Institute of Adult Education, led to the national campaigns of the 1970s (see radio study campaigns).

References

GRABE, SVEN, Tanzania: An Educational Program for Cooperatives, in Ahmed, Manzoor and Coombs, Philip, 'Education for Rural Development', New York, Praeger, 1975, pp. 589-616. This article considers correspondence education along with all the other activities of the Centre.

MWAKATOBE, R.Y. and KAGARUKI, G.E., 'The Role of Correspondence Education in Cooperative Training in Tanzania', paper presented to the African Adult Education Conference, April 1971. A brief paper by two senior staff of the Centre explaining its policy and methods.

MWAKATOBE, R.Y., 'The Use of Distance Teaching in Cooperative Training in Tanzania', paper presented to the Dartington workshop on distance teaching and rural development, Cambridge, International Extension College, September 1977. A brief but comprehensive study by the director of the CEC's correspondence section.

Radio study campaigns

Occasional projects, dealing with a topic of major interest to the country's adult population. After some experiments in the late 1960s, the campaigns have been as follows:

1970 'Uchaguzi ni wako' (The Choice Is Yours) - over 90 groups

1971 'Wakati wa furaha' (A Time for Rejoicing) - 75 000 groups

1973 'Mtu ni Afya' (Man Is Health) - 2 000 000 group members

1975 'Chakula ni Uhai' (Food Is Life) - over 1 500 000 group members

For each campaign, a radio programme is broadcast weekly over a period of three or four months. Groups listen to the programmes together, discuss the issues raised with the help of a printed study guide and decide what action to take. Each group has a leader, who is given brief training for the job. Preparation for each campaign takes many months.

References

HALL, BUDD L. and DODDS, TONY, 'Voices for Development', Cambridge, International Extension College, 1974. An account of the pilot projects and the campaigns until 'Mtu ni Afya'. Looks at both the positive and negative sides of the methods.

MBUNDA, FR D., 'Education Mass Campaigns: Tanzania Experience "Chakula ni Uhai"', paper presented to the International Council for Adult Education conference, Dar-es-Salaam, June 1976. An account of the 1975 campaign.

HURLY, PAUL, Re-examining National Radio and Mass Media Cam-

paigns, 'Convergence', iv, 1976, pp. 79-80. A constructively critical article on the campaign approach, based on experience of 'Chakula ni Uhai' and the 1976 Botswana campaign.
MATIKO, J.M.M., 'Radio Campaigns for Adult Education in Tanzania', paper presented to conference on communication policy and planning for education and development, Stanford University, 1976. Lists and discusses some evaluation findings from the campaigns, particularly the 1975 one.
GRENHOLM, LENNART H., 'Some Campaign Considerations', University of Dar-es-Salaam Institute of Adult Education, studies in adult education no. 2, 1974.
GRENHOLM, LENNART H., 'Radio Study Group Campaigns in the United Republic of Tanzania', Paris, Unesco, 1975. Two similar, largely descriptive studies up to the 1973 campaign.
MALIYAMKONO, L., ISHUMI, A., KLEES, S. and WELLS, S., 'Health Education for Development: A Case Study of Tanzania', Palo Alto, EDUTEL, May 1978. A retrospective analysis of the 1973 and 1975 campaigns, looking particularly at costs and attempting to assess long-term effects.

Institute of Adult Education, Correspondence Education Department

Started in 1970, the department produces correspondence courses to serve a number of needs: 'mass' courses at a basic educational level in important subjects; academic courses for secondary-school subjects for adults, including many teachers; and professional courses. Some supporting radio programmes are broadcast, and tutors occasionally visit regions to meet students. At the end of 1976 there were about 30 000 students. Future plans include extending the opportunities for group and face-to-face study.

In addition since 1976 there has been an annual intake of 15 000 young people training as primary school teachers. This is to meet the needs for extra teachers for universal primary education. The trainees teach about two days a week, as they learn by correspondence. They are organised in groups of up to 12 attached to local centres, each with a tutor. Each student studies three subjects each year, with a weekly radio programme in each as well as a correspondence text. After three years each trainee will have a qualification equivalent to that given after two years' full-time training.

References

ERDOS, RENEE P., 'National Correspondence Institution, 1970-1975', Dar-es-Salaam, Institute of Adult Education, 1975. A thorough report, including a great deal of generally useful information on administration of correspondence course units.
MASAWE, NATHAN and LISASI, JANICE, 'Tanzania Case Study', unpublished paper presented to the 1977 course on distance

teaching in developing countries, London, International Extension College/Institute of Education. A brief general account.

NTIRUKIGWA, E.N., 'Distance Education and the Training of Primary School Teachers in Tanzania', paper presented to the Dartington workshop on distance teaching and rural development, Cambridge, International Extension College, September 1977. Written shortly after the start of the teacher training project.

See also: radio study campaigns.

Literacy campaigns

Adult literacy work in Tanzania since 1968 has used distance teaching methods when appropriate. The campaigns included a pilot and operational phase.

1 1968-72 pilot phase: the work-oriented adult literacy project. Experimentation and gradual expansion of literacy work, based round the production of specific agricultural products. Primers were written for use in groups and for additional support to students, supplementary reading materials produced, rural libraries set up and rural newspapers started. Radio programmes provided stimulus to learn. Nearly 500 000 adults learnt to read by the end of 1973.

2 1972-5 Operational phase. During this period nearly 2 000 000 people learnt to read. The techniques and materials developed during the pilot phase were used, together with revised and new materials.

References

VISCUSI, MARGO, 'Literacy for Working: Functional Literacy in Rural Tanzania', Paris, Unesco, Educational Studies and Documents no. 5, 1971. An account of the pilot phase, including a lot of background information, with some samples of materials.

OKEDARA, J.T., The Planning and Implementation of Functional Literacy Programmes, in International Cooperative Alliance, 'Functional Literacy and Cooperatives', report of a seminar at Ibadan, London, ICA, 1975, pp. 41-5. A systematic account of the pilot phase.

SINGH, B.N. and MBAKILE, E.P.R., 'Tanzania-UNDP-Unesco Functional Literacy Curriculum: Programmes and Materials Development Project; Final Evaluation, Report (July 1973-June 1976) 1976)', Mwanza, Tanzania, June 1976. A thorough and detailed report on the major phase of the campaign.

MALYA, SIMONI, Creating Literacy Surroundings in Tanzania, 'Literacy Discussion', winter 1977-8, pp. 1-68. An extended study of strategies for maintaining literacy.

Arusha Appropriate Technology Project: Local Production Program

Started in 1976, the project encourages villagers to take part in the production of teaching materials. These are then used in discussion groups on local problems.

The Local Production Program provides a central support service to a number of existing and new projects. Among those are the Kipsigis Homesteads Cattle-dip Management Program in Kenya. Started in 1970, models, photobooklets and slides have been developed to encourage better understanding of dipping methods. Cassette recorders are also used to help discussion. Cattle deaths from tick-borne disease have dropped in the area. Other projects are with women's groups, and recent work has included extensive use of cassette tape recorders with discussion groups.

References

LUNDEEN, BRUCE and ALISA, Village-Made Educational Materials: Three Experiments That Worked, 'Development Communication Report', no. 23, July 1978, pp. 14-15. The authors of this article conclude from their survey that 'small media can play a leading role in adult education'.

CLEARINGHOUSE ON DEVELOPMENT COMMUNICATION, Kipsigis Homesteads Cattle-Dip Management, 'Project Profiles', Washington, CDC, July 1978. Facts about the project, and a list of seven notable features.

LUNDEEN, ALISA, MOLLEL, MARTHA and STANLEY, JOYCE, 'Audio-Cassette Listening Forums', third quarterly report, May 1978 through July 1978, Tanzania, Arusha Appropriate Technology Project, 1978. Looks at progress and future plans for work with women's groups.

Thailand

Schools Radio

In 1957 the decision was taken to teach some subjects to primary schoolchildren by radio alone. The subjects chosen were English, music and social studies. The teachers had printed notes on the lessons and class activities, a weekly radio programme of advice and a little training on using radio in class.

References

SCHRAMM, WILBUR, Educational Radio in Thailand, in Schramm, Wilbur (ed.), 'New Educational Media in Action: Case Studies for Planners', vol. 1, Unesco/International Institute for Educational Planning, pp. 83-103. A case study which draws out implications for similar ventures.

Functional Literacy and Family-Life Planning Program

Started in 1970, this scheme aimed to improve the teaching in adult classes. Classes are now discussion-centred, under the guidance of trained leaders. Learners use lesson cards, each containing picture and text on a topic of local importance. Group leaders also have posters to use in discussions.

For newly literate people, libraries and village newspaper reading centres are provided, as well as government-sponsored radio and correspondence courses. Those who successfully complete the scheme receive certificates equivalent to lower primary school graduation qualifications.

The scheme now operates in over 40 of Thailand's 72 provinces.

References

CLEARINGHOUSE FOR DEVELOPMENT COMMUNICATION, Functional Literacy and Family-Life Planning Program, Thailand, 'Project Profiles', Washington, CDC, July 1978. Description and results, mainly on the first few years of the project.

SUDRAPRASERT, KAMOL, PATANAK, VORAPHI and FULLER, W.P., 'Distinguishing Real from Imaginary Learner Needs for Broad-based Adult Education Programmes: A Report of a Village Survey in Thailand', Bangkok, National Education Commission Adult Education Division, January 1975. This paper describes in action the survey technique used in the programme. It emphasises the way that villager participation can refine ideas or expose prejudices.

Radio Farm Forums

Forums were planned in 1968 but not started until 1975. By 1978, 15 provinces were involved. Weekly radio programmes are backed by printed materials. Each group submits a weekly report, and local extension officers are expected to deal with some of the problems defined in these. The groups also occasionally go on trips to places such as seed stores. The forums are also linked with an FAO project to improve irrigated agriculture in northeast Thailand.

References

CLEARINGHOUSE ON DEVELOPMENT COMMUNICATION, The Radio Farm Forum Pilot Project, Thailand, 'Project Profiles', Washington, CDC, June 1977. Gives basic facts, analyses results and lists four notable features.

Togo

Radio Clubs: 'L'heure rurale'

In 1964 clubs were started in 16 districts. Members were usually illiterate. A 20-minute radio programme was broadcast on six nights a week, giving information and raising questions about national policies and problems. Each evening's programme was prepared by a different ministry in turn. Once a week the programme was devoted to readers' letters. By 1966, 152 clubs existed and 635 more were planned. The programme still goes on, but is now only broadcast three times a week. Each programme is broadcast in French and two local languages. Group leaders are trained at regional workshops of two or three days, and also attend refresher courses. They have manuals to help them, and, irregularly, return weekly report forms to the radio station.

References

KAHNERT, FRIEDRICH, Radio Togo's Educational Programme, in Schramm, Wilbur (ed.), 'New Educational Media in Action: Case Studies for Planners', vol. 2, Paris, Unesco/International Institute for Educational Planning, 1967, pp. 209-26. Covers the background, organisation, costs and educational value of the project and states the problems facing attempts to expand it.

Trinidad and Tobago

Breastfeeding Campaign

The campaign took place for six weeks in 1974 and was due to be repeated in 1977. Private and government agencies together used television programmes, radio spots, posters, newspapers, magazines and films to promote breastfeeding. Discussions amongst schoolchildren, community groups, clinic patients and fathers were also encouraged.

References

CLEARINGHOUSE FOR DEVELOPMENT COMMUNICATION, Breastfeeding Campaign, Trinidad and Tobago, 'Project Profiles', Washington, CDC, June 1977. Gives the basic facts about the campaign.

LESLIE, JOANNE, Five Nutrition Projects That Use Mass Media, 'Development Communication Report', no. 20, September 1977, pp. 4-6. Looks at a number of evaluation reports on the project and notes that effects on knowledge and practices fell short of the campaign objectives, while data is lacking on any differences in the incidence of nutrition-related diseases amongst infants.

Tunisia

Radio and film for agricultural extension

Radio programmes for farmers, most of whom are illiterate, have been broadcast daily for some years. They are between 5 and 15 minutes long, except for a 30-minute weekly magazine programme. Television was also used from 1968, but since 1973 video cassettes of farming programmes have been taken round in mobile vans. An extension worker is present at the showing so that discussions can take place. Local material can be edited in to films, which can be shown several times over at one performance if requested.

References

AGENCE DE COOPERATION CULTURELLE ET TECHNIQUE, La Vulgarisation agricole en Tunisie, 'Direct', June 1974, pp. 32-3. A brief factual account, which claims great success for the project but unfortunately quotes little evidence in support.

Uganda

Experimental radio listening group campaign, University of Makerere Adult Studies Centre

An 11-week campaign in 1966, where students, mostly teachers, worked in groups. They listened to 15-minute radio broadcasts, studied correspondence texts, and had occasional meetings with a tutor. The objectives of the campaign were a greater understanding of national development policies and better attitudes towards immigrants.

References

THEROUX, PAUL, 'Education by Radio: An Experiment in Rural Group Listening for Adults in Uganda', occasional paper no. 6, University of Makerere Adult Studies Centre, n.d. This report contains data on the listening skills of participants and the organisation of groups.

University of Makerere, Centre for Continuing Education: newspaper courses

The project ran from May to December 1967 after experiments with the use of radio and television for adult education in 1965-6. A four-page supplement containing a lesson of each of three correspondence courses was published as part of the weekly paper the 'People', over 30 weeks. Only 565 students were accepted: those who could cope with material near 'O' Level standard. Correspondence exercises for each subject were submitted to a tutor every third week. Some students attended weekend courses. During the last two months radio programmes were broadcast, where tutors discussed some of the students' problems.

References

CLARKE, R.F., 'Correspondence Education through a National Newspaper', Centre for Continuing Education, University of Makerere, 1968. The first part of this report describes the operation of the courses. The second reports on students' reactions to the course, derived from a questionnaire. The third part uses the experience gained to reflect on education and the press. There are also some samples of the materials.

Makerere teacher training project

Started in 1967, to upgrade 1000 teachers of the lowest grade.

Vacation courses, correspondence lessons and radio programmes were linked. At the end of 1970, 876 of the original 1000 passed the exam. Only just over 50 had dropped out. A second course for a further 1000 teachers started in 1970. A three-year course for 'licensed' teachers - teachers with 8 years' formal education but no professional training - started in 1971.

References

KAYE, ALBERT E., Upgrading Teachers in Uganda, in Kabwasa, Antoine and Kaunda, Martin (eds), 'Correspondence Education in Africa', London, Routledge & Kegan Paul, 1973, pp. 65-70. Describes the projects, methods and evaluation.

Upper Volta

Projet experimental d'égalité d'accès des femmes à l'éducation

This project started in 1967, to find out the educational needs of rural women and, during the pilot phase, to discover ways of meeting them. One pattern that emerged was discussion groups focussed round radio programmes. Women were trained as leaders on a four-week course, and supplied with a variety of audiovisual aids.

There have been a number of problems in developing and extending the system. But by 1976 over 100 000 villagers had had some contact with the project, and countrywide expansion is now under way involving five government ministries.

References

CLEARINGHOUSE FOR DEVELOPMENT COMMUNICATION, Project for Equality of Access to Education for Women and Young Girls, 'Project Profiles', Washington, CDC, January 1978. An up-to-date summary of the project's development.

SOCK, BOUBACAR, 'Projet experimental d'égalité d'accès des femmes à l'éducation', Paris, Unesco, 1972. A consultant's report, outlining a number of difficulties and suggesting ways that efforts could be better integrated.

Venezuela

Instituto Nacional de Cooperación Educativa (INCE)

Started in 1959 to organise and support vocational and practical education, particularly for young people. In 1966 the correspondence department of INCE launched its first course, a 12-part modular course in motor mechanics. By 1973 there were over 20 courses and 25 000 correspondence students, with an expectation that this number would more than double over the next five years. Students have access to a network of advice centres, and mobile field units travel round, providing face-to-face teaching for the correspondence students. Most written work is passed to tutors and back to students through study centres. Practical work is arranged where necessary; for example the motor mechanics' apprentice does 800 hours theoretical work and 3000 hours practical. In 1978 INCE was planning a major expansion of its programmes.

References

FAKES, J. (ed.), 'Technical Education at a Distance', Cambridge, International Extension College, Cambridge, 1973. Includes a brief case study on INCE.

WEDEMEYER, C.A., 'Report of Assessment and Development - INCE's Department of Correspondence Instruction', University of Wisconsin, 1973. An evaluation report, including some information on students' performance and recommendations for improvement of the system.

El Instituto Venezolano de Teleducación (IVT)

IVT aims to offer supplementary education to adults, using television, radio, print and film. It is particularly concerned to provide basic education. It is designed to be a low-cost system.

References

RIVAS, JOSE E., El Instituto Venezolano de Teleducación, in Oficina de Servicios para América Latina, 'Las Escuelas Radiofónicas en América Latina', Sutatenza, 1972, pp. 209-21. This article is little more than a list of objectives, programmes, staff and costs of the Institute; but since the lists are fairly detailed it gives a general picture of activities.

Western Samoa

Schools Radio

This small project in 1945 was an early attempt to train teachers at a distance. At that time the primary schools were poor and old-fashioned, and teaching was very formal. Radio was used to inject some quality teaching into the classroom and give existing teachers a good model to copy. A radio set was provided for every classroom and key lessons broadcast daily. Teachers had a monthly guide of instructions for supporting classroom activities.

References

BEEBY, C.E., 'The Quality of Education in Developing Countries', Harvard University Press, 1966. Beeby was directly involved in this project.

Zaire

Tele-Star

An open broadcast system, unusual for Africa in that it is privately run. Started in 1963 by Protestant and Catholic missions as a radio production centre, in 1966 it started producing television programmes too. When private broadcasting stations were banned in 1967 it was allowed to continue, and has received the support of external aid agencies and the Zaire government. In 1970 it became a nonprofit organisation and in 1972 a new production centre in Kinshasa was opened. Tele-Star produces adult education programmes of all kinds and has a very wide following in Zaire: 10 000 letters are received from listeners each year.

References

HEAD, SYDNEY, W. (ed.), 'Broadcasting in Africa', Philadelphia, Temple University Press, 1974. Two brief sections on Tele-Star give the history of the organisation, but little information on content of programmes or their evaluation.

MCANANY, EMILE, 'Radio's Role in Development: Five Strategies of Use', Washington, Information Center on instructional technology, 1973. Tele-Star's radio doctor programme is briefly described in this paper.

Zambia

Ministry of Education Correspondence Course Unit

The Unit started in 1966 to provide secondary-level courses for those unable to get places in secondary schools. School leavers are provided with tutorial support in urban study centres, where monitors are available to advise them. Radio has occasionally been used to support courses. Correspondence texts are also used in evening classes for adults.

References

EL-BUSHRA, JUDY, 'Correspondence Institutions in the Commonwealth, 1976', London Commonwealth Secretariat, 1976.

HEAP, WILFRID, Correspondence Education: Zambia is different, 'Zambia Educational Journal', vol. 1, no. 2, January 1972, pp. 12-13.

EDINGTON, A.B., GRIMMETT, G.V.H., GRAVES, DIANA and MARRIOTT, FLORENCE (eds), Correspondence Course Unit, Ministry of Education Zambia, 'New Media in Education in the Commonwealth', London, CEDO/Commonwealth Secretariat, 1974, pp. 246-52.

KABWASA, A. and KAUNDA, M. (eds), 'Correspondence Education in Africa', London, Routledge & Kegan Paul, 1973.

All these are very brief reports.

Radio farm forums

Weekly radio programmes in a number of local languages are broadcast to groups of about 15 farmers. They discuss the programme and send in report forms. Forums started in 1967, with about 600 in existence in 1973. The forums supplement the work of agricultural extension officers.

References

EDINGTON, A.B., GRIMMETT, G.V.H., GRAVES, DIANA and MARRIOTT, FLORENCE (eds), Zambia: Radio Farm Forums and Literacy Broadcasting, 'New Media in Education in the Commonwealth', London, CEDO/Commonwealth Secretariat, 1974, pp. 206-12. A brief but detailed case study.

Functional Literacy Project

A pilot project started in 1971 in two provinces with 252 classes. Three thousand farmers took part. The programme was in three parts: one in the classroom, with discussion, radio broadcasts and reading materials; the second, consisting of practical work on a demonstration plot; the third, consisting of individual work on a personal half-acre plot, putting into practice the methods learnt. The first stage of teaching was March to October; then four months from November to rest before a second six month period.

References

AHMED, MUSHTAQ, Country Report: Zambia, in Muller, Josef (ed.), 'Functional Literacy in the Context of Adult Education', Bonn, German Foundation for International Development, 1974, pp. 345-79. Comprehensive account of the beginning of the project.

NATESH, A.M., 'Zambia Rural Broadcasting (Literacy) December 1969-1972', Paris, Unesco, December 1972. An account of how experience from Zambian farm forums broadcasting was used to develop programmes for literacy.

SECTION 2 DISTANCE-TEACHING INSTITUTIONS IN DEVELOPING COUNTRIES OPERATING AT DEGREE LEVEL ONLY

Colombia

Universidad de Antioquia: Proyecto Universidad Desescolarizada

ARBOLEDA TORO, JAIRO, LONDONO RESTREPO, GUILLERMO and RESTREPO GOMEZ, BERNARDO, 'Proyecto Universidad Desescolarizada: Un experimento sobre Educación a Distancia', Medellin, Universidad de Antioquia, Facultad de Educación, April 1976.

ARBOLEDA TORO, JAIRO, LONDONO RESTREPO, GUILLERMO, RESTREPO GOMEZ, BERNARDO and ANGEL OSPINA, GUSTAVO, 'Proyecto Universidad Desescolarizada: Informe final', Medellin, Universidad de Antioquia, Facultad de Educación, 4 vols, 1976.

Costa Rica

<u>La universidad estatal a distancia de Costa Rica</u>
PACHECHO, FRANCISCO ANTONIO, 'La universidad estatal a distancia de Costa Rica y la Transferencia de Tecnologia', paper presented to Seminario Interamericano sobre Transferencia de Tecnologia en Educación, Chile, 1978.

Hong Kong

<u>Chinese University of Hong Kong, Department of Extramural Studies</u>
EL-BUSHRA, JUDY, 'Correspondence Institutions in the Commonwealth 1976', London, Commonwealth Secretariat, 1976.

India

There are at present <u>32 universities and institutions offering correspondence courses</u>. These are listed and described in:
SINGH, MANJIT (ed.), 'NCCE Souvenir', New Delhi, National Council for Correspondence Education (India), 1978.
See also:
EL-BUSHRA, JUDY, 'Correspondence Institutions in the Commonwealth 1976'.
UNIVERSITY GRANTS COMMISSION, 'Correspondence Education in India', paper presented to the fifth commonwealth education conference, Canberra, 1971.
UNIVERSITY OF RAJASTHAN, 'PRASĀR', vol. 2, April 1974. Special issue on Education through Correspondence.

Malaysia

<u>University of Malaysia off-campus academic programme</u>
EL-BUSHRA, JUDY, 'Correspondence Institutions in the Commonwealth 1976', London, Commonwealth Secretariat, 1976.

Mexico

<u>Universidad Nacional Abierta</u>
HOOPER, RICHARD, Some Recent Mexican Educational Developments, 'Educational Broadcasting International', September 1976, pp. 43-6.

Nigeria

University of Lagos Correspondence and Open Studies Unit
PERRATON, HILARY (ed.), 'Food from Learning: International Extension College 1971-76', chapter 5, Cambridge, International Extension College, 1976.
OLUMIDE, 'YINKA, 'COSU in Perspective', Lagos, University of Lagos Correspondence and Open Studies Unit, 1977.

Papua New Guinea

University of Papua New Guinea Department of Extension Studies
EL-BUSHRA, JUDY, 'Correspondence Institutions in the Commonwealth 1976', London, Commonwealth Secretariat, 1976.

Venezuela

Universidad Nacional Abierta
PINDAR, KATHARINE, Open University in Venezuela, 'Open Line', no. 19, September 1978.

Zambia

University of Zambia Correspondence Department
EL-BUSHRA, JUDY, 'Correspondence Institutions in the Commonwealth 1976', London, Commonwealth Secretariat, 1976.
KABWASA, ANTOINE and KAUNDA, MARTIN (eds), 'Correspondence Education in Africa', London, Routledge & Kegan Paul, 1973.
HOPPER, M.W., 'Correspondence Studies at the University of Zambia, 20 June 1966-30 June 1968', Paris, Unesco, 1968, mimeo.
EL-BUSHRA, JUDY, 'Correspondence Teaching at University', Cambridge, International Extension College, 1973.

SECTION 3

Australia

Distance teaching
There are a large number of distance teaching units in Australia, operating at all levels. The first reference gives an outline of 14 of these. The additional selected references give further information on specific projects.
EL-BUSHRA, JUDY, 'Correspondence Institutions in the Commonwealth 1976', London, Commonwealth Secretariat 1976.

CUNNINGHAM, K.S., Growth and Extent of Correspondence Education in Australia, in Butchers, A.G. (Intr.), 'Proceedings of the Third International Conference of Correspondence Educators', Wellington, New Zealand Education Department's Correspondence School, 1950, pp. 1-5.

EAKINS, C., The Use of an Itinerant Teacher Service by the Correspondence School in Western Australia, in Butchers, A.G. (Intr.), 'Proceedings of the Third International Conference of Correspondence Educators', Wellington, New Zealand Education Department's Correspondence School, 1950, pp. 197-201.

KINANE, K., Australia's Correspondence Schools with Supporting Broadcast Programmes and Radio University, in Schramm, Wilbur (ed.), 'New Educational Media in Action', vol. 1, International Institute of Educational Planning, Paris, Unesco, 1967, pp. 169-203.

UNIVERSITY OF QUEENSLAND, 'Proceedings of the Inter-university Conference on Part-time Teaching in Australian Universities', Brisbane, Department of External Studies, May 1967.

KIMMEL, PAUL, Educational Radio and Television in Australia, in Kimmel, Paul, Kies, Naomi E. and Lyle, Jack, 'ITV and Education of Children of Migrant Farm Workers, Indians, and Inner City Poor: Cross-cultural Comparisons of International Uses of Media', vol. 2, Washington, American University, January 1971, pp. 3-44.

BRAITHWAITE, BERNARD and BATT, KEVIN, Open Learning: The Australian Contribution, in Mackenzie, Norman, Postgate, Richmond and Scupham, John (eds), 'Open Learning', Paris, Unesco, 1975, pp. 95-120.

WALKER, M., 'Towards a True Community College', Bentley, Western Australian Institute of Technology, 1975.

Canada

Farm radio forums

SIM, R. ALEX, Canada Farm Radio Forum, 'Fundamental Education', vol. 2, no. 4, October 1950.

NICOL, J., SHEA, A. and SIMMINS, C.J.P., 'Canada's Farm Radio Forums', Paris, Unesco, 1954.

SCHWASS, RODGER, Radio in Canadian Adult Education, 'International Journal of Adult and Youth Education', Paris, Unesco, vol. XVI, no. 1, 1964.

Télévision éducative du Québec (TEVEC)

MINISTERE DE L'EDUCATION, 'TEVEC: documents, études et recherches', Gouvernement du Québec, 1970 and 1971. Rapport no. 8, 1971 (final report) and numerous technical annexes.

DODDS, TONY, 'Multi-media Approaches to Rural Education', Cambridge, International Extension College, 1972.

LALLEZ, R., 'The Tévec Case: An Experiment in Adult Education Using the Multi-media System', Paris, Unesco, 1973.
AGENCE DE COOPERATION CULTURELLE ET TECHNIQUE, Les systèmes multi-média utilisés pour l'éducation, 'Direct', January 1975, pp. 34-7.

France

Centre national de télé-enseignement

CROS, LOUIS, 'Enseignement par Correspondance, France', Strasbourg, Conseil d'Europe, 1968.
GLATTER, RON, 'Education by Correspondence in the Netherlands, West Germany, East Germany and France', University of Manchester, Department of Adult Education, 1968.

West Germany

Telekolleg

TRU COMMISSION, 'Distance Education Systems in a number of Countries', Stockholm, August 1975.

Japan

Senior correspondence high school (NHK Gakuen)

SCHRAMM, WILBUR, Japan's broadcast-correspondence high school, in Schramm, Wilbur (ed.), 'New Educational Media in Action', vol. 1, International Institute of Educational Planning/Unesco, Paris, 1967, pp. 135-67.
KATO, HIDETOSHI and POSTGATE, RICHMOND, Open Learning in Japan, in MacKenzie, Norman, Postgate, Richmond and Scupham, John (eds), 'Open Learning', Paris, Unesco, 1975, pp. 231-51.
TRU COMMISSION, 'Distance Education Systems in a Number of Countries', Stockholm, August 1975.
LYLE, JACK, The NHK Gakuen of Japan, in Kimmel, Paul, Kies, Naomi and Lyle, Jack, 'ITV and Education of Children of Migrant Farm Workers, Indians and Inner City Poor: Cross-cultural Comparisons of International Uses of Media', vol. 2, Washington, American University, January 1971, pp. 127-60.

New Zealand

Distance teaching

Four institutions are described in the first reference. The other references are selected.

EL-BUSHRA, JUDY, 'Correspondence Education in the Commonwealth 1976', London, Commonwealth Secretariat, 1976.
FORDE, C.S., The Radio in Correspondence Education - New Zealand, in Butchers, A.G. (Intr.), 'Proceedings of the Third International Conference of Correspondence Educators', Wellington, New Zealand Education Department's Correspondence School, 1950, pp. 218-21.
EWING, J.L., The Use of Radio by the Correspondence School of the New Zealand Department of Education, in Schramm, Wilbur (ed.), 'New Educational Media in Action', vol. 3, International Institute of Educational Planning/Unesco, Paris, 1967, pp. 79-94.
KIMMEL, PAUL, Radio in New Zealand Schools, in Kimmel, Paul, Kies, Naomi and Lyle, Jack, 'ITV and Education of Children of Migrant Farm Workers, Indians and Inner City Poor: Cross-cultural Comparisons of International Uses of Media', vol. II, Washington, American University, 1971, pp. 161-78.
GARNER, J. and FORDE, C.S., 'The Correspondence School: Golden Jubilee History, 1922-1972', Wellington, New Zealand, 1972.

Norway

NKI Skolen

REKKEDAL, TORSTEIN, Correspondence Studies - Recruitment, Achievement and Discontinuation, 'Epistolodidaktica', no. 2, 1972, pp. 3-22.

Sweden

General

TRU COMMISSION, 'Distance Education: An Outline of the Present Situation; and some Organizational Alternatives for Post-secondary Education', Stockholm, August 1975.
PROSSER, ROY, Adult Education in Sweden, in Edström, Lars-Olof, Erdos, Renee and Prosser, Roy (eds), 'Mass Education', Stockholm, Dag Hammarskjöld Foundation, 1970, pp. 63-87.

Hermods and Brevskolan

KÖKERITZ, H., Sweden's Leading Correspondence School, in Broady, K.O. (Intr.), 'Proceedings of the Second International Conference on Correspondence Education', Lincoln, University of Nebraska, 1949, pp. 151-5.
GLATTER, RON and WEDELL, E.G., 'Study by Correspondence', London, Longman, 1971.
EDSTRÖM, LARS-OLOF, The Study Circle and its Relevance to Africa, in Edström, Lars-Olof, Erdos, Renee and Prosser, Roy

(eds), 'Mass Education', Stockholm, Dag Hammarskjöld Foundation, 1970, pp. 256-62.
'Folkbildningsarbetet', nos 6-7, 1976. Special issue on study circles. Available in English.

United Kingdom

BBC listening groups
BRIGGS, ASA, 'The Golden Age of Wireless', London, Oxford University Press, 1961.
OHLIGER, JOHN, 'Listening Groups: Mass Media in Adult Education', University of Boston, Center for Study of Liberal Education for Adults at Boston University, 1967.
National Extension College
JACKSON, BRIAN, 'National Extension College 1967: Four Years' Work and the Future', Cambridge, NEC, 1967.
NATIONAL EXTENSION COLLEGE, 'After School English', Cambridge, NEC, 1967.
PERRATON, HILARY, 'Broadcasting and Correspondence', Cambridge, NEC, 1973.
FREEMAN, RICHARD, 'The Invisible Students: A Survey of National Extension College Students', Cambridge, NEC, 1976.
NATIONAL EXTENSION COLLEGE, 'Annual Reports'.
The Open University
THE OPEN UNIVERSITY, 'Report of the Vice-Chancellor', Milton Keynes, Open University Press, annual.
TUNSTALL, JEREMY (ed.), 'The Open University Opens', London, Routledge & Kegan Paul, 1974.
FERGUSON, JOHN, 'The Open University from Within', London, University of London Press, 1975.
TRU COMMISSION, 'Distance Education Systems in a Number of Countries', Stockholm, 1975.
SCUPHAM, JOHN, The Open University of the United Kingdom, in MacKenzie, Norman, Postgate, Richmond and Scupham,John (eds), 'Open Learning', Paris, Unesco, 1975, pp. 322-64.
MCINTOSH, NAOMI E. with CALDER, JUDITH A. and SWIFT, BETTY, 'A Degree of Difference: A Study of the First Year's Intake of Students to the Open University of the United Kingdom', Guildford, University of Surrey, SRHE, 1976.
THE OPEN UNIVERSITY, 'Teaching at a Distance', Milton Keynes, journal, three issues per year.

USSR

Correspondence education
ZHAMIN, V. and REMENNIKOV, B., USSR: Comparative Costs and

Efficiency of Full-time and Part-time Education, in International Institute of Educational Planning, 'Educational Cost Analysis in Action: Case Studies for Planners', vol. 3, Paris, Unesco, 1972, pp. 303-14.
GLATTER, RON and WEDELL, E.G., 'Study by Correspondence', London, Longman, 1971.
KUZNETSOV, VALENTIN, Correspondence Education in the Soviet Union, in MacKenzie, Norman, Postgate, Richmond and Scupham, John (eds), 'Open Learning', Paris, Unesco, 1974, pp. 313-20.

United States of America

General

WADE, S., Hagerstown: A Pioneer in Closed-circuit Televised Instruction, in Schramm, Wilbur (ed.), 'New Educational Media in Action', vol. 1, International Institute for Educational Planning/Unesco, Paris, 1967, pp. 59-82.
GAUMNITZ, W.H., Correspondence Education in the United States, in Broady, K.O. (Intr.), 'Proceedings of the Second International Conference on Correspondence Education', Lincoln, University of Nebraska, 1949, pp. 123-34.
WEDEMEYER, CHARLES A. and CHILDS, GAYLE B., 'New Perspectives in University Correspondence Study', Chicago, Center for the Study of Liberal Education for Adults, 1961.
MACKENZIE, OSSIAN and CHRISTENSEN, EDWARD L., 'The Changing World of Correspondence Study', Pennsylvania and London, the Pennsylvania State University Press, 1971.
TRU COMMISSION, 'Distance Education Systems in a Number of Countries', Stockholm, August 1975.

ABBREVIATIONS

ABU	Ahmadu Bello University, Nigeria
ACPH	Honduras Popular Cultural Action (Acción Cultural Popular Hondureña), Honduras
ACPO	Popular Cultural Action (Acción Cultural Popular), Colombia
AIR	All India Radio
ALER	Association of Latin American Radio Schools (Asociación Latinoamericana de Educación Radiofónica)
ATC	Advanced Teachers College, Nigeria
BA	Bachelor of Arts
BBC	British Broadcasting Corporation
BEd	Bachelor of Education
CCU	Correspondence Course Unit, Kenya and Zambia
GNP	Gross national product
IEC	International Extension College
INADES	African Institute for Economic and Social Development (Institut africain pour le développement économique et social), Ivory Coast
INCE	National Institute of Co-operative Education (Instituto Nacional de Cooperación Educativa), Venezuela
LDTC	Lesotho Distance Teaching Centre
MCA	Mauritius College of the Air
NCE	Nigerian Certificate of Education
PEPA	Primary School equivalency Programme, Honduras
PPA	Programme of Agricultural Promotion, Honduras
RER	Rural Educational Radio (Radio éducative rurale), Senegal
RSM	Radio Santa Maria, Dominican Republic
TANU	Tanganyika African National Union
UNDP	United Nations Development Programme
Unesco	United Nations Educational Scientific and Cultural Organisation

UNRWA	United Nations Relief and Works Agency
USAID	United States Agency for International Development

BIBLIOGRAPHY

AARONS, A. and HAWES, H.W.R., 'An African Primary Curriculum Survey: Country Profile: Swaziland', Department of Education in Developing Countries, University of London, August 1976.

AGENCE DE COOPERATION CULTURELLE ET TECHNIQUE, Les Systèmes Multi-média utilisés pour l'éducation des adultes, 'Direct', January 1975, pp. 34-7.

AGENCE DE COOPERATION CULTURELLE ET TECHNIQUE, Niger - télévision scolaire en marge, 'Direct', September 1975, pp. 15-49.

AGENCE DE COOPERATION CULTURELLE ET TECHNIQUE, Samoa: échec à la mesure des espoirs, 'Direct', no. 3, 1976, pp. 19-35.

AHMED, MANZOOR and COOMBS, PHILIP H. (eds), 'Education for Rural Development: Case Studies for Planners', New York, Praeger, 1975.

AHMED, MUSHTAQ, Country Report, 'ZAMBIA', in Muller, Josef (ed.), 'Functional Literacy in the Context of Adult Education', pp. 345-79.

ANDERSSON, GUNNAR, The Study Associations in Sweden, 'Folkbildningsarbetet', 6-7, 1976, pp. 5-10.

ARNOVE, ROBERT F., Sociopolitical Implications of Educational Television, in Arnove, Robert F. (ed.), 'Educational Television', pp. 1-21.

ARNOVE, ROBERT F. (ed.), 'Educational Television: A Policy Critique and Guide for Developing Countries', New York, Praeger, 1976.

BALL, JOHN, Beginning Science: A Radio Series for Primary Schools in Africa, 'Educational Broadcasting International', vol. 5, no. 2, June 1971, pp. 79-82.

BATES, TONY and ROBINSON, JOHN (eds), 'Evaluating Educational Television and Radio', Milton Keynes, The Open University Press, 1977.

BECKETT, P.A. and O'CONNELL, J., Social Characteristics of an Elite-in-Formation: Nigerian University Students, Zaria, Department of Government, Ahmadu Bello University, 1972, mimeo.

BEEBY, C.E., 'The Quality of Education in Developing Countries', Cambridge, Mass., Harvard University Press, 1966.
BENOR, DANIEL and HARRISON, JAMES Q., 'Agricultural Extension: The Training and Visit System', Washington, World Bank, May 1977.
BIENFAIT, ARLETTE, L'Ecole et la télévision, vol. 1 of Ministère de la coopération, 'La Télévision scolaire du Niger, 1964-71'.
BIENFAIT, ARLETTE, Recherches pédagogiques, vol. 8 of Ministère de la coopération, 'La Télévision scolaire du Niger, 1964-71'.
BRIGGS, ASA, 'The Golden Age of Wireless', London, Oxford University Press, 1965.
BROADY, K.O. (Intr.), 'Proceedings of the Second International Conference on Correspondence Education', Lincoln, University of Nebraska, 1949.
BRUMBERG, STEPHAN F., Colombia: A Multi-media Rural Education Program, in Ahmed, Manzoor and Coombs, Philip (eds), 'Education for Rural Development', pp. 1-60.
BRUNER, JEROME S., 'The Process of Education', Cambridge, Mass., Harvard University Press, 1960.
BURGESS, TYRRELL, 'Education after School', Harmondsworth, Penguin, 1977.
BUTCHERS, A.G. (Intr.), 'Proceedings of the Third International Conference of Correspondence Educators', Wellington, New Zealand education department's correspondence school, 1950.
BYSTRÖM, JAN, The Study-Circle as a Pedagogic Situation, 'Folkbildningsarbetet', 6-7, 1976, pp. 14-19.
CABEZAS ESTABAN, ANTONIO, 'Documento Informativo sobre Radio Santa Maria', paper presented at a seminar at Santo Domingo, 3-12 April 1975, mimeo.
CARNOY, MARTIN, The Economic Costs and Returns to Educational Television, in Arnove, Robert F. (ed.), 'Educational Television', pp. 22-73.
CASSIRER, HENRY R., Radio in an African Context: A Description of Senegal's Pilot Project, in Spain, Peter L. et al. (eds), 'Radio for Education and Development', vol. 2, pp. 300-37.
CASTLE, E.B., 'Growing Up in East Africa', Nairobi, Oxford University Press, 1966.
CENTRAL ADVISORY COUNCIL FOR EDUCATION, 'Children and Their Primary Schools' (Plowden Report), London, HMSO, 1967.
CENTRAL ADVISORY COUNCIL FOR EDUCATION, '15 to 18' (Crowther Report), London, HMSO, 1959.
CHAMBERS, ROBERT, 'Managing Rural Development: Ideas and Experience from East Africa', Uppsala, Scandinavian Institute of African Studies, 1974.
CHU, GODWIN and SCHRAMM, WILBUR, 'Learning from Television: What the Research Says', Stanford, ERIC, 1968.

COOMBS, P.H. and HALLAK, J., 'Educational Cost Analysis in Action: Case Studies for Planners', Paris, Unesco/International Institute for Educational Planning, 1972.
CROWLEY, DAVID and KIDD, ROSS, 'Radio Learning Group Campaigns in Botswana', paper presented to the Dartington workshop on distance teaching and rural development, Cambridge, International Extension College, September 1977.
CUNNINGHAM, K.S., Growth and Extent of Correspondence Education in Australia, in Butchers, A.G. (Intr.), 'Proceedings of the Third International Conference of Correspondence Educators', pp. 1-5.
DE KADT, EMANUEL JEHUDA, 'Catholic Radicals in Brazil', London, Oxford, University Press, 1970.
DODDS, E.R. (ed.), 'Collected Poems of Louis MacNeice', London, Faber & Faber, 1966.
DODDS, TONY, 'Multi-media Approaches to Rural Education', Cambridge, International Extension College, 1972.
DODDS, TONY, INADES - A Case Study, in Kabwasa, Antoine and Kaunda, Martin (eds), 'Correspondence Education in Africa', pp. 13-30.
DODDS, TONY, 'The Mauritius College of the Air: The First Two Years', Cambridge, International Extension College, 1975.
DODDS, TONY, The Mauritius College of the Air, in Perraton, Hilary (ed.), 'Alternative Routes to Formal Education'.
DODDS, TONY, PERRATON, HILARY and YOUNG, MICHAEL, 'One Year's Work: The International Extension College 1971-1972', Cambridge, International Extension College, 1972.
DORE, RONALD, 'The Diploma Disease: Education, Qualification and Development', London, Allen & Unwin, 1976.
DUMONT, R., 'False Start in Africa', London, Deutsch, 1966.
EAKINS, C., The Use of an Itinerant Teacher Service by the Correspondence School in Western Australia, in Butchers, A.G. (Intr.), 'Proceedings of The Third World International Conference of Correspondence Educators', pp. 197-201.
ELLIOTT, K., 'An African School', Cambridge, Cambridge University Press, 1970.
ERDOS, RENEE (ed.), 'Proceedings of the Eighth International Conference of the International Council on Correspondence Education', Chicago, American School and Paris, Unesco, 1969.
FAFUNWA, A.B., 'History of Education in Nigeria', London, Allen & Unwin, 1974.
FAKES, JENNY (ed.), 'Technical Education at a Distance', Cambridge, International Extension College, 1973.
FORDE, C.S., The Radio in Correspondence Education - New Zealand, in Butchers, A.G. (Intr.), 'Proceedings of the Third International Conference of Correspondence Educators', pp. 218-21.

FOSTER, PHILIP, 'Education and Social Change in Ghana', London, Routledge & Kegan Paul, 1965.
FREIRE, PAULO, 'Pedagogy of the Oppressed' (trans.), New York, Herder, 1968.
FREIRE, PAULO, 'Education for Critical Consciousness' (trans.), London, Sheed & Ward, 1974.
FREIRE, PAULO, 'Education: The Practice of Freedom' (trans.), London, Writers' and Readers' publishing cooperative, 1976.
GAUMNITZ, W.H., Correspondence Education in the United States, in Broady, K.O. (Intr.), 'Proceedings of the Second International Conference on Correspondence Education', pp. 123-34.
GRAHAM, L., Pupil Participation in the Teaching of Languages by Television, 'Educational Television International', vol. 1, no. 4, December 1967, pp. 267-71.
GREEN, C.H., 'The Story of the In-service Teacher Training Project of Swaziland', Manzini, William Pitcher College, n.d., mimeo.
GRIFFITHS, V.L., 'Teacher-Centred: Quality in Sudan Primary Education 1930 to 1970', London, Longman, 1975.
GUNBY, JENNI, The Open University, 'Cambridge Review', vol. 89, 15 October 1966, pp. 21-3.
HALESWORTH, B., Radio Broadcasts for Schools - Some Lessons Learnt, 'Educational Broadcasting International', vol. 5, no. 1, March 1971, pp. 56-9.
HALL, BUDD, 'Adult Education and the Development of Socialism in Tanzania', Nairobi, East African Literature Bureau, 1975.
HALL, BUDD and DODDS, TONY, 'Voices for Development: The Tanzanian National Radio Study Campaigns', Cambridge, International Extension College, 1974.
HAWES, H.W.R. and HAWES, C.R., Réformes des enseignements primaires, 'Recherches, pédagogie et culture', vol. VII, no. 31, September-October 1977, pp. 4-18.
HAWKRIDGE, DAVID, KINYANJUI, PETER, NKINYANGI, JOHN and ORIVEL, FRANCOIS, In-service Teacher Education in Kenya, in Perraton, Hilary (ed.), 'Alternative Routes to Formal Education'.
HILL, E.D., 'Final Report on the Francistown Teacher Training Project', Botswana, Francistown Teacher Training College, 1972, mimeo.
HOOPER, RICHARD, Education and the Mass Media, 'Educational Development International', vol. 2, no. 2, 1974, pp. 78-81.
HORNIK, ROBERT C., INGLE, HENRY T., MAYO, JOHN K., MCANANY, EMILE G. and SCHRAMM, WILBUR, 'Television and Educational Reform in El Salvador: Final Report', Washington, AID Studies in Educational Technology, August 1973.
HUNTER, GUY, 'Modernising Peasant Societies: A Comparative Study in Asia and Africa', London, Oxford University Press, 1969.

INGLE, HENRY, Reconsidering the Use of Television for Educational Reform: The Case of El Salvador, in Arnove, Robert F. (ed.), 'Educational Television', pp. 114-39.

INTERNATIONAL COMMISSION ON THE DEVELOPMENT OF EDUCATION, 'Learning to Be', Paris, Unesco, 1972.

JACKSON, BRIAN and MARSDEN, DENNIS, 'Education and the Working Class', Harmondsworth, Penguin, 1966.

JAMISON, DEAN T., 'Radio Education and Student Repetition in Nicaragua', World Bank, May 1977, mimeo.

JAMISON, DEAN T. and ORIVEL, FRANCOIS, The Cost-effectiveness of Distance Teachings For School Equivalency, in Perraton, Hilary (ed.), 'Alternative Routes to Formal Education'.

JAMISON, DEAN T., KLEES, STEVEN J. and WELLS, STUART J., 'The Costs of Educational Media', Beverly Hills/London, Sage Publications, 1978.

KABWASA, A. and KAUNDA, M.M. (eds), 'Correspondence Education in Africa', London, Routledge & Kegan Paul, 1973.

KAHN, A.W., 'A.I.R.'s Non-formal Education Broadcasts for Rural Development', paper presented to the Dartington workshop on distance teaching and rural development, Cambridge, International Extension College, September 1977.

KATZ, ELIHU and LAZARSFELD, PETER F., 'Personal Influence: The Part Played by People in the Flow of Mass Communications', New York, Free Press, 1955.

KAYE, ALBERT, Upgrading Teachers in Uganda, in Kabwasa, A. and Kaunda, M.M. (eds), 'Correspondence Education in Africa', pp. 65-70.

KAYE, A.E., The Ivory Coast Educational Television Project, in Arnove, Robert F. (ed.), 'Educational Television', pp. 140-79.

KENYATTA, JOMO, 'Facing Mount Kenya', London, Secker & Warburg, 1938.

KINYANJUI, PETER E., Kenya: The Use of Radio and Correspondence Education for the Improvement of Teaching, in MacKenzie, Norman et al. (eds), 'Open Learning', pp. 254-72.

KI-ZERBO, J., Education and Development, in Ward, F. Champion (ed.), 'Education and Development Reconsidered', pp. 94-115.

KÖKERITZ, H., Sweden's Leading Correspondence School, in Broady, K.O. (Intr.), 'Proceedings of the Second International Conference on Correspondence Education', pp. 151-85.

KUMAR, N., 'Educational Radio in India', New Delhi, Arya Book Department, 1967.

LA BELLE, THOMAS J. (ed.), 'Educational Alternatives in Latin America: Social Change and Social Stratification', Los Angeles, UCLA Latin American Center Publications, 1975.

LASLETT, PETER, Teaching by Television, 'Where', no. 11, 1963, pp. 4-5.

LEE, J.A., 'Test Pattern', University of Toronto Press, 1971.

LESOTHO DISTANCE TEACHING CENTRE, 'Learning from a Booklet:

An Experiment with Individuals and Groups in Lesotho', Maseru, Lesotho Distance Teaching Centre, 1978.
LYLE, JACK J., The In-service Training Programme for UNRWA/ Unesco Teachers, in Schramm, Wilbur (ed.), 'New Educational Media in Action: Case Studies for Planners', vol. 2, pp. 179-208. Also reprinted with Postscript - April 1969, in Erdos, Renée (ed.), 'Proceedings of the Eighth International Conference of the ICCE', pp. 346-71.
MCANANY, EMILE, 'Radio Clubs of Niger', University of Stanford, Institute for Communications Research Reprints, 1972.
MCANANY, EMILE, 'Radio's Role in Development: Five Strategies for Use', Washington, Information Center on Instructional Technology, September 1973.
MCANANY, EMILE, Radio Schools in Nonformal Education: An Evaluation Perspective, in La Belle, Thomas J. (ed.), 'Educational Alternatives in Latin America', pp. 238-54.
MACE, JOHN, Mythology in the Making: Is the Open University Really Cost-effective?, 'Higher Education', vol. 7, no. 3, August 1978, pp. 295-309.
MACKENZIE, NORMAN, POSTGATE, RICHMOND and SCUPHAM, JOHN (eds), 'Open Learning', Paris, Unesco Press, 1975.
MASLAND, LYNNE with MASLAND, GRANT, Some Cross-cultural Implications of Educational Television: The Samoan ETV Project, in Arnove, Robert F., 'Educational Television', pp. 180-202.
MAYO, JOHN K., MCANANY EMILE G. and KLEES, STEVEN J., 'The Mexican Telesecundaria: A Cost-effectiveness Approach', Washington, Academy for Educational Development, 1973.
MINISTERE DE LA COOPERATION, 'La Télévision scolaire du Niger 1964-71', 10 vols, Paris, December 1974.
MULLER, JOSEF (ed.), 'Functional Literacy in the Context of Adult Education', Bonn, German Foundation for International Development, 1974.
MURPHY, PAUD, Study Centres, 'BLSCC Newsletter', no. 3, May 1975, pp. 16-20.
NICOL, J., SHEA, A. and SIMMINS, G.J.P., 'Canada's Farm Radio Forums', Paris, Unesco, 1954.
NYERERE, JULIUS, 'Freedom and Development', Dar-es-Salaam, Oxford University Press 1973.
NYERERE, JULIUS, Declaration of Dar-es-Salaam: 'Liberated Man - the Purpose of Development', 'Convergence', vol. IX, no. 4, 1976, pp. 9-17.
OFICINA DE SERVICIOS PARA AMERICA LATINA, 'Las Escuelas Radiofónicas en América Latina', vol. 1, Colombia, Sutatenza, September 1972.
OHLIGER, JOHN F., 'Listening Groups: Mass Media in Adult Education', Boston University, Center for the Study of Liberal Education for Adults, 1967.
P'BITEK, OKOT, 'Africa's Cultural Revolution', Nairobi, Macmillan, 1973.

PERRATON, HILARY (ed.), 'Alternative Routes to Formal Education: Distance Teaching for School Equivalency', Washington, World Bank, forthcoming.
PERRON, WILLIAM and KIRST, MICHAEL, Organizational and Administrative Considerations, in Arnove, Robert F. (ed.), 'Educational Television', pp. 74-113.
PHILLIPS, H.M., 'Educational Cooperation between Developed and Developing Countries', New York, Praeger, 1976.
PIRES, E.A., with BARTRAM, B., Teachers for Refugees: The UNRWA/Unesco Institute of Education, Beirut, Lebanon, in MacKenzie, Norman, et al. (eds), 'Open Learning', pp. 273-94.
POPPER, KARL, 'Unended Quest: An Intellectual Autobiography', Glasgow, Fontana, 1976.
REID, SHIELA, Study Centres - a Report on a Seminar, 'BLSCC Newsletter', no. 4, November 1975, pp. 6-12.
REKKEDAL, TORSTEIN, Correspondence Studies - Recruitment, Achievement and Discontinuation, 'Epistolodidaktika', 2, 1972, pp. 3-22.
ROGERS, EVERETT M. and SHOEMAKER, F. FLOYD, 'Communication of Innovations: A Cross-Cultural Approach', New York, Free Press, 1971.
RUTILIO SANCHEZ, P. JOSE, Escuelas Radiofónicas de El Salvador, in Oficina de Servicios para América Latina, 'Las Escuelas Radiofónicas en América Latina', vol. 1, pp. 145-9.
SCHRAMM, WILBUR, Educational Television in American Samoa, in Schramm, Wilbur (ed.), 'New Educational Media in Action: Case Studies for Planners', vol. 1, pp. 11-57.
SCHRAMM, WILBUR, Ten Years of the Radio Rural Forum in India, in Schramm, Wilbur (ed.), 'New Educational Media in Action: Case Studies for Planners', vol. 1, pp. 105-34.
SCHRAMM, WILBUR, 'Big Media, Little Media', Washington, AID Studies in Educational Technology, March 1973.
SCHRAMM, WILBUR, 'Instructional Television in the Educational Reform of El Salvador', Washington, AID, March 1973.
SCHRAMM, WILBUR (ed.), 'New Educational Media in Action: Case Studies for Planners', Paris, Unesco/International Institute for Educational Planning, 1967.
SCUPHAM, JOHN, 'Broadcasting and the Community', London, Watts, 1967.
SEARLE, BARBARA and SUPPES, PATRICK, The Nicaragua Radio Mathematics Project, in Bates, Tony and Robinson, John (eds), 'Evaluating Educational Television and Radio', pp. 78-82.
SPAIN, PETER L., JAMISON, DEAN T. and MCANANY, EMILE G., 'Radio for Education and Development: Case Studies', Washington, World Bank, May 1977.
TRENAMAN, JOSEPH M., 'Communication and Comprehension', London, Longmans, 1967.
TRU COMMISSION, 'Distance Education: An Outline of the Pre-

sent Situation and Some Organizational Alternatives for Post-secondary Education', Stockholm, August 1975.
TRU COMMISSION, 'Distance Education Systems in a Number of Countries', Stockholm, August 1975.
UNESCO/UNDP, 'The Experimental World Literacy Programme: A Critical Assessment', Paris, the Unesco Press and United Nations Development Programme, 1976.
WAGNER, LESLIE, The Economics of the Open University, 'Higher Education', vol. 1, no. 2, May 1972, pp. 159-83.
WAGNER, LESLIE, The Economics of the Open University Revisited, 'Higher Education', vol. 6, no. 3, August 1977, pp. 359-81.
WARD, F. CHAMPION (ed.), 'Education and Development Reconsidered', New York, Praeger, 1974.
WHITE, ROBERT A., The Use of Radio in Primary and Secondary Formal Education: The Radio Santa Maria Model in the Dominican Republic, in Spain, Peter L., et al. (eds), 'Radio for Education and Development: Case Studies', vol. 1, pp. 172-98.
WHITEHEAD, ALFRED NORTH, 'Adventures of Ideas', Harmondsworth, Penguin, 1942.
WOEFEL, N. and TYLER, I.K., 'Radio and the School', Yonkers, World Book Company, 1945.
WORLD BANK, 'Education Sector Working Paper', Washington, December 1974.
WORLD CONFERENCE OF MINISTERS OF EDUCATION ON THE ERADICATION OF ILLITERACY, 'Final Report', Paris, Unesco, 1965.
YAZIDU, IMRANA, 'The Study of Radio as a Means of Communicating Agricultural Information to Farmers in Northern States of Nigeria', Ahmadu Bello University, unpublished thesis submitted for MSc degree, n.d. (1973?).
YOUNG, MICHAEL, 'Multi-media Education in Swaziland', Cambridge, International Extension College, July 1973, mimeo.
YOUNG, MICHAEL, 'Note on the Honduras Radio Schools (ACPH - Accioń Cultural Popular Hondureña)', paper presented to the Dartington workshop on distance teaching and rural development, Cambridge, International Extension College, September 1977.
ZHAMIN, V. and REMENNIKOV, B., USSR Comparative Costs and Efficiency of Full and Part-time Education, in Coombs, P.H. and Hallak, J., 'Educational Cost Analysis in Action', vol. 3, pp. 303-14.

INDEX

For Product Safety Concerns and Information please contact our EU representative GPSR@taylorandfrancis.com
Taylor & Francis Verlag GmbH, Kaufingerstraße 24, 80331 München, Germany

www.ingramcontent.com/pod-product-compliance
Lightning Source LLC
LaVergne TN
LVHW021038011026
849160LV00008BA/493
* 9 7 8 0 4 1 5 8 4 7 0 9 4 *